WYN BRAMLEY

THE MATURE PSYCHOTHERAPIST

Beyond Training and Ideology

FREE ASSOCIATION BOOKS

First published in 2017 by
Free Association Books

Copyright © 2017 Wyn Bramley

The author's rights are fully asserted. The right of Wyn Bramley to be identified as the author of this work has been asserted by her in accordance with the Copyright, Designs and Patents Act 1988

A CIP Catalogue of this book is available from the British Library

ISBN: 978-1-9113831-1-6

All rights reserved; no part of this publication may be reproduced, stored in a retrieval system, or transmitted, in any form or by any means, electronic, mechanical, photocopying, recording or otherwise, without the prior written permission of the publisher. Nor be circulated in any form of binding or cover other than that in which it is published and a similar condition including this condition being imposed on the subsequent purchaser.

Typeset in Sabon 10pt by
www.chandlerbookdesign.co.uk

Printed and bound in Great Britain by
4 Edge Limited

Dedication
This book is dedicated to my fellow psychotherapists.

CONTENTS

To the Reader   1

1. The Therapeutic Alliance Revisited   5
2. Personal Reactions to the Patient   20
3. Mature Play Between the Therapy Couple   39
4. The Mind at Play: Defence Mechanisms   53
5. The Self Revolution: Personality Disorders   71
6. The Self Revolution: Core Concepts   90
7. The True or False Psychotherapist?   108
8. Working With Couples: Why Do It?   125
9. Working With Couples: Techniques and Anxieties   138
10. The Developmental Perspective   157
11. Assessing the Patient   184
12. Self-Supervision / Note Taking   206

To the Reader   231
Biography   245

Note on the text

To maintain textual clarity and ease of reading, the therapist has been given a female gender and others, where either sex could be applicable, a male gender. No bias is intended.

The terms counsellor and psychotherapist are interchangeable, as are couple and marital. "Patient" also refers to client or service user.

All anecdotes and case material are based on real people but disguised and/or combined with similar cases to protect anonymity. Only particular aspects have been selected; no case is discussed in its entirety.

TO THE READER

You deserve a medal. You've completed years of training, put yourself under the microscope of personal therapy, read the scholarly tomes of your School's founding fathers and mothers, and acquainted yourself with all its latest theoretical and clinical developments. On qualifying, you have continued to have your work with patients regularly supervised, while participating – sometimes at great expense – in CPD (continuing professional development) programmes. You have subjected your work to the stringent scrutiny of a national accrediting body that will monitor you again and again for re-accreditation. What else, you may legitimately ask, could possibly be required of you in order to mature as a therapist?

Once you get your hands on that medal, it will from time to time require a good polish. This book is about the polish that comes from long *experience*. I am not referring here to the amount of time served, though that undoubtedly improves technique and builds confidence. I mean rather the wisdom and what I call 'safe daring' that can grow through long and varied practice in the field. I hope to provide some illuminating examples in the following pages, though I have to admit that wisdom is not a directly transferable commodity. You have to grow your own!

I aim to refresh theoretical concepts and ways of handling them in the consulting room, through the lens of my long and varied career. I will try to cross all therapeutic disciplines, though my own ideas and practices are deeply rooted in the psychoanalytic tradition. (Many colleagues and patients would raise their eyebrows at this, so unconstrained by orthodoxy have I become. But my heart still lies with the Unconscious – the nine tenths of our mental lives that lie outside our awareness). The Unconscious operates in all our consulting rooms, whatever name the different schools give it, and however much or little we engage with it. You can ignore it but it won't go away. And that includes the therapist's unconscious too, as I trust some of the case material will demonstrate.

The rules, prohibitions, boundaries and ethical codes espoused by all reputable trainings and accrediting bodies are there for good reasons. In any training courses or workshops I have run, I have ensured that these core principles are thoroughly absorbed. 'Wise and safely daring' does not mean sloppy and irresponsible. In all training programmes proper conduct should be emphasised and examples given of therapeutic failure when such stipulations are breached. The 'rules' exist to protect both patient and therapist and, while they can be discussed and even challenged in training, the novitiate, in their own interest, should always respect them. We trainers and supervisors should ensure trainees are provided with salutary examples.

A pair of examples

Trainees need to read about all the amazing successes accomplished by the leading lights of their particular school and feel encouraged. But they should learn too about the disasters: the otherwise ethical therapist who falls in love with her patient – how easily it can happen when two conducive selves meet. How she finds herself struck off following a malpractice claim by the patient. Perhaps she had realised her mistake and tried to get the therapy back on course, or maybe she justified her behaviour by saying the therapy had ended when she allowed a personal involvement. Nonetheless she had totally underestimated the patient's reaction to her implied or actual withdrawal from him and now her career is over.

Another common example of well-meaning but misguided therapy is when the therapist allows herself to contaminate the working relationship by getting involved with her patient's court case. She doubles as a biased social worker and risks herself being sued by husbands or parents for revealing material about them reported to her by the patient, but for which they have not given consent. She stands accused of breaking confidentiality.

Putting therapeutic material in court reports always changes the relationship in the consulting room. The therapeutic frame has been broken and it is irreversible. Becoming a champion for the patient's cause risks blinding them both to the therapeutic endeavour, which concerns his inner life – his feelings, motives, defences, the *understanding of himself* – leaving others, better qualified, to fight the good fight in the external world. So, rule of thumb to all trainees: never write anything for the court unless subpoenaed so to do!

Safe Daring

With the wisdom that comes from long experience, the mature therapist can risk bending or breaking the rules, but *only in the interests of her patient,* whilst keeping the therapeutic pair and the therapy frame safe from harm. (The frame refers to the physical and psychological setting, Therapeutic Alliance and any contract within which the work occurs). To safely dare is to think, feel, manage and react differently to all the bread and butter concepts and techniques we have absorbed from our training and more or less take for granted. This is not about breaking the rules for the sheer hell of it like some rebellious teenager; or a wish to be seen as some maverick genius who is above normal procedure: it's more to do with seeing those norms in a different light, testing them, amending or reshaping them, or doing something entirely new, to make a break-through when all usual therapeutic resources have failed.

As the years roll by, much of our training will seem outdated to us as different types of clinical picture emerge out of our culture that is also constantly changing. And never so fast as today. There is absolutely no point in treating today's patients as if they had stepped out of hysteria-ridden, sexually repressed, hierarchical, male dominated turn of the century Viennese society. We are not Freud's clones. Dynamic therapy along with all the others has developed almost beyond recognition, compared with my early training half a century ago. Whilst retaining tried and tested ideas about how humans in pain deal with that pain, we need to adventurously build on what we have learned ourselves, alone in the consulting room year after year, eventually growing into what I call *Mary Smith therapists*. Let me explain.

Putting aside fashion, fads and old beliefs dressed up in new language, we still need to develop our theories and practices into something more relevant for our times. This sometimes means leaping into the dark with your patient, trusting to your experience (though you will probably have fingers crossed behind your back). If it goes wrong, the Alliance (more anon) that you have built and nurtured will see you both through. You are developing out of your cradle of Jung, Freud, Gestalt, Systems, Group Analysis, Transactional Analysis, Integrative, Object Relations or whatever, into a mature type of therapist so unique that your way of going about things can only be properly described by your *own name*. You are no longer restricted to the doctrines of that supportive but sometimes stifling nursery to which you once belonged. You offer to your patient a wise but flawed human being, not membership of a cosy religion.

I have kept reading material to the minimum. This is not a textbook or training manual and there are no examinations to pass. I hope to lead the reader in the direction of *how* not *what* to think, to encourage them to trust their inner professional resources rather than scouring academic books for easy answers. All the same, that which I have learned in my own trainings and built on since, is based on seminal writers to whose work I owe a great debt, so it is only fair they should be mentioned. Many of you will already be familiar with some of these works but a re-perusal might surprise you, now you have the professional experience to more deeply appreciate the theory. Or you may ignore most of the recommended reading. That's fine with me, given the book's objective is stimulation and enjoyment rather than to be an endurance test.

CHAPTER ONE

THE THERAPEUTIC ALLIANCE REVISITED

One of the first theoretical concepts taught on every reputable training course is that of the Therapeutic Alliance. Alas this vital notion has become somewhat formulaic. It's easy isn't it? "The healthy, functioning part of the patient's (or client's) personality allies with the professional part of the therapist's, in a shared attempt to look at and treat the disturbed part of the patient and make him better." But the mature therapist knows from experience that this is far from simple. In contemporary, as opposed to traditional, psychotherapy, the neurotic or troubled aspects of the treater are just as important as that of the treated. The difference of course is that whilst the patient tries to be open and honest about his unhappiness or conflicts because he wants them fixed, the therapist has an obligation to at least appear sane, knowledgeable and authoritative, even when perplexed and worried by her patient's utterances, or her own inner promptings. (This is what is meant by professionalism in the above oft-used definition).

In today's therapeutic climate (largely 'Relational'; see chapters 5 and 6) the therapist's own private preoccupations and relationship difficulties can often be drawn from to facilitate a good outcome for the patient. She must however be thoroughly *aware* of her own issues and use that understanding to help her see what is flowing between her and her patient below the surface of their rational dealings with each other. What patterns of relating may (or may not) be getting repeated as their two psychic histories interlock? All this interpersonal activity, gradually becoming available (conscious) to her for investigation of its meaning, goes on above the safe bedrock of the Alliance. Without that Alliance, the therapy risks descending into chaos.

Where there is no repeating of old patterns with his therapist from the patient's side, are they being repeated with other key people in his life outside the consulting room? Even so, separating out her own private preoccupations and history from those of her patient is still necessary, to avoid contamination of the material brought by the patient. As a supervisor I frequently come across therapists who do not realise they are trying to sneak in their own therapy along with the patient's! Other supervisees feel they have failed if it is not they who have a starring role in the patient's repeated patterns of relating (his *transference* as the dynamic therapists have it). Basic rule is: go wherever the transference is active. It may not be directed to you. It might be to his bank manager, boss, wife, or in-laws.

It goes without saying that under no circumstances should the therapist or counsellor share with or foist upon the patient her own problematic experiences. The Alliance is not a friendship and the patient must not be seduced into thinking it is, thus developing expectations that cannot be met.

In trying to 'get on' with a patient, not just taking a thorough history or rushing to make telling links in his story to show him how insightful she is, the therapist is trying to build trust. That trust should be sufficient that under conditions where both are temporarily confused, fed up, bored, or lacking faith in the therapy's progress, or even in each other, it is the Alliance that will see them through. The patient cannot trust someone who doesn't properly listen to and *hear* – even if they don't yet understand – his distress. The mad dash to understand and interpret is usually an expression of the therapist's own anxiety about not doing a good job, or being perceived as a fraud. Being aware of this anxiety as it happens helps her to control it and concentrate on the listening. Humanistic therapists will fully appreciate this need for 'tuning in' to the feeling, tone, language, and culture of the patient so as to be 'alongside' him in the session, rather than addressing him from on high in priestly psycho-speak.

If the therapist is not fully attuned to the patient's way of being and his need to fully express himself before he can make space to receive her input, how can she expect him to listen to *her*? This *pacing* is a vital part of Alliance building. The prevalence these days of short-term therapy means that often the Alliance is sacrificed in the interests of saving time, putting yet more stress on the therapist, trying to squeeze the work into the number of sessions dictated by the institution. It is no wonder many short-term therapists suffer from anxiety and exhaustion: they are forced to work at high rise without a safety net!

Sadly one cannot will an Alliance into existence. Some patients are too agitated, depressed or suspicious to do this at first. Others jump at the chance. Indeed their over-willingness to engage trustingly with anyone and everyone might be part of their problem! Yet without a strong, reality-based bond, there is a risk of absenteeism, relapse and loss of hope, as practitioners of short-term therapy, especially, will testify.

The Alliance cannot be magically contrived, but true attention, genuinely empathetic noises, responses in language and body posture with which the patient feels comfortable all help to bring it about. Looking right into each other's eyes – not too much and not too little – is a fast bond builder. As the Alliance is forming I often find myself becoming aware of how my body position has moved to imitate that of the patient's, or I find myself scratching my head or chewing my lip just the way he does.

Sometimes unpredictable events in the early days of therapy, if handled well, can mark the emergence of quite deep, reality-based contact between treater and treated.

The Accidental Alliance

A middle-aged woman came to see me because her husband had just left her in the most callous way imaginable. She was an attractive, normally self-possessed person, at the very top of her profession. She was not usually given to emotional display but she had been utterly devastated by this betrayal and wept copiously in the first session. She appeared to be in a state of utter collapse. But at the end she got her hankie out, staggered to her feet and tried to pull herself together.

At that time my consulting room was a small bedroom in a cottage where all the old wooden doors and cupboards were identical, floor to ceiling. Before I could stop her, she opened the door that was in fact my partner's wardrobe. She confronted twenty years' worth of train magazines and an assortment of shirts and decrepit gardening jeans, all threatening to tumble out. Horrified, I looked into her tear-stained face. She looked back. We were both in shock for a second. I caught her eye – not just her face any more, but specifically her eye. We both burst out laughing.

It was the first time we truly met as two women on equal terms. She had been too upset and in need of offloading to think about whether she was getting on with me, or if I was going to be any use to her. But staring together into that gaping wardrobe, bulging with my partner's private things, my horror turned to hilarity as I saw she had seen the funny side. It was the first stage in our bonding.

I have to admit it could have gone terribly wrong. She might have felt humiliated or angry, let down that I hadn't saved her from embarrassment. For my part, I could have played safe and delivered a full professional apology, which the occasion certainly warranted, but I would have lost that chance to respond to her twinkling eye and make the first step towards a rewarding Alliance. This is the Mary Smith therapist in action. She can bend the norms, dare to do what as a novice she never would, and for which her supervisor would rightly chastise her.

The Mistaken Alliance

The Therapeutic Alliance is not the same as the contract, which refers to all agreements made about time, place, fees where relevant, holidays of both parties, and how absences will be handled. These agreements need to be crystal clear. In fact a good contract will implicitly emphasise the collaborative aspects of the therapy and demonstrate fair play on the part of the institution or therapist offering the service. This paves the way for the Alliance to develop, for the patient is given the chance to discuss or modify the contract before agreeing the terms. Already he senses the respect he is being accorded as an adult, despite any sense of shame, inadequacy or persecution he may be privately experiencing, and which has brought him for help. Contracting therefore contributes toward the establishment of an Alliance, but is not the Alliance itself.

The Pseudo Alliance

I saw a young woman once who had been in therapy for three years with a well-known London analyst. Her difficulties revolved around her marriage and previous boyfriends. There was a repeated pattern of her men being cold and withholding after initial fiery passion, and of them subsequently complaining she was a control freak.

I asked her why she had left the analysis. She insisted he was a lovely man, soothed her, made her feel at peace with herself, so different to her husband who made her angry and miserable. It seems that after a year or so of not getting very far with the marital issues, both analyst and analysed had fallen into a state of mutual reverie. Each week she would report her dreams – escapist dreams from what I could deduce, for they never concerned conflict or her husband or anyone who might stand for her husband or men in general. They would discuss symbolism, the pursuit of wholeness and such, but not the concerns over her femininity that brought her for help. I felt very angry that she had been let down by her analyst but she went on and on, insisting he was 'a dear' and that they had a special understanding.

This analyst had certainly made a deep and lasting bond with her but, despite not doing her any good, she clung to her pseudo alliance with him in her mind, whilst coming to me for help with the marriage. It became clear to me that he had been using a lot of technical terminology which had impressed her and made her and her dreams feel special. This collusive attachment, though cosy, was as unhelpful as it was expensive. The Alliance was being used not in the service of therapy but in avoidance of it.

One can't help wondering what might have been going on in the analyst's mind. Was there something about the woman that so disturbed his equilibrium he had to whisk her away to this fool's paradise? Why could he not persist with her issues around men?

This clinical snippet clearly illustrates how the Alliance runs in parallel or intertwined with transference and counter-transference strands in the therapy (see chapters 2 and 3). Her distortedly positive perception of the analyst kept her and the therapy happily stuck, until some healthy part of her realised she needed help of a different sort. The Alliance is a relationship of mutual regard deeply rooted in everyday reality, whilst the patient and therapist *simultaneously* relate subterraneously in ways which derive from their respective attachments to significant people in their pasts. It is the therapist's job to disentangle the one type of relating from the other.

Take the lady who walked into the wardrobe. Within a split second of eye contact, there was mutual recognition of a very intimate kind. Our most personal and undefended selves *met* and greeted. At the same time, looking back on it, she had a twinkle very like my older sister's, with whom I was out of contact for many years. The warmth and welcome I felt from her was true I think on the transference *and* Alliance front. Did I represent someone else for her? I don't know. Her material was just as harrowing the next week as she talked more about her husband's desertion. This was not the time to follow her transference to me. I was not important. The mature therapist never takes up leads just because they are interesting, and she knows when to fade into the wallpaper and give every inch of space to her patient.

The Undissolved Alliance

As a new person walks into my consulting room I often find a single word describing them and their effect on me leaping into my mind. With Trevor, the word was *famished*.

This story began thirty or more years ago. Trevor was in his mid-thirties, myself just a few years older. He was thin but wiry, wearing a too large but clean, conventional jacket. He looked at me, *studied* me, wary yet pleading at the same time, his eye contact anxiously intermittent.

What had brought him to therapy was a long career of beating up women. He'd had social workers, counsellors, psychiatrists, probation officers, and even AA, though he swore he wasn't an alcoholic. He said that no therapist was interested in a nasty violent man with such a long history, and he could understand why. But it had taken all these years, a messy divorce, and the court's refusal to allow him access to his daughter, for him to see there was something terribly wrong with him. His reading had at last led him to see he needed psychotherapy. He supposed I would be like all the others and refuse to help.

I confess my heart sank. In addition to my NHS work, I was at that time seeing a few private patients one afternoon a week at home, to help with the mortgage. The house was empty in the day and neighbours on both sides were out at work. I was well aware of one of the tightest rules of private practice: never see a patient with a history of violence alone in a place where no help can be immediately summoned. I was going to have to refuse help.

All the same it seemed fair to hear him out, which would also give me time to work out how and where on earth I could refer him, given the many refusals he had endured.

His story, which he reported without a shred of self-pity, was full of loss and negligence. Dad had left early, Mum died when he was six. He was fostered by several families and he and his siblings were split up. There was a period in a children's home when he started to steal and generally misbehave, but he was never aggressive to the male staff. As a teenager and young adult, there were many girlfriends whom he hit whenever he felt they were mocking him or cheating on him.

Trevor had idealised memories of his mum and was always on the lookout for the girl he would marry and with whom he would make a big, big family. The mother of the first child he fathered left because of his violence to her, and all his efforts to have access to the daughter were thwarted. He found me after a long period of depression and sessions in the public library reading up on violent men.

At the end of his account he practically begged me to take him on. He said I needn't worry about his hitting me because he had only ever hit women with whom he was sexually involved. Of course this was little comfort to me as I knew how easily sexual transferences could develop, and his violent behaviour was clearly linked to his being thwarted by women.

Common sense told me not to start working with him, but I was moved by his sincerity in wanting to give up his behaviour. The dynamic formulation was clear: here was a man with low confidence and self-esteem, resulting from his lack of any secure attachments. He idolised his dead mother who nonetheless he could scarcely remember and dreamt of finding her again in marriage, meanwhile seeking temporary comfort with equally damaged partners he called tramps. They all frustrated his longing to reconstitute his original family, with himself this time as *paterfamilias*, and so he lashed out at them for disappointing him.

I was still worried about my own safety though, and he saw it in my face. I confessed my doubts about taking him on and he rushed to reassure me. I crossed my fingers and offered him a contract in the same direct style he used. "We will start once a week and see how we go, but if you ever so much as raise your hand to me, you will be out on your ear. No excuses, no second chances." His face lit up. "Deal," he said. "When do we start?"

The therapy was long and unconventional. I worked the dynamic formulation over and over with him, in order to let out his grief then get him to face the facts that he could not simply replace what had been lost, and that no woman would ever live up to his maternal ideal. He unconsciously selected damaged women who were bound to let him down. Thus his rage at the world that had so denied his every need could justifiably be expressed while he continued his eternal wait for the return of his mother.

There was also much social skills education, plain comfort and understanding when he was in despair, and anger management of a CBT kind whenever he got a new girlfriend. There was a long period when he tried yet again via the courts to get access to his daughter and begged me to write reports on his good behaviour since being in therapy. I longed to acquiesce but declined; it was his solicitor's job to provide this information for the court. For a time the Alliance wavered, but in the end it saw us through.

Eventually he met a woman with whom he lived and had two more children, telling me she wasn't "the one" but she kept him steady and was a good mum to their kids. She would do for the time being. More children arrived and the relationship began to look increasingly permanent.

After several years Trevor left the therapy. I was satisfied he was as well and free from violence as he would ever be. Every year Christmas cards came, and I sent one back, keenly aware of his lack of original family at this difficult time of year. I fully expected that soon they would trail off and I could let the whole matter go. But thirty years later they still come.

Many therapists reading this will feel that I did not terminate the therapy properly, that the maternal transference to me had not only been left extant, but I had also encouraged it by sending him Christmas cards. I beg to differ. If the cards Trevor sent were a symbol of continuing dependence he would have tried to phone, or contrive a social meeting, or send me messages from time to time. But all I ever received was a Christmas card with his latest family news, the achievements of his now four children, rapidly turning into adults.

I believe that, though elements of transference may well have lingered, what really lasted and will continue to last, is the Therapeutic Alliance. He is under no illusions. We are totally different people with hardly anything in common except the therapy experience we shared. In thirty years he has never asked for more therapy or tried to contact me. But that special *reality-based* bond is indissoluble. For once, against all the odds, someone believed in him. It is that bond we mark, when we exchange cards.

Incidentally, there were undoubtedly aspects of mother in his distorted perceptions of me during our early work. But the dominating transference was to his older sister, who had been torn from him so cruelly when he was little. I think it is she, as well as my real self, who perches on his mantelpiece each Christmastide. If the rules say I am wrong, then to the devil with the rules.

The Dip In, Dip Out Alliance

Half a century ago therapeutic culture dictated that treatment was a long-term business, aimed at deep personality change. The patient was instructed not to make any life-changing commitments – marriage, jobs, travel – until the treatment was over. He would see his therapist intensively, sometimes four or five times a week. The NHS didn't provide talking therapies in those days, so private practitioners had all the free time at their disposal to offer to their patients. Therapy was a very specialised, arcane field, available only to the well-off.

Only medically trained personnel – with literally three or four famous exceptions – were permitted to train. It sounds almost incredible now, when therapy schools proliferate and just about anyone can apply to train. In those days no one over fifty-five could be analysed: they were too old. Therapy then was regarded as a kind of pilgrimage into the soul. It encompassed every nook and cranny of the subject's psyche and had a beginning, middle, and end phase, by which time the patient should be a thoroughly rounded human being as well as cured of any pathological symptoms or behaviours. Certainly no concept existed of focal or short-term therapy, and behavioural conditioning was still in its infancy. Carl Rogers and The Encounter Movement was only just on the horizon, treated with much suspicion and distaste by the UK therapeutic elite, coming as it did from the United States, that far distant land of wild and dubious ideas.

The Therapeutic Alliance as a concept was developed and accordingly thoroughly accepted in psychoanalytic circles, but was never as critical to all psychotherapeutic enterprises as it is now, when the luxury of a long-term commitment is unavailable and only the experience of a strong Therapeutic Alliance engenders hope in short-term patients that they can return again one day, to make use of this rare and special provision.

Therapy, thank goodness, has become democratised, enriched by many new schools of thought other than the analytic, but alas it has also become impoverished by many inferior trainings and enthusiastic but amateurish practitioners who have taken shortcut qualifications that do not involve their own therapy. Sadly some patients have to endure several inadequate treatments before finding reliable help. A good Alliance with one practitioner can foster belief in the system despite failures elsewhere.

Making available quality talking therapies sufficient to meet the demand and need is profoundly problematic. Would-be patients often complain that by the time they have jumped all the NHS hurdles in their way to finally reach a properly qualified practitioner, they will have either recovered or died. As the suicide and self-harm rates attest, there is truth in this claim. The Alliance therefore needs to be cultivated in every therapy, enabling those who need more to tolerate the long wait.

If short-term work fails to bring about the improvement required for optimal functioning, the patient will have to dip in and out of therapy provision as it becomes available in the future, often with different therapists. On occasion, benefits can accrue from the variety of styles and standards offered, but this is largely a matter of luck. Sometimes a focal treatment will help with a particular area of the patient's life, but he will need to return later to work on some other troubling issue, joining the queue for the NHS or finding the funds to 'go private'. The Therapeutic Alliance conceived in one therapy, therefore, needs to be strong and enduring enough for the patient to be able to transfer it to a new therapy. In private practice the same therapist is likely to treat the patient more than once, and it is the old Alliance that brings the patient back.

The Alliance I refer to here is not only an individual's Alliance achieved in one course of therapy, but an Alliance with 'Therapy' as a whole. The belief and trust developed out of a positive experience with one therapist, can not only be transferred to another, but can sustain the patient while he waits, sometimes for months or a year, to get a first appointment in a new town or clinic.

In these days of busy lives, multiple occupations and obligations, and work or leisure related globe-trotting, long-term work seems out of the question anyway, even if it could be afforded. There is a convincing argument for accessing therapy the way one attempts to see one's GP, i.e. when there is a pressing need. Our therapy techniques are constantly adapting to this dip in, dip out kind of focal therapy. My worry is two-fold. First, many training courses are still so steeped in historical techniques and theories that when the student emerges into the real dip in, dip out world she finds herself unable to cope with the fast-paced short-term work in which she is expected to excel. Our trainers, no matter how senior, dedicated or well-read, need to get out there and feel what it is like at the non-private 'coal face', if they are to equip their trainees to operate in the contemporary world and not the one in which they themselves were trained.

My second concern is for the therapist striving for bigger and wider results than can be expected. In attempting to speed up the therapy she ignores any Alliance building and just hopes some previous practitioner has imbued her patient with enough faith to stay with the new therapist through thick and thin for however many sessions have been contracted. Such a therapist would be better advised to shrink her therapeutic ambition (her desire for omnipotence), build a good Alliance where the auspices for one are good, and then find a local area of upset in the patient on which they can both concentrate, leaving other areas to be investigated by other practitioners later on.

Too many therapists feel obliged to do it all. This self-inflicted pressure not only leads to burnout, but also results in the abandonment of the undervalued Alliance. When difficulties arise, especially in the distorted world of the transference, there is no basic bond to help the therapeutic pair to weather it. Fearful of just this eventuality, many therapists avoid the transference altogether and resort to kindly chats that help no one. It is no exaggeration to claim that such abandonment and avoidance can ruin the patient's confidence in talking therapy to such an extent that he deprives himself of its help for the rest of his life.

The mature therapist is humble enough to do what she can and what is possible in the time available. At the same time she enables her patient to internalise an affirming experience of being Allied with his therapist as a fellow adult, and with the therapeutic movement as a whole. She trusts her future colleagues to pick up where she left off and carry on with the good work.

When the Alliance *is* the Therapy

A scowling forty-year-old Cathy plonked herself down on the sofa and I thought: *bitter.*

"I'll tell you straight I've no time for this therapy malarkey. I'm only here because my mate Norman's been gobbin' off about it again, thinks I'm heading for a nervous breakdown. To be sure I'm pissed off with everybody, can't be bothered to wash hardly – what's the point? Even breathin' is an effort. S'all right for you sitting there all smug and superior, rakin' in the money…"

Cathy sang in a folk band and Norman was the fiddler. She had a rapid-fire acid tongue so it took me two sessions to get a grip on her background. She hated her Irish Catholic parents – called them peasants. Mother was very beautiful but always having "attacks of the vapours", whilst Dad waited on his adored wife hand and foot. There were several younger siblings. Cathy complained bitterly about being used as a substitute mother for them, fetching and carrying, shopping for groceries, cooking and cleaning etc. while her mother "mooned about like a sick cat". Dad had no time for her. She rebelled at thirteen – drinking, staying out late, promiscuity.

By sixteen she realised she was gay and, in a row, threw this fact at her father, whereupon he called her "worse than a whore, a pervert" and she stormed out, never to return. Mother barely noticed and the next sister down took over Cathy's servant role.

Cathy lived with an older woman for a while but was abandoned by her because the woman could not stand her contemptuous attitude to their other friends, claiming Cathy was jealous and clingy. This woman had introduced her to the world of busking and folk clubs. Cathy discovered she could scrape a living through singing in pubs, at festivals, and outside theatres.

Twenty years on, doing rather well with her band, her only pal was Norman the fiddler, who had been on drugs but was now clean. He said he owed it largely to his counsellor.

In the early sessions Cathy tried everything to drive me away. She was sometimes late and sometimes tried to stay over time. She dropped hints of self-harm if I didn't acquiesce to her demands to change an appointment, or let her bring in chips to eat. I held my line whilst interpreting this behaviour to her as her trying to test me, prove I was as bad as all the rest. She was sure I would treat her as her only love had treated her all those years ago – "used me up and spat me out!"

On the fifth or sixth session she announced she had to have a fag, and started to shout at me when I asked her to wait till after the session. I was a bully and a fascist, just like the nuns at school. She got out her cigarette papers and started to roll them.

What to do? Not give in certainly, but not pull rank either. I felt sorely tried. "Look, you can't smoke in here. But if you're so desperate you can't wait, please go into the garden and come back when you're ready."

She looked at me, momentarily dumbstruck. Was the old bat actually compromising? Then: "You will add on the missed time at the end won't you? I'm shelling out good money for this."

"Nope. You're pushing it, Cathy."

She didn't really want to go and I suspect she didn't need a fag, but she slunk out and returned, banging the front door, a few minutes later. She stared at the floor, mutinous but silent.

That silence granted me space, at last. I tried to show her how she spent her life treating other people, including me, the way she herself had been treated. She felt used and abused, disrespected, manipulated and always, always in the end, rejected. So she rejected and abused first, then wondered why she felt miserable rather than triumphant.

"'Cept for Norman. He's decent, fair, puts up with it. If you really cared about helping me, if you were a proper therapist, mebbe you would put up with it as well."

"I'm still here aren't I? I have put up with it." (Cathy waved her pack of Rizzla papers under my nose – liar. I had to smile.) "Well, I put up with most of it. Because I wanted to understand it, why you have to be like this when it doesn't make you happy."

"How else should I bloody well act? Is there a secret formula for getting people to treat you right? To show a bit of respect? And what difference would it make? Doesn't make any odds. They'd still treat me like shit, because… because…"

"Because you *are* shit?"

Her eyes were full of unshed tears. To stop me witnessing them, she stormed out.

I toyed with the idea of emailing her, worried she might not show up next time, but in the end decided against.

When she arrived for her next appointment she was actually smiling. I felt that we had turned a corner and now the real work could begin. The fact that she had turned up indicated to me that we had an Alliance, albeit a grudging one, at long last.

Then she delivered a shock. This was to be her last session. She'd told Norman what had transpired with me and he said it was just what he'd been trying to tell her all along. They'd worked out a plan whereby he would give her feedback on her behaviour as it happened, and she would try to mend her ways. She'd seen the light she said, recognised the enormity and destructiveness of her defence mechanism.

She insisted on leaving though I told her I thought we had only just begun the work. She had made progress and that was cause for celebration, but the solution was not simply to smile and be sweet to people. She didn't have to go about *earning* love: the point was to find a way to love herself. Then any sweetness would come naturally from her poise and self-confidence. She didn't have to act the goody-goody, now she had seen the destructiveness of the baddy. She didn't have to *act* at all.

"Bah, psychobabble," she snorted, and left.

Over the next ten years she returned four times, each time staying longer and making more progress. Her dipping in and out stopped when she met the woman she eventually married.

She fought me hard for several weeks, trying to drive me away or subdue me, her two methods of relating to people she secretly longed to get along with. Once our Alliance was born she took it with her into her social world, afraid for the moment to stay and trust me further. It was the Alliance too that brought her back into therapy when the social world inevitably disappointed her.

Norman remained her best friend even after her marriage. I reckon that between us, Norman and I did a reasonable job, though he did most of the donkey work.

This case shows how vital the Alliance can be, more crucial than observation, interpretation or clever analysis. Without the Alliance, Cathy would never have returned. Therefore, during our first set of sessions, the Alliance *was* the therapy.

CHAPTER TWO

PERSONAL REACTIONS TO THE PATIENT
(The Counter-Transference)

There can be no understanding of counter-transference without an understanding of transference. So let us refresh and update. In human beings, how and when did transference start? We must go back to the newborn, or even further, to the foetus.

The primary aim of any living species is to survive. For *homo sapiens* this means we must learn from the very beginning to adapt to ever-changing circumstances and personal relationships. Without social/family networks life cannot go on. How to make use of them when at birth and even before, we have no language, no intellect, no insight, we are totally helpless to look after ourselves?

The infant inside and outside the womb does have a rapidly developing brain though, a collection of neural pathways waiting to be filled with experience, experience that will be registered and re-registered with embellishment after embellishment, as the new is inscribed on top of the old. The body will remember all that impacts on it long before the capacity to conceptualise or consciously memorise those impacts has arrived. These 'codes', written in nerve cells, are just prototypes. They are but crude models which the infant's organism will use to make sense of future experiences while the ability to actually think is gradually forming.

The models will be refined, honed into a more sophisticated shape with each new experience until we see a more developed and relatively stable *characteristic*, a way of absorbing and then responding to the world which we might call the beginnings of personality formation. It will go on developing as much in the so-called body as in the so-called mind: they are one and the same. And the babe is still only weeks or months old.

The newborn in its mother's arms may feel securely held or dangerously unsafe, even though he lacks any idea of what mothering or danger or arms are all about. Drinking from the nipple may be blissful or extremely frustrating without the infant understanding what bliss or pain means. His total universe is subjective, experienced through his senses and through his body – blood, nerves, gut, muscle and skin. All register what he will later identify as warmth, wetness, smell, touch, pain, hunger. The brain, receiving messages from the body, records. A neuro-chemical template is set down so the baby's whole organism has an expectation of what the next experience is going to be like and prepares for it. When it arrives, the template is then added to or modified, after the comparison between *now* and *then* is completed. The more or less finished template, call it *expectation based on previous experience* if you like – is then *transferred* to the next milestone faced by the infant or toddler. His mind is just emerging; it is his body doing most of the work.

We all seek the known and the familiar in order to feel safe *even if the familiar is terrible*. Better the devil you know than the one you don't! The growing infant's body knows from previous experience that he has survived pain, anxiety, rejection etc., so it can be a relief to be visited by these horrors again. At least he has a template, a reassuring model to refer to. It is the *Un*known, *change*, that's really terrifying. A contented, well-nurtured child is lucky, but even an unhappy child can survive by creating defence mechanisms against expected tribulation. So long as there isn't too much change and his familiar miseries keep on coming, he'll cope. This is why many people can't deal with sudden happiness, pleasure or love – they're simply unprepared for it, have no resources practised over a lifetime on which to draw.

If the baby has continuity of experience in his early days, *even if this is bad experience*, he will quickly build a repertoire of responses that ensure he copes. He will *transfer* any lessons learnt to the next stage of development, or the next personal relationship, each subsequent experience being met with an increasingly sophisticated and confident set of responses, be these embracing in nature or defensive. We begin to see his unique personality traits – his *Life Style* as Alfred Adler would say.

A new situation crops up for our infant, say the desire for solid food, the urge to walk or talk, the need to allow father into the twosome he's so far enjoyed with mum. All this may be exciting but it's also worrying because it's new, different. In a fresh set of circumstances the puzzled but curious human animal tries to make sense of them by bringing past experience to bear. What elements in this situation are similar to old ones? How I coped then might be useful here. Anxiety increases when new elements cannot be easily fitted in to old experience. The toddler twists and turns the new situation around to try and force it into the old familiar shape. A well-adapted youngster eventually gives up, abandons his template and faces *change*, with all its associated threats. He tolerates ignorance and fear until he learns something new to add to his store of old lessons. The less well-adapted, more fearful child shrinks from change, the biggest of terrors. In later life we see him desperately trying to keep safe by avoiding learning anything new. Or he just insists on processing every new situation in terms of the old. This is the person imprisoned by transference as opposed to using it experimentally, healthily, a mere tool to help fathom out some new set of conditions.

The Therapeutic Attitude

What you initially feel about your patient, or indeed anyone, is dictated by similarities or differences in temperament and interests, in social and educational background, political allegiance, and moral values. However, the patient is not being interviewed for the post of friend. This much all therapists understand, but it is surprising how often I notice as a supervisor that aspects of many therapists' own personalities and preferences colour their interactions with patients, completely unintentionally. The lesson here is: Therapist, know yourself; watch yourself; give this priority over collecting letters after your name or getting published.

It seems logical that the more senior and self-aware the therapist, the wider the range of people will be with whom she can make a swift and firm Alliance. Thus she provides a foundation for the more complex work of sorting out the patient's appropriate and inappropriate mode of relating, both with her and with significant others. Putting it bluntly, she is increasingly open to people who may not be to her taste.

Many therapists claim to be very tolerant, but for tolerant I read 'prepared to put up with'. This is not good enough. There needs to be true openness to, and a frank investigation of, the patient's view of things, in order to come to a joint understanding of why he thinks and feels that way. 'Tolerance' implies an evaluation has *already* occurred – the therapist is prejudiced, whether in favour of or against the patient's own opinions and attitudes. This will make her either hesitant/aversive or overenthusiastic and blind. Passing judgement, however unintentionally, gets in the way of the digging about function of therapy. No archaeologist avoids excavating a site, or digs too recklessly, just because they do or don't approve of the primitive customs practised by the folk who used to live on it. They just want to know what's down there!

I believe that no one can be entirely free from prejudice and preference, but practitioners are obliged to be mindful of theirs, to try to stick to doing therapy, not try to convert or consciousness-raise in their sessions. Does this mean they should accept racist, sexist, classist attitudes? Or should they bite their lip and instead analyse together with the patient the roots of the hatred and/or fear, as well as the social and familial conditioning that underpins such views? This is especially the case perhaps if those very views, or any activities resulting from them, are repeatedly wrecking relationships.

Where is the boundary between joint psychological work in the session, and political/ethical debate among friends in the pub? Is it a hard or soft line? Has the mature therapist a clear position on this, a position of her own, not that of the ideological school from which she graduated? Or does she hide behind the views of her old orthodoxy?

What if your patient fails to present you with convenient symptoms or syndromes you have thoroughly studied in training? In today's consumerist, narcissistic society, with more riches and more poverty than the previous generations ever saw, I see more and more patients, even – perhaps especially – the conventionally successful ones, complaining of lack of purpose, drive and direction. This state of mind often (by no means always) underlies presenting pictures of chronic fatigue, depression and substance abuse. Once the base feeling state is identified, work can begin.

But what if the long serving therapist holds a similar negative view of the contemporary world? What if she has given up on politics, grieves over the inevitability of wars, believes the human animal, despite its fine aspirations for a better world, is doomed by its intrinsic nature to repeat the mistakes of the past? (Despite this she has become a healer, so there must be hope somewhere!)

The point is whether the session descends into a non-therapeutic but interesting, even gripping and satisfying, discussion for both parties, reinforcing their shared view; or whether the therapist sticks to the task and explores with her patient the antecedents of his philosophy, conscious that those precursors may be very different from her own? When an outlook is so negative, has it been intensified by depressive, perhaps cyclical and/or situational features that, on lifting, enable the patient (or therapist!) to hold more balanced perceptions of good and evil? Sometimes a wait and watch policy enables a better assessment of the patient than hasty diagnostics based on outdated clinical categories. In this situation, the therapist needs the quiet confidence that comes from long experience, in order to bear her ignorance and go on properly *attending* instead of resorting to panic or wild hunches. She does not have to feel inadequate if she does not yet have the answers. Toleration of uncertainty or even temporary confusion without self-blame is another professional quality that cannot be taught, but can be striven for!

Always, the mature therapist is in sensitive touch with her mood level as she starts her day. It is her responsibility to take care of that mood, not her patient's. Many trainees and newer therapists, not yet comfortable in their professional skin, unconsciously use their successful cases to bolster their self-esteem, lift their mood, or evaluate their worth as practitioners. If we rely on our patients to make us feel good about ourselves, what chance do the more difficult, forgotten ones have? All too often they are speedily referred, kept too long on the waiting list, or even denied therapy from the start, being deemed unsuitable for this particular unit's methods. Feeling rejected, sent elsewhere and medicated while they wait, it would not be surprising if they quickly deteriorated, thus apparently justifying the early assessment of unsuitability.

It is not my place to lecture readers on who they should and should not treat, but to draw their attention to the persuasive power of self-interest. Therapists exist to help patients feel better about themselves, not the other way round.

I am all for further training and carefully chosen (not prescribed) CPD. Everyone appreciates the need to keep abreast of the latest developments in the field. Some reticence though may be a good thing. We are bombarded with workshops and courses on obesity, self-harm, dementia, trauma, gender, computer porn, bullying and so on. No therapist can know and do everything. Perhaps some judicious selection is in order here.

Many of our brighter young therapists, eager to be accredited and then employable at a high level – not to mention keen to deliver top class therapy – all too often rush indiscriminately to any further training on offer, especially if it concerns the latest trend. However, a balance needs to be struck. All the courses in the world cannot replace the good therapist's capacity to be fully present, allowing the patient to impinge on her receptivity whilst deploying calm observation, introspection, and the patience to wait for possible links to announce themselves. This comes only through long practice and self-discipline, neither of which can be taught. Extra diplomas, however useful in themselves, are no substitute.

We are looking here at the *therapeutic attitude* which parts company with the academic one threatening to dominate therapy culture. Time should be taken to acquire both. How much time? This is a matter for the individual, self-aware practitioner who should neither be press-ganged nor force herself to take up extra trainings before she is ready, and before the proper therapeutic attitude is firmly fixed.

Once the therapist is comfortable with her ability for stillness and can model it for her patient, she is ready to look at her own reactions to the person in front of her without anxiety or self-criticism. She can use her self-observations in the service of deep therapeutic work that is for the benefit of the patient. We are not talking about self-indulgence here, but the kind of introspection that leads to creative shared exploration.

Let us review and redefine what dynamic therapists call *counter-transference* then, and see some examples of it as it manifests in the consulting room.

How is Counter-transference Understood Today?

This concept has a long, controversial history, but nowadays counter-transference is seen in the literature as an umbrella term, covering *all* emotional responses to the patient, both conscious and unconscious, by the therapist. In day to day practice though, therapists use 'counter-transference' as a shorthand way to describe exaggerated or out of the ordinary emotional reactions by either party to the other, the kind of reaction that would make an observer wonder what on earth might be going on. Of course, this phenomenon also happens between people outside therapy all the time, but isn't deliberately focussed upon or studied by the persons generating it.

Counter-transference is an interpersonal, not a solitary, process. The therapist and patient facing each other in the consulting room are bound to have *reactions* to one another, but whether we call these transferences and counter-transferences, as opposed to mere reactions, depends on the amount of distortion wrapped up in those responses. Both parties need to become *aware* of their distorted perceptions and, so far as is possible, the *origins* of them; how past experiences with other key people in their lives are intruding upon/colouring the here and now experience in the room.

Hopefully the therapist knows her own emotional history well enough through her own therapy to be relatively free of transference pitfalls whilst remaining empathetic and intuitive enough to pick up the patient's transference issues.

Even though she may not let it show, when the working therapist finds herself intermittently or constantly more aroused – more angry, cold, sexy, impatient, disapproving than is usual for her in her day to day life – she is experiencing her own *transference* to the patient, which she needs to privately and speedily analyse, lest she is tempted to act on it at the expense of her patient. But it is a *counter-transference* if it arises in response to some specific stimulus – something he's just said or done, the way he looked at her, his body language, smell, an incident he reports that affects her strongly. *Counter* just means in response to some input from the other. This means the patient too may have an ongoing or wax/wane transference to his therapist, seeing her, say, as an idealised mummy; but he may also have a *counter*-transference to her when an intervention from her cuts across this exaggerated or distorted perception and challenges it.

It gets complicated when the therapist finds herself churned up by the patient's transference to her. Maybe she doesn't feel comfortable being hated, envied, adored, judged. She needs to explore the origins of these discomforts rather than enact the distorted (transferential) feelings aroused in her by her patient. Otherwise he will counter-transfer to her transference and she will then counter-transfer to his counter-transference, and so on *ad infinitum*, spoiling any attempt at genuine communication. It should be stressed there's nothing bad or wrong in feeling this way, providing it is allowed into full consciousness rather than falling into the trap of guilt followed hastily by denial.

It is important to scotch any idea here of transference – and counter-transference – *versus* so-called reality. All reality is transference and counter-transference in the sense that we learn through bringing past mastered lessons to any present new situation and then we test them out for congruence. Mentally healthy folk drop past solutions that no longer work and face the challenge of having to make new adaptations, whereas insecure and fearful people cling onto many of the old lessons, or avoid facing change and growth altogether. They remain prisoners of their comfort zones.

Most people lie somewhere between these poles, their perception and emotional responses sometimes totally appropriate to the new situation, however objectively threatening or strange, and at other times way off-beam even when the new situation isn't especially externally threatening. It is this off-beamness we call *transference and counter-transference*, some accumulation of past disturbing experiences distorting the person's perception of what is happening now.

It is inaccurate and reductive to classify a piece of therapeutic material as *either* transference *or* reality, for it is bound to be a nuanced shading in and shading out of the two. In the course of one therapy session there could be transference and counter-transference produced from both sides – barely perceptible, totally absent or suddenly bursting in dramatically, a sudden jolt in the otherwise smooth process of predominantly accurate mutual perceptions. Both parties can transfer a bit, a fair amount, a lot, or hardly at all, from moment to moment. It's the practitioner's job to track all this in herself as well as in the patient, whilst dealing with the 'ordinary' conversations that make up the session.

No one can scientifically measure the exact degree of accuracy or distortion in either party's perception of the process going on in the consulting room. Many patients hotly defend themselves against interpretations of the session material by their therapist that they feel are unfair or show them in a bad light. The therapist may be technically correct, according to her training manual, but if this is the reaction she gets she has timed the intervention prematurely or tactlessly, or she may have fallen victim to *reciprocal counter-transference*.

Reciprocal Counter-transference

In situations of reciprocal counter-transference the pair have quite unconsciously adopted complementary roles. He grew up with critical parents, attended a critical school, married a critical wife and labours under a critical boss. He has a chip on his shoulder that makes him think the world is conspiring against him. Is it? Or has he reinforced his victimhood by going out of his way to find critical relationships to justify his theory of the world as a nasty judgemental place? His well-meaning therapist may be trying to show him how he avoids seeing the truth about his way of maintaining/reinforcing that chip, but all he experiences is her persecution of him. This is the story of his life. He may have subtly and unknowingly solicited this response from her and she has taken the bait. It is this unconsciously adopted *process* that needs their joint understanding rather than her banging on with her sterile interventions.

There are many other gruesome twosomes like this, gruesome only if the shared understanding of them is missed. Take the guru and acolyte for example. This reciprocal counter-transference may be pleasurable and flattering for both parties but if they get stuck in these roles no therapeutic work gets done. All that is manifesting is a mutual admiration society – fine for other settings but not for the therapeutic one where change of mental habit, not intensification of it, is being sought.

The same goes for authority/dependent couples, rescuer and rescued ones, controller and controlled, and of course the erotically entrapped. These are re-enactments of early relationships or compensations for inadequate ones that the therapist is failing to understand. Something in her own history has been caught in the patient's web of memories, associations, reports of current problematic relationships, and she is *obliging* his unconscious requirements instead of helping him *understand* them. This serves to reinforce rather than free him from his habitual modes of relating that do not help him grow.

This is where the distanced view of an external supervisor can save the day.

Two Brief Examples

I recall two well-qualified supervisees. One had a rather superior, patronising university professor on her hands, the other a consultant pharmacologist with a similar disposition to the professor. The first supervisee felt intimidated and deskilled and longed to refer the professor to "someone more senior". The other supervisee became competitive and tried to impress the pharmacologist with all her psychodynamic knowledge. Amazingly, neither therapist realised they were gripped by counter-transference, that their patient was doing what they always did to lesser mortals and needed the help of their therapist to see it! Both supervisees were so engaged in dealing with their private imagined inadequacies – one by proving her intellect, the other by running away – that neither appreciated that their patients were probably alienating friends and family, just as they had frightened them. This had to mean a *loneliness and isolation* in each patient that both supervisees were perfectly equipped to treat, if they could only get past their respective transferences to powerful men.

Mrs. Jones and Mrs. Smith

Counter-transference involves a relation *between* two people as well as *inside* each of them. Mrs. Jones meets Mrs. Smith at a dance class and they establish a superficial friendship. Something inside Mrs Jones sees something in Mrs. Smith that, without her realising it, triggers her past. She feels compelled to deepen the acquaintance. Mrs. Smith responds positively. She could cool the friendship, indifferent to Mrs. Jones's transference to her. Her choice of staying around indicates a degree of fit in their histories – for example Mrs. Smith becomes the kind of mother Mrs Jones never had while Mrs Jones stands in for a loved daughter long since flown the nest. This is not to deny that they may have similar hobbies or other affinities but it is the reciprocated transference that will keep them bound together, possibly for life.

Transference and Counter-transference Outside the Therapist/Patient Relationship

Imagine a therapy where there is no degree of fit, very little counter-transference from either side, no personal dramas from the past gripping either of the pair. Dry indeed. Which is why it is vital you don't only concentrate on yourself when scanning the material the patient is presenting. The patient stays in a job that doesn't fulfil him. Why? What is being re-enacted? Why does he seemingly fail on purpose then complain about others never giving him a chance? Where has this bit of behaviour come from? To what conflict is it a solution (albeit a destructive one)? Furthermore, why did he marry the woman he married? How come he quarrels so much with his son? Who does he fantasise about in private? There are rich transference and counter-transference pickings here which have very little to do with you. I always say to trainees and supervisees: go wherever the transference/counter-transference is hot at the moment, and remember it may not involve you.

Projective Identification

When a person unwittingly disowns a quality in themselves and transfers (projects) it onto another, accusing him of the quality being disavowed, the disowning party may identify with the quality he's dumped on the other person so much that wherever the dumpee goes he must go too. They are tied together in his mind. There is usually a grain of truth in the projector's perception of the other person. This is projective identification, a concept much favoured by the Kleinian school, but borrowed by other disciplines, though used to a much lesser extent.

Sometimes only one person is projecting, but sometimes it is a reciprocal phenomenon. It is clearly seen in marriage, or in the hothouse of the workplace.

Mary and John's marriage

Mary met John at university and was drawn by what she saw as his intellectual brilliance and deep spirituality. Her own father had been a hard-drinking unemployed bully and she had always sought refuge in learning and sacred music. Her early infatuations were with her teacher, the local vicar and then her tutor at university. She transferred all her own aspirations to John and in so doing lost a part of herself. So wherever he went, she had to go too and very soon they were married. She quickly discovered John was overly reliant on her social skills as he had none of his own, and his spirituality was non-existent. He was simply introverted and inhibited. Mary was terribly angry and disappointed as well as frightened and lonely when she went into therapy. She had to learn to retrieve what she had given away, take back the projection with which she had identified, and make her own spiritual and academic way in the world. She divorced John and went back to university to do a doctorate. She stopped expecting her men to do her life's work for her, work that she'd been too scared and lacking in confidence to do for herself.

Projection and Mental Illness

Projection is close to transference. Transference is the past intruding on the present, affecting one's perceptions, and projection is often the next step. A man may have become a secretly angry, rivalrous, fearful or passive person as a result of years of self-reinforcing distorted perceptions. He finds a particular quality in himself unacceptable, damaging to his self-regard. He rids himself of it by turning it into a mantle that he drapes round someone else's shoulders, given any opportunity. This is someone who reminds him, however remotely, of the original perpetrator, and who is competed with, blamed, loved, hated, with the same intensity. (Love is included here because celebrity worship, for example, happens when idealised rather than negative qualities are projected. Something similar occurs in stalking. A longed for personal quality once belonging to, or dispensed by, some central figure in his life, is projected onto the recipient and in the mind of the projector cannot be disentangled from that person).

As already hinted, there is usually some truth, if only a small amount, in what he attributes to the other person, unless he is quite ill and cannot distinguish one person's personality from another; he throws the same dark cloak over everyone's shoulders. In extreme cases the therapist has before her a patient with paranoid delusions. She will have to forgo any thoughts of working with the transference or any other psychodynamic construct and instead turn her mind to psychiatric assessment. After consultation with the psychiatrist, it may be decided that therapy with limited supportive aims, along with medication, is the best course of action. Or the best plan may be to wait until the patient is well enough, and receptive to, what she can offer. A delusional person has no insight but can cleverly hide his false beliefs in the early stages. The therapist can easily become part of the conspiracy against him if she turns a blind eye to what at first seems merely odd, but eventually shows itself as an approaching psychosis. In these circumstances only sheer omnipotence, incompetence, or ideological fanaticism will drive a therapist to attempt the impossible or to decline a second opinion.

After skilled assessment, modified psychotherapy of most types can successfully operate with *relatively* ill people in combination with medication, management strategies and family or NHS support services. But the therapist must abandon the purist approach of her training, let go of some of her central tenets, such as prioritising the unconscious dynamics of her relationship with the patient, or getting him to set future goals. The treatment plan, whether a thought-out, holistic package as described above, or an exclusive twosome, supported by the GP, should always be trimmed to fit the patient's coping level now, not to support the ideology of the therapist or the institution providing the help.

Other patients can benefit intermittently in states of remission. This is where goodwill and collaboration between therapist and the medical team are vital. Premature therapy can be worse than no therapy at all, and late therapy provision can be too late. We have to accept too that psychotherapy is not universal balm and does not suit everyone.

Summary

Psychodynamic concepts are not tidily precise and separate, but are more like changeable, different currents flowing into the same river, one current stronger at this time, and another current stronger at that – transference, counter-transference, projection, projective identification and so on. Different therapy trainings may not use these technical terms but all therapists will be familiar with the clinical pictures that result from them. Let us look at a not unusual example.

Hannah

Hannah has a strict, nit-picking boss. Due to cruel parents and bullying experiences at school, Hannah attributes sadistic qualities to this boss, who is profoundly offended and insulted at these accusations. She claims she treats everyone the same and though she has high standards she has never persecuted anybody. She says Hannah is imagining things and just being paranoid. Hannah eventually files a complaint and the whole thing deteriorates until finally there's a tribunal, dividing the workforce as everybody takes sides, costing a lot of time and money, and almost driving both Hannah and the boss to nervous breakdowns. Either party could have asked for a transfer, or mediation through HR, or they could have changed their jobs, but neither did. Indeed, they were driven by their counter-transference responses – their identification with each other – to pursue things to the bitter end.

This is mutual projective identification. They hate each other but can't separate. Like many a marriage!

There's a degree of truth/reality in this 'fit' between Hannah and her boss. The boss is indeed somewhat brutal. And Hannah hounded the boss via the complaints procedures as much as the boss hounded her. Transference, counter-transference, projection and projective identification are normal, common interactions between persons: we all do it. However, illness or pathology comes about when these interpersonal processes are more or less constant, indiscriminate and dominating the life or lives of the people involved. As with Hannah and her boss, when two persons identify with the persecutor they have introjected in childhood and then projected onto the other in adulthood, a whole department's culture can be disrupted, and productivity drops dramatically.

Positive Transference

This chapter cannot be concluded without a mention of positive transference. If reciprocated, this is so pleasant, lulling, for both therapist and patient that its dangers can be easily missed. Arthur's case is a clear example. Personal details that could identify him have been pruned away, and everything here reported took place decades ago.

Arthur

Arthur came from an East End, Jewish background, and had enjoyed what seemed an unremarkable but sun-filled childhood. The last of six boys, he was rather petted and spoilt by his mum and dad, though they were always busy with the brood and their little carpentry business. Mum was constantly washing, cooking, sewing and cleaning but always found time for Arthur who was somewhat prone to every bug around, pale, thin, off school a lot, but affectionate and cuddly.

He came to me aged forty-five, long divorced but 'good mates' with his ex. He had four grown boys of his own now. He'd become a very rich and generous businessman, set the boys up in business, owned a yacht and several souped-up cars, had a girl in every port, belonged to all the best clubs, but his life seemed empty and meaningless. "I've made it, but is that it?" he asked me despairingly. "Is that all there is?"

Now in those days, working full time, I always dressed for the long clinical day in trousers and tops, loose and comfortable, homely even. I only realised much later that this was probably reminiscent of his mum. I became very fond of him and for a while felt somewhat guilty at seeing him as my special patient. (And so I should: I was so busy enjoying my transference to my 'son' that I skated over his transference to me). I was responding to his little boy lost appeal, beneath the macho man-about-town exterior. I felt privileged to see the 'real' Arthur. He saw me as someone with whom it was safe to be his true self. We co-created our own little island of content, but very little insight or movement really happened for quite some time.

One day, I was due to give a formal lecture at a prestigious conference in London and was somewhat nervous. I dressed very carefully that morning, for I would have to dash off after Arthur's lunchtime session to catch the London train. I put on Dior black stockings, heeled shoes and a skirt with matching tailored jacket that had cost me a fortune. Arthur came in and went pale. I thought he was going to faint. He was always one for a quip and in a few moments he recovered himself enough to say: "Hey, the lady's got legs!"

Then he fell silent for a long time. Stupidly, it had never occurred to me that he would react to my change of attire. (My only excuse here is that I was still a young therapist, not yet 'mature'.) I eventually prompted with: "What's up then?" He sighed heavily. "It's no use Wyn, I can't talk to you in that power get-up. You scare the shit out of me." I explained the reason for the change of clothes and assured him I was still the same underneath, but he was having none of it. "I feel betrayed. How will I know next week when you turn up in your usual scruff that it's the real you? *This* could be the real you and the casual pants are just to stop me feeling threatened. You really *could be* my headmistress and Maggie Thatcher combined – only, ha-ha, better looking of course."

Now this is the ignoble bit. I'm ashamed to confess that in the counter-transference I felt a moment of glee. Triumph. If *he*, top brass international millionaire businessman, was intimidated by my smart outfit, I would create the perfect impression at the conference! And hadn't my relationship with Arthur become rather cosy of late, with little new material emerging? Maybe I should get a couple of other new outfits as well, show him I'm a woman, a woman who gives lectures, can be powerful and sexy, a woman with legs as well as just a snuggly momma!

Fortunately I noticed this bit of narcissistic fantasising, and fell to wondering what it could mean in terms of Arthur's treatment. We were of a similar age but there had been no hint of eroticism in his material.

Directed by this self-supervision, I enquired in his next session about his many past – and often simultaneous, – girlfriends, and his ex-wife. I had always imagined them to be glamorous status or power symbols like most other things in his life. I assumed top models, actresses. But no, they were all short and dumpy with cheery Barbara Windsor grins and enormous boobs. He readily agreed he associated the boobs with maternal warmth and protectiveness, not sex. The crux of his problem, part of the dynamic formulation if you like, was that Arthur had never left his dear old mum, sought her everywhere, even in the consulting room. Actually, he'd never had an adult relationship with a woman in his life!

It had taken my reaction to his shock at my change of clothes to make me see the central problem that had brought him to treatment. When he had said "Is that all there is?", referring to his wealth and phenomenal achievements, what he was really asking was "Where's my mum?"

I tested this new hypothesis by asking him about the sex act. (Every dynamic formulation should be checked against evidence from the patient). Sex was okay, it turned out, but he did it largely to please the woman while secretly enjoying the skin to skin maternal warmth of her body before moving on to the next body. He was terrified they would catch him out snatching a bit of mothering and be disgusted, so he never stayed around for long. It was shame that had made him so promiscuous, not lust!

I'm glad to report that the therapy moved on swiftly after that, on the understanding that I would give him advance warning each time I was going to "do a Joan Collins", as he put it.

Some years after the therapy he wrote to tell me that he was content with life and had met and married a fellow businesswoman. "Be assured Wyn," he wrote, "your work was not in vain. She wears skirts and proper stockings and I don't mind a bit!"

Conclusion

It is incumbent on therapists to scan themselves as well as their patients for transference and counter-transference manifestations in the session, but not so intensively that all other material falls by the wayside.

These terms are but technical concepts for day-to-day interpersonal exchanges. It is important not to pathologise them but where relevant to educate the patient about how he is affected or dominated by them. Neither should they occupy all the time available. The Alliance will from time to time need a boost. Defence mechanisms (see chapter four) also need highlighting as they arise *in vivo* as well as in reported accounts of interactions outside the therapy. These too are normal psychological features that become problematical only when running the patient rather than him running them. The sensitive practitioner will notice her own defence mechanisms when they are touched upon by the patient, though she will almost always keep quiet about them.

Space should also be allowed for catharsis, empathy, compassion, companionable silence, the odd shared joke. Most of all, the patient should be encouraged to express himself fully without being interrogated or told what he 'really' means, the moment light dawns on the clever therapist. A halting, detailed, all-round-the-houses self-expression may seem tedious to the therapist who has already spotted what the patient's unconscious is up to. But she should always remember that such self-expression is rarely possible for him outside her consulting room. It is in itself relieving, Alliance-building and hence therapeutic. She should not grab all the restorative work for herself – the patient has his own part to play!

A note of caution: no one is so interesting to us as ourselves. Whilst monitoring transference related upsurges in ourselves, we must not become besotted with our own functioning to the detriment of the suffering person in whose interests we are deploying this introspection. It is a self-evident truth, sometimes lost, that the treatment exists for the enlightenment of the patient. Any benefit accruing to the therapist is secondary. Yet the furthering of her insight into herself arguably provides a postgraduate training superior to any other.

Suggested reading:

Adler, A. (Reprinted 1999). *Individual Psychology*. New York: Harper Perennial (Torchbooks).

Bramley, W. (1996). *The Broad Spectrum Psychotherapist*. London: Free Association Books.

Breuer, J. and Freud, S. (2004 revised edition). *Studies on Hysteria*. Harmondsworth: Penguin Modern Classics.

Casement, P. (1985). *On Learning from the Patient*. London: Social Science Publications (Methuen).

Coltart, N. (1993). *Slouching towards Bethlehem*. London: Free Association Books.

Heimann, P. (1950). On Counter-Transference, *International Journal of Psychoanalysis,* 31: pp. 81-4.

Little, M. (1951). Counter-Transference and the patient's response to it. *International Journal of Psychoanalysis,* 32: pp. 32-40.

Segal, H. (1964). *Introduction to the work of Melanie Klein*. London: Heinemann.

CHAPTER THREE

MATURE PLAY BETWEEN THE THERAPY COUPLE

It's a freezing December morning as you prepare for your first patient. You wrap a zig-zag patterned, fringed poncho round you, hands tucked inside. Jake comes in rubbing his own hands together against the cold, sees you and grins. "You look like an old Indian squaw," he says. As his therapist, what do you do now?

If this had happened to me when I started out as a psychoanalytic devotee, I would keep a poker face and wait. He may go on to free associate round the image, giving me more data about his transference to me. He may change the subject (in which case, why?) He may dismiss me as humourless, cold (so who else in his life was cold towards him?)

If this had happened a couple of decades later when the *zeitgeist* permitted the odd question or prompting, time was short in the NHS, and focal therapy was much in vogue, I might have asked what Indians and squaws reminded him of.

Had it happened just a few years ago, with Self-Psychology in the ascendant (see chapters five and six) I might have rapidly scanned myself thus: why did I choose to wear this ethnic looking garment? I had plenty of other warm clothes. Or I may have hazarded a guess at the transferential meaning behind the squaw joke and consulted him about it. I had been rather firm with him lately. Perhaps he was expecting to be scalped? I must then wait for confirmatory or disconfirmatory evidence in the material that immediately followed my comment. Oh, and did I resent being called old? Mustn't forget to monitor my own feelings, must I?

What I actually did was give a little laugh to acknowledge the truth of his picture of me (this to support the Alliance), then waited. He continued the session from where we had left off last time. The joke had meant nothing. (As Freud once famously said: "Sometimes a cigar is just a cigar").

Nonetheless this tiny example shows how much technique is affected by the ideological culture in which it is set. The Mary Smith therapist is conscious of the ideas and values permeating the therapy movement during her own training, but is not overly tied to them and can break from them when necessary.

Trainees often ask me if we old 'uns truly adopted a 'blank screen' face, if we sat sphinx-like till we were possessed of a complete and certain Interpretation (preferably 'mutative') of the material, before addressing the patient. It seems incredible now, but it is indeed how we were trained.

Whenever the spirit of the times morphs yet again, one aspect of therapy – the exciting new – always dominates, becomes a temporary fashion. With her long and varied experience the mature therapist can synthesise into a coherent whole old and new trends that make sense to her without over or underestimating either. Many dated concepts are as central to competent practice today as they were in the heyday of analytic innovation back in the 1940s and '50s. However, they do need revising in light of clinical and theoretical developments, as well as the vast changes in the way therapeutic treatments are delivered. In this book I aim to demonstrate the importance of combining old and new concepts without falling prey to the thrill of the new, or chucking out the baby with the bathwater in dismissing the old.

When Jake made his joke about my poncho, he was *playing* with me. I knew him well and long enough to be able to judge this. Had another patient said the same thing I may have understood the comment very differently, or seen it as material for shared exploration. An experienced therapist does not refer to the *zeitgeist* or her training to decide if it is play or not, but to her own independent and mature assessment.

Jake's ability to feel relaxed and make a spontaneous joke speaks well for the Alliance. But my previous firmness with him had been due to his *overly* relaxed attitude, his continuing reluctance to look inside himself. There is more than one meaning to playful activity in the consulting room, and part of Jake's play could well have been defensive, a screen behind which to hide. Therefore my laugh at the squaw remark was kept short. I could see from his face he had registered my friendly response, but also my resolve not to let the joke go on too long. Without any exchange of words we understood one another over this matter. In my view, non-verbal communication, as with body language, is not awarded nearly enough attention in most kinds of psychotherapy.

What is 'Play' Exactly?

Being serious and being playful are usually seen as antithetical states, a huge mistake in my view. Many erudite definitions for play exist, but I'll take the simple one from the Oxford Pocket Dictionary: "shift about, have free movement *within limits*" (my italics).

As we all know, Freud's self-professed aim was not to make people happy but rather to free their capacity "to love and to work". I suggest that without a capacity to play neither of these indicators of mental health can be fully achieved. Play therefore is a very serious business.

What then are these limits within which it is possible to enjoy "free movement?" Play may happen within one person's mind or in the external world but there's always something that delineates the field within which the play occurs. Otherwise it's not play but something more sinister, anarchic. Watch kids in their playground: the form and rules of the game are essential for it to succeed; but rules and form will themselves alter, soften or harden according to which children are playing. In order to satisfy the need for a sense of security and belonging in the group, roles and hierarchical positions are constantly changing. Otherwise the dissatisfied participants would simply stop playing. The game orders what they do with each other, but their adjustments and alterations refashion the game. There's an identical interplay between society's institutions and its members.

Without toys or company, is play possible? Yes. Even in solitary confinement, we know of people surviving through mental games with themselves, refusing to allow certain thoughts in (making safe operational limits for themselves) but allowing other thoughts, fantasies and memories to arise, interconnect and become elaborated. Some have written political, mathematical or philosophical treatises in their head, their enforced isolation obliging them to either go crazy with terror or to playfully swim and dive in the widest and deepest ocean of ideas, before refining their explorations into a piece of original work. It is said that Einstein's elegant formula $E=Mc^2$, which, written out mathematically for his students, would cover a dozen blackboards, was in fact the result of intuitive reverie, a *playing* with 'extreme', 'daft', 'impossible' out-of-the-box ideas and putting them together into a hypothesis that came to *him* rather than the other way round, as in non-intuitional thinking. Only after the event did he set about proving that his lightbulb moment had scientific merit. Play, then, is often the forerunner of creativity.

It can also be a source of self-help without the lone player noticing. 'Idly' thinking, doodling, choosing to read a book with characters one can identify with, watching soaps on television – these are all ways of escaping the ever pressured present and turning inward, there to play with what Object Relations therapists call 'internal objects'. Inside us are conflicts, fears, joys and hopes that have come about as a consequence of past experiences with the figures that once shaped our worldview and which still reside in us, 'pressing our buttons'. These internal icons may not accurately represent the way such figures really were, objectively speaking; they are more a construct we have made from our *subjective* experience of our interactions with them. Some of these figures will be labelled 'damaged' in our unconscious minds or 'powerful' or 'critical and undermining', or idealised so 'impossible to live up to'. When we 'idly' play on our own we are often trying to rework these figures into more manageable form, seek our revenge on them, mend them if they are broken, or return to a lost paradise of loving union with them.

If this is hard to believe, ask yourself why certain types of stories, film, pictures, or music can be guaranteed to hold your interest and others leave you cold.

Children at Play

So, play is contained within some kind of mental or physical setting: the safer the setting, the wilder and more fruitful the play can be. A toddler's playpen is often construed as cruel and restrictive, but it can also be seen as protective (hot saucepans, the busy street beckoning, sharp furniture and electric sockets). Play (and its concomitant *learning*) can be facilitated by the pen or completely shut down, especially if there are no toys inside it and/or mother never comes to check up and encourage. Compare this with the playpen that is the consulting room: how vital it is to have a safe, predictable, regular setting with a not too intrusive, but not too distant, therapist mum – a mum who lets her charge play independently (with his thoughts, emotions, words, fantasies) when required, but who can also play *with* him when invited, without having to know exactly where they are headed. She doesn't need to have control of every scrap of material but rather joins the patient in behaving spontaneously when the consulting room has become imbued with an atmosphere of playfulness.

However, the therapist is sufficiently observant to call a halt when play threatens to become dangerous; for instance when an inexperienced player risks edging into psychosis or melancholia.

As a supervisor I have found that the prospect of straying from comforting ideology and solid training into this free play area is really scary for most therapists. Afraid to go there, their treatments, though technically correct, often lack charge, vitality. Sudden breakthroughs are rare.

When the toddler plays with external things – trains, bricks, dolls – they may or may not mean trains, bricks and dolls to him. For example, he may grab the leg of a doll and point it like a gun! Toys can symbolise exciting or troubling ideas or things, or parts of things; or represent people or situations lost to conscious memory. Juxtaposing toys in what may seem to adults totally illogical ways, the toddler may be playing with internal figures past and/or present, turning them round and over, rearranging them and their relationship to him and to each other in new experimental ways. Thus he can ease his anxieties while building confidence and self-esteem. He can effect change in his internal world; he has *agency*. An inhibited child that can't play is already at a terrible disadvantage, unable to soothe himself, resolve gnawing conflict, safely let rip justifiable or unjustifiable rage, or just celebrate being alive.

A patient who can't play – 'free associate', just let whatever is on his mind flow out of his mouth – is similarly crippled. The first job of the therapist may be to enable, coach, permit, model for him, how to *play with* rather just aridly *report* thoughts, ideas, feeling and fantasy without fear of censure. He may be fearful of his 'ancient voices' that never allowed play, or his therapist who he is sure will echo them. Her attitude and behaviour in the session contradicts his expectations. Learning to simply express himself may have to come before treatment *per se*. In therapy as elsewhere one has to learn to walk before one can run.

Neither should it be forgotten that the therapist too has a history-filled internal world, in which, due to her own therapy, training and experience, she can privately play and come to understand the meaning of that play. If she freezes at the prospect of outward play with her patient, or plays recklessly without understanding what she is playing *at,* she should stop at once and consult her supervisor. Meanwhile she can fall back on the reliable disciplines of her training. She is not yet ready to 'safely dare'.

The sketchy account above of the toddler at play describes the type of findings made by Melanie Klein and her post-war colleagues at the Tavistock Clinic. They attempted to analyse children by studying them at play in the consulting room, sandpits and toys provided. As a consequence of these researches many therapy training courses insist on child/infant observation as part of the curriculum. Like watching games in the playground, observation and thinking for ourselves can often teach us more than the academic textbook which by its very nature transmits only second-hand and pre-digested information. We must find time to 'stand and stare' if we aspire to become a Mary Smith mature therapist.

As baby becomes a toddler, then a young child, play takes on huge significance for the adult he will one day become. Playing (in effect pretending) with carers and pals, teaches him to distinguish between internal and external reality, moving on from the pre-existing developmental stage wherein both are felt to be the same.

Pretending Daddy is a monster and slaying him is great fun when you know he isn't 'really' the dreaded dragon: Daddy scowling and growling actually experienced *as* the monster is thoroughly traumatising! A child will enact – through games, language, demands for stories – his fears and assumptions about what his own and others' minds consist of, assuming he has reached the stage through earlier play of realising that other minds, different to his, do exist. If adult playmates can playfully join in the child's various scenarios without getting too anxious, disapproving or irritated, they can soothe and reassure the child just by their implicit affirmation that the proceedings are not dangerous. Children will dismember or kill off dolls representing real human people with guiltless abandon, because 'mere play' is permissible. Thus relief from intolerable inner stress is achieved and calm restored to the child's sense of a self who would never in a million years murder anyone in 'reality'. Imagine the grown-up version of the child who never learned to make this comforting and vital distinction!

Much complex experimentation in a safe environment with safe people who will send back images to the child at play that his activities are very much okay is required by the child for him to master the ability to symbolise, then decode, others' symbols – in other words to communicate reliably. We are not born with this facility, only the potential to learn it given the optimal conditions. The child needs to grasp that symbols – the manner in which others choose to display themselves to him (in language, dress, gifts etc.) – represent that person's reality but are not the reality itself. Similarly, behaviours exhibited by his pal at nursery do not necessarily mean what he means when he does that behaviour. Thus he discovers the world of motives and manipulation: what might lie behind the symbolic shields people wear.

Current thinking is that good attachment relationships create opportunities for the child to make speedy and efficient use of the human predisposition to develop the ability to understand and interpret his own and others' minds. Neuroscience tells us that this tendency has already been laid down in infants' brains during evolution. It needs Nurture to flourish and develop, but Nature has already taken the first step. The child comes to see the various compartments inside and outside his mind where certain thoughts, feelings and behaviours belong and can be appropriately expressed. It dawns on him that others too have minds with compartments. Their minds, like his, regulate what may and may not cross the boundary between inside and outside; what is allowed to be seen and what is secret – and what might be negotiable between consenting parties. This knowledge enables him to navigate social interactions more easily and rewards him with satisfying relationships, in turn motivating him to make more. Clearly such a person stands a better chance in life than the one arrested at the early part of this process we all go through of getting to know our own minds. What will happen to him if the mind project, the playing with inner and outer reality to discover its nature, is never concluded properly?

Some patients need long-term help in order to learn to play, so they can begin to recognise what they are feeling and how that relates to their until now censored, edited or projected (disowned) thoughts. Many patients with a personality disorder diagnosis have little idea what they are truly feeling at any given moment so it is little wonder their relationships are chaotic. The tragedy is that their peers have made these discoveries that most of us adults take for granted, decades ago. Accordingly those friends and acquaintances are more emotionally fluent and introspective, making *their* therapist's job much easier.

In enabling patients to acquaint themselves with their own minds, the phrases 'What if…?' and 'It's as if….' and 'Let us for the moment pretend…' are often used in the consulting room. Trying to rush such a treatment where only a handful of sessions are on offer is counterproductive. Whatever the inadequacies of early attachment figures were, the trauma that their absence or failure to mirror caused will only be repeated by a too hasty practitioner inadvertently bullying the patient. It is arguable that no therapy offer, and the patient's subsequent reliance on what defences he has managed to scrape together, is preferable to a re-traumatising therapy.

Trainees at Play

Play in itself is neutral, not good or bad. It all depends on how it's mediated. Within one set of limits (boundaries, or confines, if you like) play can be socially sublimatory and helpfully cathartic, as in boxing or football. It can facilitate learning and skills acquisition through experiment and practice, or can lead to the production of artworks or scientific discoveries. It can lead to relaxation, a clearing of the cluttered mind to allow space for insight, as with Sherlock Holmes and his scratchy violin, his ear-splitting playing nonetheless helping him focus on murder cases. But when the setting is absent or not congruent with the play, when there's no organising principle as represented by teacher, nurse, mother, or peer code among the participants, play can turn very nasty indeed and at worst lead to destructive anarchy, as in Golding's *Lord of The Flies*.

Let me take you into a trainee's nightmare. Recall your own trainee days. You've paid a fortune to attend a workshop on 'Play and its Relevance for Therapy'. There is no timetable and no introductions. The coffee is cold and the loos are miles away and filthy. The staff claim they're giving you 'play space' and troll off to the common room for 'consultations' while you are all left to stare at one another. They return, eventually, only to lock you all in the library with a sack full of Lego, dolls, teddies and crayons and instruct you to 'Find out about play. See you at five...'

Granted, this is a wild exaggeration, but some experiential groups and training sessions are run very close to this model. On the other hand, many training staff so fear a playfulness that could get out of hand they resort to an almost doctrinaire reliance on Theory, which becomes an impediment rather than a stimulus to shared exploratory thinking (intelligent playing). Whenever theory is taught didactically, the trainees must then be enabled to play with it, not just swallow it.

Domestic, Social and Cultural Play

What about play in the everyday family and social sphere? One of its major functions must be *mastery*, starting with the nipple play of babies, whose very survival depends on it. Later the play itself, without the necessity of the milk flow, becomes pleasurable and is transferred into love play later in life. As baby pulls at his toes and throws his rattle out of the pram, he's mastering his musculature but also learning about boundaries, where 'I' ends and the rest of the world begins, how his arm sticks to him even as the rattle careens through the air. He's mastering the basic principles of science: why doesn't my rattle jump back at me? And he learns to master others through their love for him, as a very tired mum or dad endlessly returns his toy from the floor.

He's having fun too! Imagine a world without pleasure, a life of toil, duty, obligation. It would not be one worth living. Pleasure aids survival in both the animal and human kingdom. It motivates us to carry on against all the odds. Why then do we so inhibit it in the consulting room?

A long-standing patient you have come to know well starts enthusiastically telling you about the book he's reading at the moment. Do you leap to the conclusion he's avoiding the painful work of therapy? Or that he's trying to be your friend instead of your patient? Or that he's testing you to see what you yourself read and whether you are intelligent enough for him? If the book's theme at first glance seems distant from his own personal narrative, why is he distracting you with small talk? What if you have read the book too: do you say so? If you loved it or hated it should you confess? This isn't a tutorial, after all. Your anxiety is mounting. What is the correct thing to do?

Does it have to be so angst ridden? Can you not share your respective views (*sharing* is so closely related to play) without feeling you are colluding in some illicit extra-therapy relationship? His thoughts on the book may lead on to new material relevant to his therapy if he is allowed time to tease out his opinions. Obviously the sharing should not deteriorate into an interminable argument, however benevolent, about the book's worth. In playing together over the book, you are both without specific goals but know from previous occasions that such play often throws up unexpected results. And if it doesn't, well you have had some *pleasure* from one another – good for the Alliance, and well, just pleasurable. Does it have to be defended?

Why can patients and therapists not enjoy each other when there is real pleasure to be had, so long as there is no collusion to avoid the work, and the therapist, even when apparently just chatting, remains the therapist, alert to undercurrents? Therapy is serious, but does the atmosphere always have to be earnest or dark? Can't there be fun too, at the proper time?

Bonding with lots of others too, also has great survival and self-esteem value, as in ritual and ceremony, a more prescribed, even sacred, form of play. Humans need to be liked, respected, admired for their talent, beauty, wisdom, or social position. Or they yearn to identify or associate with someone who represents their ideal. Look at our obsession with sport – so preferable to dealing with competitive impulses by clubbing others into submission and then being feared, avoided and left to play alone! There is mastery over oedipal rivalry as kids play mums and dads, over sexual anxiety as they take up roles as doctors and nurses. The enactment of fear of abandonment or rejection in children's play – lost in a dark wood in dread of the Wolf or the Wicked Witch – makes the threat shareable and faceable, and eventually attenuates it.

Our minds play with us in dreams too, sending teasing messages to us that hint at, but disguise, meaning. Under the apparent chaos there are warnings or consolations, wishes or fears not spoken of or even thought about during the day. The code is a protection from a too direct communication from our deeper, knowing selves that's too unsettling or perhaps guilt-inducing to tackle head-on. In dreams we can risk private play with our hidden aspirations and terrors, the daytime necessary weight of taboo momentarily – but only partially – lifted.

Foreplay isn't only for, well, the fun of foreplay. It has huge social and cultural relevance. Not only does its denouement ensure the species carries on – rape or intercourse without foreplay could achieve that. Successful foreplay leads to a deeper trustful bond such that – all other things being equal – the pair will remain together long enough to healthily *rear*, not just produce, the next generation. Foreplay is also about how to help the partner surrender control and control surrender (in other words be able to lose but find themselves again). We ought not to metaphorically rape or seduce our clients, or go straight into therapeutic intercourse without some foreplay – in other words, adequate and sensitive acclimatisation. If therapeutic foreplay isn't forthcoming, patients may well 'freeze up' or just leave.

If we extrapolate foreplay to a community level, we are in the realm of ceremony and ritual. Look, say, at a coronation, the investiture of a tribal chief, a wedding, a Saxon ship burial, the World Cup football fans' wild costumes – all highly arousing to the senses and the spirit, conducive to a potent sense of belonging, to group excitement yet a corporate experience of safety. And does not all ceremony have its climax, the crown placed on the king's head, the communion wafer eaten, the ring slipped onto the bride's finger? These are the shared symbols of physical and emotional union, be this between two people or between a leader and his followers. This is theatre, a *play*. The stage may be bigger than the family one, and certainly greater than the first platform of mother's encircling arms, but it is theatre all the same.

More than anyone, Donald Winnicott, in his vast body of work, understood and communicated to us the importance of play – in early childhood, in the consulting room and in wider society. Between fantasy and reality, between the inner world of limitless space and the outer world of restricting materiality, there lies for the mother and child a 'potential' or 'transitional' space. (Later, this intermediate area of experiencing will be extrapolated to adult participation in and appreciation of cultural and creative activity). And it all starts with the first carer and baby playing peek-a-boo. There is an area between mum and child that belongs neither to her, nor him nor both, but which is a notional place where they can uninhibitedly play together via songs, toys, chat or just looks and touch. She will put something of herself in that space, be it fantastical or real, and baby will do the same. Each may then psychologically draw out something quite new from this melting pot of both their productions and add to it, before returning it to the pot for further embellishment. All this newness is absorbed and mentally played with by baby, creating fresh ideas, concepts and fantasies to lodge in the developing neurones.

Unless the attunement between them goes badly wrong, this communicative play is accompanied by feelings of delight and self-regard that new learning brings. We are here in the area of mutual projection and introjection, mirroring. It is also the stage at which the differing degrees of Winnicott's False and True self are laid down, should attunement consistently falter. (Winnicottian readers will already know the theory. A requirement is placed on us all as children to comply, in order to be rewarded with the love and approval we all want. This is in stark contrast to, and conflicts with, our wish to resist compliance, to act spontaneously, authentically and become our own person, not our parents' or society's.) I shall explain this important concept further in chapter five.

Play as Theatre

"All the world's a stage, and all the men and women merely players" quoth the Bard in *As You Like It*. And, in *Hamlet*, "The Play's the thing, wherein to capture the conscience of a king". In *Theatres of the mind*, written more than thirty years ago but still fresh today, the late great therapist Joyce McDougall introduces the theatrical lens through which she sees psychological problems. I have tried and failed to put her central proposition into my own words but cannot hope to express it as well as she does (pp. 3-4) so I quote it here:

> *Each of us harbours in our inner universe a number of "characters", parts of ourselves that frequently operate in complete contradiction to one another, causing conflict and mental pain to our conscious selves. For we are relatively unacquainted with these hidden players and their roles. Whether we will it or not, our inner characters are constantly seeking a stage on which to play out their tragedies and comedies. Although we rarely assume responsibility for our secret theatre productions, the producer is seated in our own minds. Moreover, it is this inner world with its repeating repertory that determines most of what happens to us in the external world. Who writes the scripts? What are the plots about? And where are they performed?*

She then explains with case material the way our minds put on plays using various stages and scenarios. For example, the body is used as a theatre in psychosomatic ailments. On the narcissistic stage all in the external world are hijacked as actors to perform in the subject's personal drama, denied any separate existence of their own. On the erotic stage, neosexualities (what used to be called perversions) are enacted in an attempt at self-healing. All this is more than just an attractive metaphor. She sees so-called abnormalities in a more positive light, as real efforts of the unconscious mind to put things right, though the play is never quite a runaway success!

Ms. McDougall subsequently wrote a book entitled *Plea for a measure of abnormality* which teases out this idea further.

Psychodynamic therapy is predominantly a *verbal* therapy, and has at times been accused of elitism, a therapy for the educated. It remains to be seen whether in the future it can incorporate some aspects of the more active modalities, especially for the less articulate patient, one who may feel threatened rather than empowered or pleasured by clever wordplay. But, for the time being, if there remains any doubt about the significance of play in our work as 'talking therapists', we have only to look to the *language* we use: play the field, play to the gallery, only playing (teasing), play up, play down, play fast and loose, play dumb, play dead, play on words, playing away (sexual cheating), play the fool, play truant, playact, playboy, make a play for, play of the light, playing cards, play along with, play a fish, play the game, play tricks... Come on reader, add some more!

Suggested reading:

Axline, V. (1990). *Dibs in Search of Self: Personality Development in Play Therapy.* Harmondsworth: Penguin Psychology.

Freud, S. (2002). *The Joke and its Relation to the Unconscious.* Harmondsworth: Penguin Modern Classics.

Golding, W. (1997). *Lord of the Flies.* London: Faber & Faber.

McDougall, J. (1986). *Theatres of the mind: Illusion and truth on the psychoanalytic stage.* London: Free Association Books.

McDougall, J. (1990). *Plea For A Measure Of Abnormality.* London: Free Association Books.

Miller, A. (1990). *The Drama of being a Child: The Search for True Self.* London: Virago.

Segal, H. (1988). *Introduction to the Work of Melanie Klein.* London: Karnac.

Winnicott, D. (1990). *The Maturational Process and the Facilitating Environment.* London: Karnac.

Winnicot, D. (2000). *Playing and Reality.* Harmondsworth: Penguin Psychology.

Winnicott, D. (2000). *The Child the Family and The Outside World.* Harmondsworth: Penguin Psychology.

CHAPTER FOUR

THE MIND AT PLAY: DEFENCE MECHANISMS

Thanks to neuroscience, we now understand something of the brain's complexity, though little as yet of its interplay with the mind, which remains an abstract rather than a biological concept. But through a century or more of close clinical observations, we can build pretty reliable theories about how the mind behaves and why. Eventually neuroscience will tell us if we were right.

So how does the defence theory work? We believe ourselves to be in charge of ourselves. We are competent, self-directed decision-makers. Yet we clinicians have seen from our work with troubled people that, like the iceberg, some nine-tenths of their mind seems to be hidden from them. They do and feel and believe things that puzzle and hurt them, things that they never chose or desired to experience: some ghostly 'other' must be responsible. What is going on?

Let's imagine our mind as a sphere. At its centre is a portrait, statue, icon or symbol (take your pick) that represents our self, *who we are* – or think we are. That picture may be faint or colourful, tattered or firm at the edges, occupying a lot or a little space in the sphere. Whatever the portrait's variation, it is fair to say that, for most of us, the picture is of an autonomous separate person, wending his way, mostly successfully, through a world of other selves, other persons. What we are blind to though, because it operates outside of our will, is the massive and constantly fluctuating force field within the sphere, in which that self-portrait is embedded.

These days it is naïve to conceive of our brain as a unitary thinking machine taking decisions under our sole direction. For within each individual's mind, that central image of the self is cosseted, preserved, defended from attack by powerful forces surrounding it that affect our perceptions, judgements, and consequently our choices. Such processes cannot help but profoundly determine the course of our relationships with others. The early analysts called these forces Mental Mechanisms of Defence. I find this a clumsy description, preferring to see our human defences not as mechanistic, but fluid, rather like the amniotic fluid swishing about inside the womb, protecting the foetus suspended in it.

Accordingly, the fluid in which our self-portrait bobs and floats should be appreciated and respected for the great service it performs. Its constituent parts, which I shall shortly describe, *protect* that image. This fluid, comprising all the so-called defences, resides in all our minds and is perfectly normal, only becoming poisonous when it drowns out the very image it purports to preserve.

The purpose of the defences is to prevent the undermining or spoiling of the picture we hold of ourselves, so that we can go on believing we are an okay person, worthy of regard, even love. Whenever the acceptable representation of ourselves is threatened, from within or without, a sense of pain or injury looms. Mood and motivation fall. In response, and without our conscious will, the energy within the spherical force field becomes charged, liberating the defences to envelop the image, keep it whole, whilst fending off the threat. If these forces fail, self-esteem, or even our sense of identity, is lost, as our internal portrait fragments. Mental and physical slow-down or even disintegration sets in... Is there a therapist in the house?

Not all theorists see defences in such a rescuing or benevolent light, and it is little wonder. For whenever a person in whose service the defences are being mobilised comes to overly depend on them, their relationships suffer. The onus is on us as would-be healers to sort out the resulting problems. These defences will continue to operate in the consulting room, resisting all our efforts to de-toxify them.

The late Donald Meltzer, a famous Kleinian, described defences as 'lies we tell ourselves to avoid pain'. This statement is true, but fails to appreciate their positive aspects. If we never, ever, told ourselves 'lies', were forced at all times to abandon self-deception, life would be intolerable. We'd be constantly confronted with the unvarnished truth about ourselves, would come to despise ourselves, unless we could recruit adoring fans to reassure us with their worship. We would be rendered unable to play, in any sense of that word.

Way back in the 1930s Anna Freud first tabulated the defences, along with illustrative clinical material, using the psychoanalytical terms of the day to explain them. Sometimes this makes the text seem dense, old-fashioned and unhelpfully mechanistic. Along with the discredited writings of her father on the seduction and penis envy theory, her work too has been unfairly overlooked in many quarters. However, the Anna Freud Centre for children and their families in London remains fully functional and successful. I would recommend a reading or re-reading of her seminal work on the defences, whatever your ideological background. Some theoretical ideas, however old, have critical relevance to all schools of therapy, and are indeed timeless. The Mental Defence is one such, though I have tried to rework the somewhat stiff language in which it was first couched.

We have all had a patient desperate for help but seemingly doing all he can to block our efforts. He just will not let us in. As we study his defence system rather than concentrating on his presenting symptoms or taking an ever more elaborate history in search of some clue, we begin to lose our irritation with him. We come to understand that the obstructive, distancing tricks he plays on us – defences for which we have till now had scant regard – are for him psychically *life-saving*. They must not be cruelly ripped away from him, even when we know it is their power that lies at the heart of the treatment. He clings to his defences as a lifeline. He is not being difficult. It is the highly charged force field within his mind, operating without his will or knowledge, that is fighting us in the consulting room, not his conscious self who desires nothing more than to cooperate and get well.

This is the mind at interdependent play. Although a portrait of the subject's self resides in his mind, so do the quite separate forces that regularly gather of their own volition to maintain that picture as intact and inviolable. We might call each defence an individual mind game, though the games do combine, flow playfully but with purpose into each other, and around the person's self-image, as we shall see.

This kind of mind play can be healing (if necessarily self-deceiving), but it is damaging to interpersonal relations when out of control. Unconscious defences deployed discriminately keep us in good odour with ourselves; but leant on too much alienate us from others who can usually see the lie to which Meltzer refers. I shall list the important ones here but it is vital that therapists do not treat them like a laundry list. The important point for the therapist when identifying one or more excessively used defences in their patient is to locate and work with *the pain that the defence is warding off*.

The worst way to deal with them is to tell the patient 'you are only doing or saying that because you are using this or that defence mechanism.' This constitutes an accusation and implies the patient is doing it on purpose. The therapist is gloating: 'I can see right through you and your games; you don't fool me.' A patient needs help to identify his image-saving defences and have them *non-judgementally accepted* so he can gently begin to deconstruct them. First he acknowledges their usefulness in the past and even feels grateful to them, but knows, perhaps with sadness as well as pride, that now he is almost ready to let them go. To achieve this state of preparedness, the *unconscious process* of protecting a vulnerable self-image has been brought into consciousness every time the process has occurred in the therapy and the underlying vulnerability faced. This has left a cleansed and realistically evaluated self-portrait in place of the old swamped one.

In my experience one of the most healing factors in any type of psychotherapy is the patient's realisation that his secret defences, once revealed, cannot drive away his therapist. He will not be judged and rejected by her as he has been by others.

It should go without saying that therapists also house defence and protective systems and need to be aware of them operating in the session. For instance, some therapists are very skilled at subtly 'putting down' the patient as they announce with relish the name of one or more games his mind is playing. But they themselves are playing games: this is contempt masquerading as insight, and is used to make the therapist feel superior. Such abuse of therapeutic privilege makes the patient feel less worthy than ever, or offends him and causes him to leave. Interpreting defences is a delicate matter and relies heavily on the Alliance as a counterweight.

Repression, Denial, and Rationalisation

Any unacceptable or painful feeling can be *repressed*, which means pushed out of consciousness – anger, grief, guilt, fear, for example. Some writers see repression as a specific defence whilst other theorists see it as underlying all of the defences: that repression occurs first and is then 'fine-tuned' by one or more of the others. A man or woman may be described as a repressed *personality* when they appear unable to display, or even experience, much feeling at all about anything. This may be due to the repressed emotions being morally unacceptable to the person, or shaming, or frightening. Such a person may have been raised in a repressed household or culture, or been subjected to continuous mental trauma resulting in extreme withdrawal from the entire emotional arena – safety at any price. In long-term therapy he can learn about emotions, come gradually to perceive these mysterious entities in himself and eventually display them in ways appropriate to his situation.

However, some people, such as the so-called high-functioning autistic, lack the *capacity* to experience certain emotions. In common parlance, they are hardwired that way. Though cognitively able, even especially gifted, they find it almost impossible to empathise, and subsequently fail to develop appropriate social skills. It can be damaging to attempt to de-repress such a mind. Repression is not the issue here and both parties end up feeling a failure. The same goes for schizoid personalities where trying to access emotions that are not there can be a dispiriting business. Therapists should always be cognisant of the personality structure, the permanent 'building blocks' making up each of their patients, so they can set realistic aims for the treatment. Some psychiatric input on training courses would greatly facilitate this.

Denial is an unconscious refusal to see what is under your nose. A loved father dies and the daughter with whom he lived still puts out a table setting for him every night. This is more than forgetting, absent-mindedness. It is a refusal by the mind's protective forces to accept the unbearable truth. Shock and denial go together. When bringing news of a death, the messenger is often faced with the bereaved person's disbelief: "but we had lunch together only yesterday…" People recover from this kind of denial of course, the defence having had a cushioning effect, giving the person time to absorb the horror of what has happened to him.

Massive denial is often seen in the military. A soldier may see massacres or executions on both sides of a conflict but he screens out any memory of them. He is not lying when he says: "Massacre, what massacre? I saw nothing. I saw only bravery, our lads doing their jobs." A soldier whose denial processes fail may be so traumatised his career is finished forever. Even in much less dramatic situations we all need some degree of denial, perhaps only temporary, in order to cope with life.

This is similar to *rationalisation*, where unacceptable feelings or memories are justified, the facts distorted and reconfigured into a more acceptable story. In this case the bad things are not denied but 'whitewashed'. A massacre may be rationalised with a sad shake of the head as "collateral damage" – so much less condemnatory!

Relocation and Blaming

My partner and I were off to a pre-Christmas lunch with a group of friends in a rural corner of the county we didn't know. My partner sees himself as an expert navigator (and usually is), so looked up a map and directions to the country inn. The weather was gloomy and squally, the lanes narrow and criss-crossed. He missed a turn, cursed, then tried to turn back. But there was no suitable turning place for miles. As his frustration and agitation increased, he again missed a turn and we were lost. I didn't mind the mistakes, I only wanted to get to the venue on time, but he was clearly in an aggrieved state. "Bloody internet, can't even draw a proper map. And no bloody signposts round here! What does the council spend its money on, eh? Look at that junction, four roads and no sign… oh yes, but covered in mud. How is one supposed to read *that*?"

He was threatened by feelings of shame, would not have been able to bear seeing himself as doubly 'at fault' having made two errors. To protect his view of himself as a good orienteer it had to be someone or something else that was to blame. He had to *relocate* the source of the problem anywhere else but under his nose.

In couples this defence can become quite dangerous. Each partner is a ready-made target for relocation and *blame*. One partner may always accept the blame, aware that they are innocent; meanwhile, underneath the spurious peace resentment grows and any intimate relations suffer. If you are constantly expecting to be blamed you tend to keep quiet and avoid the blamer. And being blamed all the time kills any sexual arousal. The absence of sex is often the presenting complaint when a blaming couple come for therapy.

Passive Aggression

Compliant on the outside but hostile underneath, the *passive aggressive* person never strikes out but gets under the skin of his foe, winding them up, sometimes to the point of absolute rage. He does this by being late, 'forgetting' promises made, being sullen and uncommunicative, sabotaging his marriage or job by 'losing' critical files or missing vital appointments, playing deaf to requests for feedback or affection. In marriage he often claims he is perfectly satisfied with the *status quo*: it is only his partner who is a discontented nag, always going on about the relationship when there is nothing wrong. The partner does indeed 'go on' because the quiet aggressor is refusing to communicate and is savouring his victory while the partner helplessly begs for better contact. Hope is lost. Loneliness, depression, or substance abuse ensues. Sometimes though, there is a rebellious extramarital affair, in which communicational as well as sexual needs are at last met. This marriage is teetering on the edge and will crash unless the passive hostility can become active, then constructively worked on between the parties.   Careers too can be wrecked by such personalities.

Projection

In *projection*, unwanted aspects of the self are disowned, attributed *unconsciously* to another, then regarded with disapproval. This defence was described in chapter two.

Reaction Formation

The subject is terrified of exposure concerning a particular personality trait, say lack of confidence, fear of confrontation, doubts about his self-worth. He copes by behaving as if the very opposite were true. He does this to such an extreme that no one ever suspects the shaming truth.

Alan

Alan fought against coming to couple therapy until his wife said she was taking out a court injunction to have him removed from the joint-owned family home. In the first session he sat scowling at the floor or studying cloud formations out of the window, while his wife told of his bullying, forcing instant unilateral decisions on her, bellowing at her if she tried to negotiate, ranting at and unfairly disciplining the children. He shouted at shopkeepers and laid into babysitters if they weren't up to scratch. He had lost his job after quarrelling with his female boss, so was now taking up casual work storekeeping at a sports centre. He had already found himself in trouble there, for yelling at the users who "pissed about" with expensive equipment.

His riposte to all this was that she and the kids were ganging up on him, deciding things behind his back, not telling him important things he should know, and excluding him from their plans whenever they could. He became red-faced and angry, unable to compete with his wife's fluency. Unable to get his words out and embarrassed by this, he marched out.

He did however come to see me on his own. It emerged that his family of origin never, but never, had physical contact and never discussed emotions, but were happy enough. He left school early, wasn't academic but did want to help people. He tried to work for charities but became disillusioned with what he saw as corruption and bad practice and eventually tried his hand as a swimming teacher, losing the post through his short temper. Currently lacking a proper job, he was doing all the shopping and cooking, cleaning, decorating, the school run, and ferrying the kids to their multiple hobbies, while his wife earned well in a successful publishing firm. With some awkwardness he admitted he really enjoyed these tasks and in another universe would have gladly been a house husband. But never, never, in this one!

Alan was a very frightening man in the couple session, but on his own, and given time to think, I found him sensitive, nurturing and home-loving to an unusual extent. He disguised what he saw as his feminine personality, which so privately shamed him, by rushing to the opposite extreme and acting like macho man in the home, at work and in public. He was terrified of losing the respect of his children and earning the contempt of his professionally successful wife. He admired his wife's abilities but was mortified by his own lack of a career and earning capacity. In short, he believed he was inadequate as a male, just "some kind of eunuch or sissy". His bossiness and bullying was an attempt to hide this.

His unpalatable behaviour, which he believed was appropriate male assertiveness, was compounded by a long depression he was unconsciously *denying* – another mark of embarrassment and self-loathing. When denial failed he *rationalised* his depressive irritability and aggression as being the result of his wife's impossible and unfair behaviour toward *him*.

Another example of reaction formation is when an older sibling takes on the over-scrupulous parenting and protection of a younger one, who he envies and toward whom he even harbours murderous feelings. This does not invalidate the care given or the mind's noble intent to repair damage before it is even wreaked. Neither does it suggest all older siblings feel this way unconsciously. It is simply an example.

Arguably this defence is preferable to the older sibling with a disabled brother or sister about whom he feels terribly guilty, as if, by being healthy himself, he has robbed the other child of life's opportunities. To assuage guilt, atone, repair, make good, he resolutely refuses to take advantage of any happy invitation that fate puts in his path. He has equalised their relationship by spoiling his life.

Splitting

In fairy tales there are murderous stepmothers and lovely wish-granting fairies. There are witches and angels, ugly frogs that turn into handsome princes, magic kisses that wake the dead, and dreadful poisons secreted in the rosiest apples. Why do children love these tales that entrance generation after generation, impervious to changing cultural and social norms? I think the answer is that in their clean division of characters and symbols into simple categories of 'good' and 'bad', they reflect, even manifest, the defensive process of *splitting,* to which the child's own mind leaps in recognition. The congruence of internal with external experience is very satisfying, a perfect mirror image.

Marco Iacoboni, a leading neuroscientist, has demonstrated the existence of mirror neurones in the brain that account for our ability to empathise with others. They show that we are not isolated beings, but are biologically wired and evolutionarily designed to be deeply interconnected with one another. I feel sure that sooner or later a similar explanation – a matching or mirroring phenomenon – for the endurance of the fairy tale will be found. Outside stimuli such as good and bad elements in a story, will be shown to exactly reflect such a split already structured into the cells of the brain.

How does a therapist 'split'? She has one patient, her secret favourite, who is eager, intelligent, insightful, fluent and thoughtful. The therapist looks forward to each session. She has another patient who is withholding, depressed, shabbily attired, and never makes eye contact. Naturally she does all she can to deliver the same care and attention to each, steadfastly believing all patients are equal. But what is happening in the force field of her mind? Let's suppose she is a recently qualified therapist, not yet totally confident of her abilities. She is anxious to prove herself, not only to others but also herself, so that she can take healthy pride in her work and herself.

Quite outside her awareness, her mind plays a clever trick on her. The 'good' patient becomes idealised, can do no wrong, whilst the miserable and uncommunicative patient becomes 'the bad one'. Now, no therapist would ever, ever do this on purpose; but by keeping the difficult patient in the negative category (she dreads the sessions), the positive, nay perfect, patient can be kept bright and shining in her estimation and reflect her own splendid therapeutic talents. The purpose of the mind's game is to keep the 'good', therapist-sustaining patient untarnished at all costs, by relocating (projecting if you like) any unappetising part of the work into the 'bad' patient. The defence is labouring to keep up the therapist's self-esteem at the expense of the patient who might need her most. Though she works hard with and for him at a conscious level, unconsciously he is a container for all the difficult, prestige threatening parts of therapeutic work she is afraid to tackle and at which she dreads failing.

In fact, she is too enslaved by her idealisation of the 'good' patient to be of any real use to him, and the 'bad' patient is experienced as practically untreatable when in fact he may have much to teach her if only she could perceive him accurately, devoid of her projections. To do this she would need the courage to accept her self-doubt, rendering the splitting redundant.

It's easy to observe splitting in a child that loves his mother. When she tucks him up in bed and kisses him goodnight, she is the saintly mummy, perfect in every way. When in the day she's cross and punishing, or when she clearly prefers to be with Dad and packs Junior off to bed, she becomes the witch mother who deserves to have her head cut off at the very least. If that happened though, he would have no ideal mother to keep him safe and loved. What to do?

A toddler will often invent two distinct mothers, a good one and a bad one. Sometimes they even have two dolls, or rabbits, or pairs of shoes whom, in their play, they address. For example: "You Naughty Shoes, you pinch me, I hate you," versus "You squidgy Soft Shoes I watch the telly in, I love you". (Mum knows both pairs fit perfectly). By keeping people or items in separate categories like this, depriving badness cannot possibly spoil or destroy nurturing goodness. He has a nice warm mum (or shoes) upon which to call at any time; yet still has an outlet for his anger and disappointment be it with the wicked stepmother in the fairy story, or the shoes that allegedly pinch.

Some people feel ugly, damaged inside, that something is fundamentally *wrong* with them. The portrait of themselves held in their mind is itself divided up into an assemblage of more, or less, dirty parts. The force field surrounding it, unable to maintain an acceptable coherent portrait because there isn't one, goes into overdrive. It generates a massive operation to support the picture's owner to trick the external environment into believing that the internal hated portrait is not the real one. It is only the outer public picture of perfection he shows to the world which must be seen and judged. Such patients unconsciously belittle themselves for failing to live up to the ideal they feel they must display to the world if the world is to tolerate them. These perfectionists cloak their damaged, deepest selves with impossible aspirations they can never meet, and as such are profoundly unhappy, restless people. They have quite unconsciously rejected the messed up, absolute *failure* they believe themselves to be and instead have demanded *outward perfection* of themselves as the only antidote.

This split between absolutely awful and absolutely perfect is too wide to ever heal without professional intervention. The genesis of the damage, hurt and dirt which they so hate in themselves must be traced before it can be faced and mourned rather than concealed. Only then will they be able to settle for being just a 'good enough' person.

Another clear example of splitting, thought to have a strong genetic component, is in manic depression, or what we call these days bipolar disorder. The high phase is used as a bastion against the threat of its opposite – serious, sometimes life-threatening depression. Medication aims to make the highs less high, so the depression is less low. The mood wave is thus flattened somewhat. The split has been chemically narrowed. The mature therapist has realised through long experience not to avoid mental illness when controlled in this way, and does not rule out therapy for other matters, or indeed help with making best use of the remission periods. Being bipolar, or having a controlled eating disorder, or being a 'dry alcoholic', does not mean you never have 'ordinary' anxiety attacks, or loneliness, or episodes of bereavement reawakening old bereavements; or that you should not access therapy for conflicts about your job or your relationships.

It lies beyond the scope of this chapter, but it's worth reminding ourselves that in non-psychotic individuals very serious splitting occurs most often in those traumatised in childhood, be this sexual or violent abuse, extreme neglect, multiple separations or constant diminishment by parents. The therapist needs to track down what lies behind the splitting, and handle it with supreme delicacy and patience.

Undoing

Undoing is making up magic rituals and behaviours that will ward off some anticipated or dreaded bad luck or disaster. As with all mind play though, when taken too far it can be extremely dangerous. It pays to try and identify your defences, drag them kicking and screaming out of your unconscious, so as to keep them in check!

Like splitting, *undoing* can become deadly, as in severe obsessional states, where the sufferer's life is totally disrupted by magical, seemingly crazy beliefs and unintelligible rituals. Fear and dread crowd out any happy or optimistic thought. There is no time for enjoyment because almost every minute is filled performing over and over the life-saving routines. Warding off certain Armageddon just around the corner has become the sufferer's entire *raison d'être*. Suicide is a real possibility.

One of my patients had recently separated from his wife. They were an educated, responsible couple and agreed to share custody of their young daughter – half a week each. Naturally it took some time for the ten-year-old to adjust to having two homes down the road from each other. Bedtimes were problematic. She developed 'magic' ways of making this difficult time tolerable, the time when she could not help but grow conscious of one parent's absence. She invented detailed and time-consuming rituals about washing, brushing her hair, story-telling, exact ways to kiss and cuddle the parent at whoever's home she was currently staying. Then the sheet, duvet and cuddly toy had to be arranged to an exact geometrical pattern. A centimetre's mistake would occasion tearful outbursts: "You're not getting it right!"

Sometimes the routines failed to work. If sleep did not come by the child's prescribed time there was a ceremonial procedure laid down for the summoned mum or dad, who had to arrive and behave in a certain way or sleep would forever elude her. If the ceremony were not performed to the precise requirements, it would have to be conducted all over again. For a time, exhaustion set in for the poor parents.

Rituals are also deployed to shoo away threatening impulses from within. It is possible that this little girl, who undoubtedly adored both her parents, was also very angry with them for parting and causing her pain, and wanted to punish them. This would mean losing their affection though, so better to neutralise any fury at them with potent ceremonies designed to kill off unwanted violent impulses. Perhaps these impulses arose on the occasions when, even after the first set of rituals, she couldn't sleep. Did she have to conjure up in reality whichever parent she was staying with, to prove to herself she had not destroyed them with her anger?

The fending off of feared catastrophe characterises this defence. The person comes to believe that the magic will actually work, though intellectually they know the contrary to be true. They crave a sense of safety that always escapes them. 'Undoing' is so called because the anticipated disaster, or at least *a* disaster, has almost always already happened, as with the little girl's parental divorce. The rituals, if perfectly performed and sufficiently often, might undo the catastrophe and/or prevent another.

Identification with the Aggressor

Little Johnny has a vivid imagination and loves animals, but is also frightened by some of them. We might suppose he projects his gentle and nurturing self into a lamb and his ferocity and will to dominate and control into a lion. Come bedtime he can't sleep unless the light is left on. Some nights he can't sleep even then. He doesn't want to look a complete idiot, but he's sure there is a glinty-eyed, enormous lion behind the long curtains. When he finally admits his fear, saying he can hear it breathing and making the curtain sort of swish, Mum explains that it's only the wind and anyway lions don't like living indoors. Then poor Johnny thinks it must be in the garden, just outside the window. And it has definitely come for him. No amount of assurance from his mum helps. The lion (embodying his denied and projected destructiveness) is definitely out there.

Norman, his big brother, arrives, is amazed by Johnny's timidity and sets about dragging him along the landing to the stairs, where he removes the protective gate, plonks him on the top step and orders "Now roar!" Johnny snivels, but adores his brother so is unsure what to do.

"You mean to tell me you're scared of that mangy, ancient, one eared, deaf old dear? One *real* lion roar and he'll be off to the woods, fast as his old legs can carry him. Now *roar!* ... Pathetic. Roar *louder!*"

The lion (in Johnny's head) flees in terror. He has *identified with his aggressor*, taken back into himself what he had projected, *become* his aggressor, and now he can sleep.

This defence explains why some victims of sexual or violent abuse become predators or bullies themselves, especially in a conducive environment such as a boarding school or prison, where alternative strategies or role models are not readily available. The first imperative in any environment is to survive: "if you can't beat 'em, join 'em." The abuse is usually justified to make the perpetrator feel better: "I got caned at school and it never harmed me. It was character-building, taught me how to be strong."

Transfer this phenomenon to the world stage. If a bully or bully organisation runs the country do you keep your head down, conform when you have to and wait till better times? Do you fight back and face certain death? Do you run away and hate yourself? Or do you tell yourself that at least the trains run on time, and, so long as you can fix for yourself and your family not to be bullied, you will join the power holders, especially if they have some convincing excuses for their brutality and the rewards to you and yours are considerable. To accomplish this, your mind must play some clever tricks if you are to go on living with yourself. *Identification* to the rescue. Imagine a few million other minds playing the same game!

This is an extremely simplistic description of the totalitarian state. There are hundreds of other factors contributing to its success. But would it, could it, survive without the majority of citizens cooperating, becoming aggressors themselves?

Summary

In this chapter I have looked at the main defences under labels accorded them by the pre-war analysts. My hope is that seasoned therapists of whatever persuasion will not be so side-tracked by their own ideological preference, or their old training, or the latest publication about the newest theory, that they devalue or ignore these critical features arising in every therapy. I make that claim because every patient and every therapist is a human being and we all have minds run on similar principles. This means we all generate these defence/protective processes, be they the 'white lies' variety that we can afford to ignore, or the ones so out of kilter with comfortable social, sexual, or colleague interaction that they cry out for exploration in the consulting room. I reiterate here the absolute requirement that it is the pain being fended off that is more important than nailing down the identity of the dominating defence.

The defences discussed here are not all inclusive. In our consulting rooms we see many behaviours and attitudes that clearly serve defensive purposes but are not discrete and static products to be added to some academic list, as some of the older writings might suggest. Rather do defences swirl about the self-image at the centre of the mind, first one dominating then the next, or combining so subtly and swiftly that there is no time to attach a label. The more active the defences are, in whatever combination, the more that pain, dread and anxiety are threatening to appear. The sole aim of the patient's mental force field is to make those horrors vanish at whatever cost. The therapist's aim is to gently and supportively tease them into consciousness for shared investigation.

Other defences appear in the person who emotes constantly, 'lets it all hang out', but who is defending against *thinking* about their unhappiness for fear of what they might discover. The opposite defence is *intellectualisation*, where the intellect is overused to avoid being overwhelmed by feeling. 'Control freaks' are often protecting themselves from unbearable feelings of helplessness or dependency. They are all the time 'making sure', making sure they will not be left exposed in all their contemptible weakness, their inability to cope. This is often seen in people in top jobs who have acquired the desired control but who are in danger of collapsing beneath the stress of maintaining their defence.

A hugely important defence, rarely spoken of, is *collusion*, especially between therapist and patient. An example was given in the first chapter, of the analyst and patient who 'agreed' (*colluded*) to award each other a very high regard, then used mutual *intellectualisation* (endless discussion of irrelevant dreams) to defend against facing the failure of the therapy. Because collusion is always an unconscious agreement to avoid shared pain, it is inimical to any treatment. A supervisor's role in this situation is vital if the enterprise is not to flounder, providing of course the therapist does not seduce the supervisor into entering the collusion. Even supervisors are not perfect, free from the defensive/protective forces within *their* minds!

Conclusion to Chapters Three and Four

Chapter three looked at the phenomenon of play in general terms, showing its importance in almost every human endeavour – so distant from the popular notion of play as 'larking about'. Chapter four turned inward, to see how the mind itself plays with our person, manipulating our image of ourselves. Whatever the truth about our real selves, the defence's job is to convince us, even if it takes some mental jiggery pokery – lying – that we can still function successfully in the societal world as well as co-exist with ourselves in our internal, private one.

As with the human mental defence, play of itself is neither childish nor mature, sick nor healthy, good nor bad. Like the unconscious that knows no morals, ethics, no time even, it just *is*. It is part of our survival equipment, like our aggression, our sexuality, our propensity for profound attachment, our capacity to think and reflect: it's a given. *We are a species that plays*. As with our aggressive instinct, it can be hi-jacked by our higher faculties for good or ill, to struggle toward health, happiness and the sense of an authentic self, or to lay waste to everyone and everything that has disappointed us. Play can be harnessed by us for cruel purposes – a weapon, a manipulation, but that is not its intrinsic nature, which is neutral.

If we could help our patients to understand that play is not just frittering away time or indulging ourselves, and that aggression is not just bashing people, then they could cast away their value-laden assumptions and begin to look at these notions afresh. Much unnecessary guilt would be alleviated and the forces of healing released from their prison of disapproval. Play is a compelling force within us that needs to be constructively channelled, no less than aggression. With either, we can make love or make war, create or destroy. If we provide for our patients a physical, mental, and verbal play space with safe boundaries round it, they will teach us, if we have the patience to watch, listen and play *with* them, what it is that truly ails them. Indeed, through discovering an ability to play, and seizing the right to be justifiably angry, many will gradually heal themselves if we can resist the temptation to rush in and do it for them.

Suggested reading:

Burgo, J. (2012). *Why do I do that? – Psychological Defense Mechanisms and the hidden ways they shape our lives.* Chapel Hill NC: New Rise Press.

Freud, A. (1966). *The Ego and the Mechanisms of Defence.* London: Hogarth Press and The Institute of Psycho-Analysis (6th impression).

Harris Williams, M. (2010). *A Meltzer Reader: Selections from the writings of Donald Meltzer.* London: Karnac (The Harris Meltzer Trust Series).

Iacononi, M. (2009). *Mirroring people: The science of Empathy and how we connect with others.* New York: Picador, Farrar Straus and Giroux.

Storr, A. (1974). *The Integrity of the Personality.* Harmondsworth: Penguin.

CHAPTER FIVE

THE SELF REVOLUTION: PERSONALITY DISORDERS

Until the 1970s mental health provision in the UK was dominated by NHS psychiatry on the one hand, and private psychoanalytic treatment on the other, two completely different worlds. Doctors had to rely on a few crude and frequently addictive drugs, electroconvulsive therapy and hospitalisation. Meanwhile Freudian, Jungian and Kleinian analysts, bunkered in their various institutes, continued their internecine rivalries, oblivious to the seismic theoretical upheaval approaching.

In the world beyond esoteric institutes, universities and psychiatric teaching hospitals, anxiety and restlessness among more junior mental health professionals was increasing. Social workers, nurses, probation officers, priests and educational welfare officers were becoming more and more frustrated by the chasm between specialist medical help – be this NHS or private – and the restricted services they themselves were allowed to offer. A whole workforce, eager to help, felt they were being wasted. What about the vast numbers of really troubled people who nevertheless were not technically ill and who distrusted 'mumbo jumbo' psychoanalysis even if they could afford it? What about all those people, desperately unhappy, but not so seriously at risk they required ECT! Clearly a new type of non-medical service was needed to breach the gap.

As time went on the demand for further training grew noisier. These non-medical professionals wanted to change from *doing* things for and to their clients, to *being* with them in a listening confidential relationship where the goal was helping them to help themselves through constructive introspection.

This idea spread rapidly across the helping professions and an inclusive term had to be found to describe it, taking care not to step on any medical or psychoanalytic toes. We now take the title 'counsellor' for granted, but many workers had to fight hard to get their new job title recognised. I, myself, did counselling in a huge polytechnic for a year or two as 'the welfare officer', before a name change was agreed! Strange now to think of counselling as 'new-fangled', but it was viewed with much suspicion back then, and many employing authorities feared 'counselling' would mean inferior psychiatry or analysis. Many doctors felt threatened or insulted at first and declined to co-operate with what they saw as an amateur army of do-gooders.

Books, gurus and workshop leaders, both analytic and Rogerian, increasingly crossed the Atlantic to inspire and coach the new, keen British practitioners. Many indigenous analysts and psychiatrists, watching this encroaching movement with suspicion and fear at first, began to examine their own theories and practises and to cast their eyes across the water to the United States where the psychoanalytic community seemed to be rethinking everything that had formerly been unquestioningly accepted and practised. What on earth was going on?

Around the same time an alarming – and some claimed untreatable – type of patient began to present in increasing numbers on both sides of the Atlantic. This type of patient was medically classed as *narcissistic personality* or *personality disorder*. Conventional treatments, both medical and analytic, failed, resulting in much self-doubt among the specialists. Were the existing approaches too narrow, too constrained by ideological orthodoxy? Or was medicine just too ignorant about the true nature of these people? Perhaps they had arrived on the scene in response to the new availability of help and concentrated attention from these counselling folk? They were certainly hoovering it up in large quantities. Had they simply lurked in corners before, disrupting their environment and themselves, but not realising their disturbance? Or had this sort of person been bred by an increasingly complex, permissive society, where quick gratification and 'doing your own thing' was starting to be seen as a right? Were we, as a society, in danger of attaching psychiatric labels to people, pathologising them, when it was our lax, too-much-freedom-too-soon culture that was sick?

Let us fast-forward now to the twenty-first century. Immersed in consumerism – drones delivering to your door ten minutes after you order; social media affording instant world access; technology churning out new gadgets faster than you can learn how to use them – is it any wonder the whole culture is obsessed with immediate gratification of every whim? Bombarded with ever more tantalising goods with which to distract oneself, or make oneself look important and desirable, where is the time or place for the personality to maintain its stability, recharge its batteries? When or where can the natural world be wondered at and absorbed, or the mind allowed to turn inward and think through its own ideas and choices without outside interference and the demand to become at least popular, and preferably celebrated – which increasingly seems to mean famous for just being famous? If the culture itself is narcissistic, is it surprising that this diagnosis in individuals is increasingly common?

As ever, American universities began pouring out challenging new psychoanalytic theories concerning these patients, and, as ever, the contents of their papers and journals crossed the water and percolated through to our own analytic establishment, before trickling down to the more receptive and well-established among the new breed of counsellors. Many counsellors, though, were still struggling to acquire quality training and supervision in their own locality, still being met with resistance and denied recognition. Neither academically funded, nor research oriented, and busy with their day to day work in clinics or privately in their own homes, many by-passed the new thinking and the exciting arguments that were currently splitting the analytic world down the middle. Some, sadly, have never caught up to this day and have lost the opportunity to incorporate Self philosophy, theory and practice into their existing mode of working.

As far back as the 1960s in Britain, Donald Winnicott's writings helped build the foundations of the new ideas about how the Self is formed, though the term *Self* with a capital 'S' would not be coined for some years yet. He concentrated on very early development indeed, the moment to moment interactions between mother and infant from birth onward. It was to this period that the new USA Self Psychologists (as they would one day style themselves) would turn, in trying to unearth causative factors of personality disorder and narcissistic disturbance in the adult. In chapter seven I will discuss some of Winnicott's work in this area, because of its singularity and relevance to all therapeutic schools.

How can senior therapists use this upheaval in analytic thinking today, especially those therapists who were trained before the new ideas took root in training programmes? Alas, trainers are often the last people to adapt to new changes, suspicious of anything that might threaten their well-established ideological views. I am not here suggesting that practitioners and trainers should abandon their stance and convert to a new ideology altogether, that of Self Psychology. No, but I do hope experienced therapists and trainers will find a way to look at their patients, trainees and supervisees in this Self Psychological *light*, along with their habitual ways of processing what happens in the consulting room. I will discuss the core concepts of the new psychology in the next chapter.

Many UK counsellors are already practising in a more Self Psychological way than they perhaps realise, because these early radical ideas have now been exhaustively debated and parts of the language assimilated into the counselling vernacular. On both sides of the Atlantic the various factions within the movement have at last more or less settled into their respective ideological camps. While the revolution waged, opposing groups tried to sort out their differences and similarities through conferences, learned papers, books, workshops and lectures. In fits and starts some of these ways of thinking about patients' very early development filtered down to the less academic counselling world. In the process some of it got badly distorted or oversimplified.

The mature Mary Smith therapist knows she needs to be doing what she's doing consciously, with deliberation, not because she has imbibed something she only half understands from the current therapy climate. As potent non-faddish ideas come onstream, she familiarises herself with them, taking what is meaningful to her way of doing therapy and jettisoning the rest. She is wise enough to pick and choose and not enrol in any school of thought that is going to stop her thinking for herself.

I will try to elucidate the central concepts of the new psychology and decipher the somewhat complicated, tongue-twisting terminology. A new discipline always struggles to birth a fresh, distinctive language for itself, but sadly this deters many busy practitioners from exploring its demanding literature. I will also look at the main opposing factions within this still advancing movement, what theoretical position they espouse, and how, at least in some quarters, the ideological split has been resolved.

What is a Personality Disorder?

Before I discuss this though, I should explain my own understanding of what *personality disorder* and *narcissistic personality* actually mean. The classification of these disorders constantly changes. For example, we are now to say *complex needs* rather than personality disorder. Well, I'm sorry, but I have complex needs and I am sure you do too, reader. This politically correct term tells us nothing of import so I am going to stick to the old one in this text.

First, a caveat. Diagnosis can be abused. It represents a value judgement: these people deviate from what is considered the social norm and so engender in their therapists disapproval, fear, awe, or a dogged determination to 'cure' against all the odds. Sometimes there is even a sneaking admiration for their tactics! However, it must be remembered that patients can be a little or a lot disordered, and can become more or less disordered under different circumstances. So caution about diagnosis is essential.

Once you label someone as narcissistic or personality disordered you may be setting them on an unchangeable psychiatric career path, the history of which will affect all future treatment plans and create all manner of prejudice amongst helpers, however well intentioned. These, after all, are what we in the trade commonly refer to as 'heart sink' patients. These negative connotations arise from our repeated failures or relative failures with such people. The fear of another failure should be faced and shared at clinical and referral meetings, not swept under the carpet.

Types of Personality Disorder

First a simple diagram to schematise the diagnostic picture. See fig 1.

FIGURE 1: PERSONALITY DISORDERS	
1. Behavioural Personality Disorders:	More social services/courts rather than GP surgery or psychotherapy
2. Borderline Personality Disorders: *(abandoned psychiatric category in the USA)*	Bipolar Schizoid
3. Narcissistic Personality Disorders:	Oral Envious Grandiose Psychopathic

Like the rest of us, these patients are unique individuals as well as being similar to one another in significant ways. Therefore the vignettes of actual cases I shall shortly describe are merely samples, not to be used as a template for any diagnoses you may be required to make.

The main difference between narcissistic and other personality disorders is one of emphasis. The narcissistic disorder is where the narcissistic aspects of the personality override all the others. All of these categories have pronounced self-preoccupation among their 'symptoms', but the bipolar and schizoid type also has a distinct leaning toward the pre-breakdown personality of these two major illnesses. The bipolar has mood swings, sometimes from moment to moment, other times in longer sequences. The schizoid is more introverted and given to fantasising about himself. He deploys a lot of projections and splitting. His perceptions are so distorted by these defences that an observer will say he is not thinking straight.

Back to the diagram. The *oral* type of narcissism shows itself in a greed for emotional supplies, a craving or demand that others should provide love, nurturance, admiration, whatever is required for the sufferer to feel whole again; for there are insufficient supplies within. The *envious* narcissist hates others who possess what he lacks: he must spoil, destroy, attack or steal qualities in the emotionally whole person who has no right to flaunt the inner security for which the narcissist so unconsciously longs. Spite and revenge are his natural territory.

The *grandiose* narcissist is a strutter, a boaster, a beautiful specimen of all that is desirable in a human. It is all a façade of course: inside he is empty, lonely and the very opposite of grand. He is addicted to the adoration of the external world to compensate for the inner void. Without an audience he will psychically wither and die.

The *psychopath* is without conscience. One day we will know if this is a neurobiochemical deficiency of some kind, a structural or developmental problem of the brain, or some extreme version of the very early interpersonal deprivation of which the Self Psychologists write. Maybe it will turn out to be a combination of factors. One thing is certain. Not a shred of genuine guilt or remorse can be found in this person.

Where there is no guilt there is arguably no treatment. How do you make an Alliance with someone unable to feel loyalty, trust, commitment (though he can act as if he can feel this way, to gain his ends)? Help is neither wanted nor sought. He may be a genius or stupid, but always he is dangerous. The meeting of his need to occupy the source of all satisfaction is ruthlessly pursued. Satiation could mean the seizure of power, sex, money, political influence, business success; it would certainly involve murder or rape if that is his taste. The creative psychopath can masquerade as a charismatic leader in a religious, political, business or psychiatric community, and, worryingly, can command total adoration – though sometimes of course he is merely(!) a narcissistic personality.

Behavioural personality disorders are included in the diagram because they cause society one heck of a problem but don't often come into contact with psychotherapists. Social services and the courts deal with them on the whole, as they cannot control their impulses. Drink and drugs feature prominently because delayed satisfaction is intolerable. They are always in trouble with the law (unlike the manipulative type of personality disordered person who appears self-restrained, even a helpless victim, although this is a stratagem to gain emotional supplies).

Profile of a Personality Disorder

Personality disorder is a diagnosis of what the patient *is*, not what he *has*, such as in cases of an eating disorder, panic attacks or depression.

Most of us enjoy a relatively well personality most of the time. We possess a fairly constant set of idiosyncratic characteristics and adaptational defences to keep us going. When occasionally these defences fail us, under excessive internal or external pressure, we become ill, or dysfunctional, 'not ourselves'. This is recognised by our family and friends and maybe the GP. Attention is given, allowances made and mostly we eventually return to our usual selves. For the personality disordered person it is their usual self that is the problem! Like other folk, they come to therapists with depression or anxiety or existential questions about their unhappiness; rarely do they come asking for help with their personality disorder. By the time the greater problem underlying the presenting one is realised, the therapist may have committed herself to a course of conventional therapy inadequate to the deeper need of the patient.

At the start the therapist may feel she is on familiar ground. The personality disorder only comes to light when a promising Alliance dramatically shatters, or the patient reacts with pique or outright anger to an intervention the therapist had felt was insightful and helpful. Is she being incompetent, badly paced, tactless, or plain wrong? This sudden lack of confidence in an otherwise good and experienced therapist is frequently a warning sign of a disordered personality. (This is not to deny that sometimes she can be downright wrong!)

These disordered people come in all shapes and sizes. They may be bright or dim, charming and likeable at first, or horrid and nasty from the beginning. So what do they all have in common? Usually the following:

1. A fat file. If you suspect this diagnosis, always go to the notes. There is frequently a long history of medical, social, employment and relationship problems. Usually many experts have been consulted and sacked. None of them appear to agree on the precise diagnosis.

2. In and out of the consulting room the person *acts* and *reacts* rather than pausing to think through what is said and done to him. The enduring of any mental pain in order to gain long-term knowledge of himself is out of the question. He is impulsive, unless of course he is impersonating the perfect acquiescent patient in order to gain favour. Therapy may seem to be going well until you offend the patient with some unpalatable observation. Before you know it, a complaint is being lodged, or he leaves in a huff or just inexplicably disappears. If there is unpleasantness it is all your fault and nothing to do with him.

3. He can be *powerful* and *persuasive*. He can make you feel the best therapist in the world, or the worst. He can make you doubt your sanity just as you were about to doubt his. He will find your Achilles heel and exploit it mercilessly. There is nothing calculated and therefore evil about this: he does it as naturally as breathing. It is how he lives, day to day.

4. He cannot tolerate *frustration* or *disappointment* but soaks up empathy and reassurance like a sponge. However gently he is confronted with some unflattering truth about himself, he will fly into a rage, dismiss it, change the subject, persuade you that you are wrong. Therapy has to be on his terms, no matter what he has officially agreed to. He is an expert at making you (and others) provide what he thinks he needs and may God help you if you fail. And if you do provide what he thinks he needs, you will fail anyway, unless you can get him to see and understand why he needs it so badly. There's no point in just joining the ranks of his other emotional suppliers.

5. He is *seductive* and *manipulative*. While his needs are met he seems just like anyone else in trouble. He is grateful, humble. It is only when thwarted that his truer colours appear. The diagnosis is almost always missed in the early stages. He does genuinely suffer and arouses compassion like any other patient. Yet in a GP surgery setting he can divide the staff and set one off against the other without any of them realising they are being 'played'. Again this is automatic rather than cunningly planned at a conscious

level. The disordered person is deploying the splitting defence mechanism described in chapter four.

6. He does not *learn from experience*. He blames others for his pain, self justifies, often turns to vengeful litigation or protracted argument to 'prove' he is right. Insight is unbearable as it offends his picture of himself. Because he is never wrong the motivation to change is virtually absent: it is others who must change. All he needs is to find the perfect environment, the right sort of people; but they all turn out to be similarly disappointing. His subsequent depression is very real.

7. He is *self-oriented*, though he may come over as the soul of altruism, a real philanthropist you can't help but admire. But he is doing it in order to be seen and loved, and to foster an image of himself that he too can love and admire. Another guise is the narcissist who seems very noble in his pronounced self-criticism and humility, such that everyone gathers round to relieve his suffering and reassure him of his acceptability, no matter what awful deeds he has done.

8. He is totally *believable* when first encountered, which is why therapists so often fail to recognise his true nature. Lying, or at least twisting the truth, to suit his own ends is easy and guilt free, for his urgent priority is the acquisition of the emotional supplies that reassure him he is still king of his internal castle. For him, that life-saving end will always justify any means. He may make a convincing Alliance early on, but in fact it is an Alliance of expedience. It is conditional upon the therapist delivering *unconditional* devotion to his narcissistic aims.

It is important to stress that personality disordered patients are not simply nasty people. They suffer horribly from an inner desolation they constantly try to assuage. When they fail they can become quite ill and even suicidal. They are as deserving of compassion, even when at their most manipulative, as anyone else.

Some Examples of Personality Disorder
Patrick
Patrick's GP referred him to me for private therapy after he suffered panic attacks in the street and was more than once rescued by a member of the public, ending up in A&E.

He was a small, agitated, sweating man of around forty, with huge, damp brown eyes, rather like a puppy. He thought I would want a history (he was being a 'good boy'), and so launched into a chronological account of his life so far. He was adopted ("but that's totally irrelevant"), was a gifted carpenter/restorer of antiques ("won several prizes, worked for Lord Bloggs once"), left school as it was too boring and slow for his quick and creative mind. He had never been married but had been betrayed by several women who let him down after he gave them everything they could possibly want. His kind of love was intense and spiritual. He was loyal, devoted, but they never seemed to compute this, always took advantage.

The current crisis concerned a woman with whom he had cohabited for five years. She had just last week walked out on him and gone to her family in Ireland. "I couldn't believe it! I had given her a home, money, clothes, let her have her silly job, making cloth toys. The house was like a factory, a real mess…"

I asked what reason she had given for leaving. Incredulous, both angry and tearful, he said that she'd called him bossy and possessive and a control freak.

Rather than examine this judgement for any grain of truth, he insisted I help get her back. She loved him really, but she had these moods when she would rebel for the sake of rebelling. But this time she had taken all her toys and sewing kit with her. What should he do?

There was no way he would talk about anything else other than how to make her return. I was starting to see his panic attacks as manifestations of an irresolvable conflict. He was so angry at her unfair desertion that he could kill her, but at the same time he wanted to beg, plead, abase himself before her, anything to make her come back. Then he would remember she was like all the others who had let him down and his rage would return, followed almost instantly by a preparedness to crawl on his knees if required. Neither solution was going to work. Begging was anathema to his self-respect, and he had not done anything wrong, anything to be sorry for. Destroying her on the other hand would bring sweet revenge, but would not fetch her home.

I had not yet detected (easy to be wise after the event!) that it wasn't the woman herself that counted here, but her function as the preventer of his personality fragmentation. She was an integral part of his self-image, an extension of him, not a person in her own right; so that without her was indeed a broken man.

He aroused so much pity in me that I decided to go along with him for a while and leave the deeper work for later, when he could finally admit she had left for good. He wanted to write a letter (she appreciated traditional things like beautiful vellum). He discussed at great length what he should say. I helped him tone down his self-justification and his subtle but pointed blaming of her, and acknowledge some of his part in the relationship failure. Under some duress he agreed to ask her for a parley on neutral territory, a step at a time. He preferred a quick reconciliation, but I convinced him such a demand would be counterproductive. I sensed this was all useless, but he was not going to calm down until every stone had been turned.

To my astonishment she agreed, and two or three more meetings were arranged over the next few weeks. Patrick was over the moon: soon she would be back!

Meanwhile I encouraged him to look inside himself if he wanted to avoid a re-run of this disaster. Yes, yes he enthused, this therapy thing was just great. He would tell me anything I asked. Let's go faster. Fast as we can.

He had looked up his original parents, now dead. They had been society people ("toffs") and his birth was the result of some scandal or other. He avoided his adoptive parents ("decent folk but uncultured, we have nothing in common"). He had no close friends, was scornful of pubs, films, pop music, and preferred to read philosophy or watch documentaries on television. Here was a proud man defending his inability to make contact with people by dismissing them as unworthy. Whereas I had become worryingly idealised. I understood him like no one else. His panic attacks had gone thanks to my help with the letter and advice about conducting the meetings with his ex. I was nothing short of a miracle worker. He was now "willing to co-operate" about anything I wanted to know.

We settled down into what felt like conventional therapy though I always had this uncomfortable feeling he was trying to please rather than truly seeking self-knowledge. He was particularly euphoric when his ex agreed to a long weekend at their home, what she called a 'trial reunion'.

Thing were progressing so well I ran a trial of my own. We had been talking about the adoption again. Ever so delicately, I put to him that he seemed to have a need to be more sophisticated, enlightened, cultured, gifted than those around him. Did he think there might be any link between that need and his being adopted? He looked shocked, paused, then said airily, "Yes, yes you're onto something as usual. Clever lady. Time's up now, so we'll come back to it next week. I look forward to it." In fact there were seven minutes left.

I never saw him again. In the meantime he had run up a month's debt on his fees. He claimed that the owner of the manor house where he was working was being audited and so his salary would not be released till the end of the following month. He had four more sessions booked in with me at which point we were due to review bookings. I wrote to remind him of these dates and said I hoped to see him. I enclosed a bill. No reply.

I phoned and wrote once more, to no avail. I then wrote to say the matter would be brought to the small claims court if payment was not forthcoming. No reply. The four booked weeks had now gone by. I applied to the small claims court which found in my favour and required him to pay me. He ignored the court, who then contacted him again threatening him with bailiffs if he refused to reply. Eventually bailiffs went in and he had to pay up to prevent them taking his television. He refused to address the cheque to me, insisting on paying the court. He then wrote to the court saying he should be compensated for my breaking of confidentiality in bringing the case. The court declined to reply.

Case summary

I was the hated, rich "irrelevant" mother who put him up for adoption, but who he longed to come through for him nonetheless – only so long as he could stay top dog of course. My offers of insightful comments were interpreted as me winning over him. He tolerated this and paid my bills as long as I helped get his woman back. During the last few weeks when it looked as if she would indeed return, the payments ceased. Then came the comment about his need for superiority. This proved an insult too far.

Patrick had re-enacted his early trauma through first depending on me utterly, then hating me for demanding payment for mother love which ought to be free. This was total rejection in his book. I had become a traitor and controller like all his other women. I am certain now that he lied about his women, about who did the dirty on whom, who was the real controller. He used denial and grandiosity as a massive defence against the humiliating experience of their and his birth mother's original abandonment.

Although I was misused and cheated, I feel sorry for Patrick because I doubt he will ever be able to tolerate self-examination. He will go on collecting and losing women who will eventually tire of his insatiable need. He will endlessly believe himself let down and abandoned, alone in a cruel universe of inferior, unfeeling people.

I also feel I was right to make him face the consequences of his behaviour. This was not so much about money. I wished rather to demonstrate that people on the receiving end of personality disordered behaviour have a right to be protected.

Tamsin

Tamsin was a thirty-year-old trainee therapist on a new and, to my mind, rather inadequate course. But at first she seemed too apathetic to do anything about it. Her therapy with me seemed an equally dreary option, as did her recent marriage which she said was a mistake, but at least she had a roof over head and food in her belly, thanks to her rather boring husband. Suicide always hovered at the back of her mind but she simply couldn't be bothered: even death seemed pointless.

It was more than a year before her depression began to lift. At least she made some efforts around that time, despite claiming that her life was still as pointless as ever. She experimented with drugs and soon tired of them. She had multiple bodily complaints which I suspected were psychogenic and these worsened with alcohol or drugs. She then tried having affairs with "the weirdest people I can find" to stimulate or feed "my dried out soul". They soon palled and she turned to literature and music. It had to be the most *avant garde*. After just a few weeks she pronounced that Art was nothing but a world of phonies and she wanted nothing to do with it.

However, Tamsin was very intelligent and would scour her inner world as relentlessly as she poked and prodded at the inadequate external world in which she felt forced to live. To cut a long therapy short, she eventually improved. Having read her extraordinary course essays and witnessed the clarity and depth of her thought once the depression lifted, I expressed my faith in her abilities and encouraged her to apply for a better training. This she did, and graduated with honours. We worked on the meaning of her earlier promiscuity and examined afresh the disillusion with her marriage, which then significantly improved. She found new delight in certain Victorian novelists that before she had treated with contempt before even opening the first page. She developed an interest in the countryside and wildlife, taking long walks with her naturalist husband.

After seven years, the time for parting approached. She found this impossible to cope with, knowing she was ready to leave and proud of it, yet hating me for 'throwing her out'. She refused to be rejected (as she saw it) and relapsed into a near psychotic state. A sophisticated psychological thinker herself, she challenged me over all manner of theory that I hadn't but should have used in our work; how sloppy and inelegant my plain English had been in the sessions. Why hadn't I deployed the latest Object Relations terminology as exemplified by this and that new writer? Why was I so out of date? She accused me of projecting my own faults onto her and analysed my character mercilessly, claiming it was I who was perilously close to psychosis.

I attempted to show her how she was using these attacks on me as a defence against her own fears of leaving. If she could prove me inadequate then she could take all the credit for her improvement herself and be enabled to go: she would no longer have a use for me. Would it not be better though, to permit herself to feel some gratitude, even loss, despite my real imperfections? For then we could disengage gradually, allowing her time to internalise the good aspects of me and carry them with her into the future alongside her own considerable psychological achievements.

The more I interpreted, and the more I declined to wilt beneath her withering review of our years together, the nearer to illness she became. (Meanwhile I was having a pretty bad time myself. There were occasions when I felt quite uncertain of myself, really frightened after the sessions. I took to keeping my next slot of the day free to recover). She was not going to give up until I admitted I was fraudulent and useless to her. She went so far as to say she believed that after seven years she had surpassed me in learning and technique. If I was as good a therapist as I thought I was, I would have the grace to admit it!

I have never experienced a completely satisfactory ending with a personality disordered patient, but I always strive to make it as bearable as possible for us both. I suggested that if she thought we were now of colleague status, perhaps we should have a final session where we eliminate the patient/therapist divide (her envy over this was palpable in the last months). We could sit back as if we were actual colleagues, and discuss the progress and process of this therapy as if we were to write a paper on it, or present it at a conference. It may have been a cop-out on my part, but this suggestion was accepted after some suspicious mutterings. Our last session gave her the equal status to perform in an adult professional way. Her rage and incipient paranoia, and her projection of her own professional doubts onto me vanished. We had a most interesting intellectual discussion in which I believe she secretly reclaimed some of the brighter memories of our work together. She said she had enjoyed the session and suggested we have a few more. I declined, reluctant to collude with her wish to deny she had ever needed me, or to support any idea of hers that it was actually she who had helped *me*.

Case summary

In order to prevent further deterioration in my patient and secure a bearable ending for us both, I flattered her, played her at her own game. I deliberately fed her narcissism to keep her self-image sufficiently intact that she could leave me without feeling dismissed or having to thank me. That would be just too galling for her. In Self Psychology this deliberate 'giving in' to narcissism is a controversial issue. You must make up your own mind where you stand if you are to avoid muddle when doing therapy with these difficult but hurting people.

Harry

In the early stages of therapy I warmed to Harry, looked forward to his weekly session. He was a big athletic man, with a thunderous laugh. His job was grounds manager of a posh local estate; he knew all about game, guns, horses, fishing. He wore a lot of tweed, a waistcoat and shiny brown brogues. Before and after his sessions with me he puffed on a pipe for a few minutes, a few yards from my garden gate. He said he was always careful not to get too close and interfere with the arrival of another patient. I suspected he was keeping an eye on comings and goings, or was perhaps defying my time boundaries, refusing to be admitted or ejected according to my dictates; but I never got any further with this and he always behaved discreetly outside my home.

He knew all the local gossip, told excellent jokes, frequented all the best restaurants, dining out with anyone who was anyone in the region. I was greatly entertained but not fooled by his cabaret act. He agreed it probably covered up 'some godawful sinister secret' but wasn't prepared to elaborate. He did come clean about his childhood though: an actress mother always on tour with some "flea-bitten, second rate ragbag of a company – to hear her you'd think it was Hollywood". When not acting, she was drunk or depressed. Busy but silent dad was out on the farm all hours while crotchety gran, a few neighbours and a plethora of sheep dogs brought him up.

In the first year he was able to grieve over the neglect, though with much shame as well as relief. Each time he opened up, he would rapidly return to his hail-fellow-well-met defence, which for a time I decided not to tamper with, for I sensed there was little else beneath it to sustain him. He was such a lovable, extraverted guy, with dozens of friends who clearly thought the world of him. I saw him as a large glittering fish in a smallish grey pond. I thought that once his mourning was done, all would be well and he could go back to cheering up everybody around him. I was going to miss him.

How wrong can you be? He arrived late one morning, purple in the face, scowling. He sat silent for a full three minutes, his now piggy eyes glittering malevolently as they devoured the carpet. I felt quite frightened but tried not to show it. His wife of thirty years had up and left the night before, gone off with one of the servants at the big house. No explanation, nothing. He'd found out from one of the junior staff after interrogating them all.

He was late because he had been hiring a contract killer to find and shoot them! For the first time I saw this man's black, all-consuming depression. Looking at his face and posture I had no doubt at that moment that he was capable of murder. I realised I was sitting with a borderline bipolar personality disordered man in an extreme mood phase.

I was silent for a time while I gathered myself. Harry fumed and fumed then started to bash the arm of his chair, then cursed and cursed in a long, low pain-filled growl. I do not to this day remember how, but I gradually talked him down. I think that what made him reconsider was my quiet insistence that if he shot her she would have won, obtained the high moral ground, despite being the offending party. She, not he, would be the centre of this tragedy. I then painted the grim picture of him languishing in prison while their suffering was over. I didn't actually say they would be sitting on gilded thrones in heaven laughing at him, but he got the message. Suddenly he whipped out his mobile, cancelled the arrangements, but asked the person on the other end to await further instructions. It seemed he needed a bit more time to invent a worse fate for the evil pair.

It transpired that the 'moodiness' which he had asked help for was in fact an understatement. This fit of black rage, emanating from an assault on his carefully constructed and perfectly maintained self-image, showed me what his wife was almost certainly fleeing from.

Once exposed, he could not get away from me fast enough. Now the marriage was over, all he wanted was to punish the miscreants and hide away where no one could see his disgrace. He could not bear to continue seeing me. My attempt at reassurance failed to persuade him. He paid his bill and cancelled all future sessions.

Afterword

A couple of years later I saw in the local newspaper an announcement of his forthcoming wedding to a distant cousin of his employer. On the surface at least, he had recovered without my help. But for how long?

Suggested reading:

Gerhardt, S. (2015, 2nd edition). *Why Love Matters: How Affection Shapes a Baby's Brain.* London, New York: Routledge.

Phillips, A. (2007). *Winnicott,* Harmondsworth: Penguin.

CHAPTER SIX

THE SELF REVOLUTION: CORE CONCEPTS

Most experienced therapists are wise enough to try and plug the gaps in their original training while keeping abreast of new theoretical developments. So far as Self Psychology is concerned, they may not have been fortunate enough to have participated in such a specific training module, or may have been put off by the vast array of literature available, its complex language and/or its internal squabbles. I can't do justice to its ideas in a single chapter, but I hope to fillet this way of looking at human development, carve out its juicy bits and hope they might tempt you into considering whether and how you might use them to develop your own kind of therapy. I am not so much concerned about your theoretical mastery of Self Psychology as your consideration of how this *way of thinking* might inform and add to your personal work style. You don't need to be a fully fledged Self Psychologist or to abandon your existing ideological background to make use of these central ideas in your clinical work.

Self Psychology has grown out of the psychoanalytic tradition, but its philosophy can blend comfortably with other schools of counselling and psychotherapy. The fundamental departure from classical analysis is as follows.

Freud's central assumption was that under our veneer of civilisation we are driven by unruly instincts we must at all costs gratify so that we can return to a state of *quietus*, freedom from excitation and frustration – a form of peaceful death wish. All human motivation and action is based on this premise. Hence the necessity for subduing the population with law and religion, or sublimating raw instinct into sport or art, or far-off war. Of course we pay for this repression in terms of neurosis, the consequence of damming the natural expression of animal instincts.

Therefore, for Freudians, sex guilt and aggression always permeated the atmosphere in the consulting room.

The Kleinians did not focus quite so much on the individual in relation to his drives, but became more interested in how the human being was always seeking *objects,* other persons who could act as recipients for his projections or who could supply mental content to compensate for or neutralise frightening fantasies in his internal world. This theory rested on the premise that relationships with others were a life-preserving necessity. You go mad if you cannot regulate yourself by evacuating and incorporating mental content. Therefore the transference to the therapist was central to the treatment in that relations with her would illumine key relationships in the patient's past.

Kleinian consulting rooms were therefore filled with discontented infants, depositing their pain into the mother analyst, in the hope that something more positive might be returned to them, that would soothe them and make sense of their inner turbulence.

John Bowlby and the *attachment theorists* took as their central tenet the theory that all human motivation at bottom is toward survival. For this, an early attachment to a secure figure and later to a group, a place and some shared belief system, is essential for healthy growth. We cease to optimally function if these attachments are broken for a significant period.

The ghost of separation and catastrophic loss always haunted the consulting room.

The Jungians' focus was on the ultimate achievement of *individuation*, the fulfilment of all the person's potential, once neurosis and illusion were analysed and given up. Spirituality took centre stage over biology, evolution, object relations, attachments and inner drives.

Self Psychology accepts the value of all these concepts, but claims they are not the fundamental issue when trying to understand

and help suffering people. The core concept of Self Psychology is that of the *Self* (capital 'S'), and the Self's *subjective* experience of his inner and outer world. That subjective, idiosyncratic experience is his alone, not in the end available to scientific observation and measurement, not explicable by theory or logic. A unique Self is doing his learning, relating, choosing, feeling, loving, hating; so a deep understanding of the patient's Self, its development, vicissitudes, its characteristic way of expressing itself, is a vital requisite for a successful therapeutic intervention. When the sense of Self is temporarily or for long periods impaired, normal social functioning is disrupted – depression, confusion and an amalgam of defence mechanisms ensue. A 'nervous breakdown' is a serious interruption of that ongoing sense of Self we normally take for granted and rarely think about.

What is a Self?

The Self is not the same as the *Ego*, for that is originally a Freudian term which describes but one of the many selves (small 's') that combine to make up the Self of the Self Psychologists. Freud's Ego negotiates between the unconscious promptings of the unruly, pleasure seeking Id, and the demands of the Superego, i.e. the conscience. Neither does Self refer to *identity*, as that is restricted to labels, roles and life postures (career, place in family, adopted beliefs, etc.). It isn't *personality* either, as that relates to a list of the Self's characteristics but misses out the subjective aspect.

Try seeing it this way: **The Self is an individual's consciousness of his own being.** It is therefore elusive, invisible. You can only know it like the Abominable Snowman, by the footprints it leaves on the surface of the snow. It is a relationship between the 'I' and the 'Me.' If 'I', that agent of action in the world, feels okay about 'Me' (that Wyn who I see myself as), then my whole Self is in a state of *equilibrium*. This means I can forget what in ordinary language is called self-consciousness, and relax. But if I go to a party and no one talks to me, or I realise I have worn the wrong clothes, I feel doubtful about my Me and my whole Self lapses into a state of disequilibrium. My I must wake up and do something about my Me to regain and maintain my sense of okay-ness.

With me so far?

Self Psychology operates on the premise that whether we are aware of it or not, all of us are continuously *building, maintaining, repairing, or in some way expressing* our sense of Self first developed in infancy. That Self was *always there* in embryonic form, as opposed to other schools of thought where a sense of who we are is entirely dependent on mother aiding and/or allowing baby to separate from a fused and boundary-less state, all mixed up with her. Self Psychology sees such a fused state as a defence mechanism, not a normal progression. It represents a choice on baby's part to use the mother as a Self strengthener, so to speak, when he feels his emerging Self to be weak. The psychic energy for all this work is coming from a would-be Self struggling to form: the infant is not passively travelling through a natural phase. Self formation and Self maintenance is part of the human condition, a given. It is allegedly pre-programmed in us.

This is a totally different and more optimistic idea than the Freudian vision of human beings tormented by aggressive and sexual instincts on the one hand and moral strictures on the other. Freud's mother has all the power, and the baby is helpless. Self Psychology's infant psychically grabs at mother, looks to her to reflect him, to help him bring his nascent Self into being. If that Self is felt to be wavering, he will go so far as to temporarily *merge* with mother so as not to lose himself.

Some Self Psychology Vocabulary

In the rest of this chapter I will italicise terms or specific concepts deployed by Self Psychologists, which you will come across all the time in the literature.

For a Self to be *cohesed* rather than *fragmented*, its environment of people, things, places and beliefs must be *attuned* to it. In other words a Self must move in a Self maintaining world of *responsiveness*. A healthy Self can solicit and receive the right kind and quantity of responsiveness if there is sufficient provision of *Selfobjects* in the environment. These *Selfobjects* (defined in the next section) are as necessary to our *Self cohesion* as are food, drink and air to the body.

But we don't eat non-stop and we eat different things and different quantities at different times, depending on need, appetite and preference. In the same way, family, workplace, partners, friends, political or moral beliefs do not have to be ever present and active, affirming and integrating the Self all the time. Such persistent obsessing over *Selfobject functioning*, consciously or unconsciously, would indicate the existence of a narcissistic personality disorder.

What is a Selfobject?

'Object' in Self Psychology is not the same as 'object' in the sense used by psychoanalysis in general or by the object relations school in particular i.e. another person to whom you are relating – you are the subject and he is the object. A *Selfobject relationship* is not between two people: it is one person's *intrapsychic* experience *of* another person, artwork, piece of music or whatever, that is profoundly necessary to keep stable the sense of a unified Self. It also refers to the intrapsychic experience of a thing, place, person etc., which enables the Self to *express* its intrinsic nature – an outlet as well as an inlet. There is very little point to life if the Self, having fought to come into being, cannot express itself. The way a person operates through his Selfobjects is called his *idiom*.

So what evokes in me a satisfactory Selfobject experience, one that allows me to idiomatically express myself, as well as feel at home with my Me? Let me think... Well, certain landscapes – deserts, mountains, wildernesses; beautiful singing, a gripping story, total silence; anything saturated with colour; a stormy sea. And, of course, the company of certain very special people. The list goes on and on.

We are not aware of these processes as they occur. It is only when our *Self cohesion* is threatened, or chances to express our individuality are blocked, that we become uncomfortable, commence once more the search for Selfobjects, the experiencing of which gives us a repaired feeling – 'I' is relieved to feel okay about 'Me' again.

Therapy for the Self Psychologist involves intuitively discovering (rather than asking the patient directly!) the patient's *idiom* and relating to him through it.

Let us clarify the three modes of relating involved in any, but especially the therapeutic, encounter.

First, think about your best friend. You may be using her to meet some specific, entirely private need to firm up your sense of Self. She is not the Selfobject experience herself, but she is necessary for it to happen. Technically then, your friendship with her is a *Self/selfobject relationship*.

You will almost certainly have a transference relationship to her in the traditional analytic sense, as well. This is the second modality. She may provide for you the mothering you never had, or represent a loved sister who died young, or enact the anger at injustice you were conditioned not to express as you grew up. Doubtless you represent something similar for her too. This old style 'object relationship' is *between* you and benefits you both, rather than one of you primarily using the other to give you a quite separate internal experience. Of course these two types of relating – traditional 'object' and Self Psychological Selfobject relating – can be intertwined, as one does tend to encourage the other.

Thirdly, there is the so-called 'real' relationship between you. Perceptions are not distorted, there is no hidden agenda and you are both there out of simple choice and presumably for enjoyment. This begs the question: what *is* reality anyway? Does it exist or is it all subjective, phenomenological? Thank goodness such questions are beyond the remit I have set myself for this book! This ordinary third dimension in friendships is a mirror to the Alliance in therapy.

It is essential to be clear about the difference between the three modalities. In the therapeutic encounter the Self Psychologist has no conscious desire to gain emotional advantage for herself, rather does she passively wait to uncover what the patient might need to solicit from her in these three ways. She allows space and time for the patient to *use* her in whatever way he wishes. The patient's Selfobject functioning – the manner in, and purpose for which, he *uses* the therapist – shows the therapist his, the patient's, *idiom*, through which the therapist will funnel her interventions. This leads to a genuine intimacy between the couple which is much, much more than being kind, patient and tolerant. This intimacy is the product of the therapist's *accurate empathy*, which has similarities to, but is not the same as, Rogerian empathy.

What is Accurate Empathy?

The Self Psychologist lets the patient tell his own detailed story rather than require he structure his rambling productions into a comprehensible narrative. At this early stage she is observing and learning how the patient makes use of her, so that she can meet his Selfobject needs sufficient to make him feel validated, understood, and *cohesed*. Inevitably the therapist will fail to meet every nuanced need and it is in this area of failure that therapeutic work can start.

This *accurate empathy* is not the treatment itself, as in the humanistic school, but is a method of data collection. Watching, waiting, and holding off from intruding allows the patient to show the therapist much about his sense of his Self, where that Self is *attuned* to its environment, and where it is not. Having thus accumulated her data she can choose whether, when, and how to meet or interpret those needs that are embedded in all that he is recounting.

There are degrees of empathy and *accurate empathy* is at the extreme end. Imagine that your patient's dog, to whom he was devoted, his only friend, has died. As a compassionate human being you will feel sorry and say so. As his therapist who knows him well and probably has warm feelings toward him, you will make the effort to imagine his pain, try to put yourself in his shoes so as to show you understand. In so doing you will probably imagine your own dog dying (assuming you are a dog lover) and get closer to his pain than would a stranger. As a Self Psychologist however, your own dog dying is irrelevant. You know what he is feeling through your knowledge of his *idiom*, his absolutely unique way of making use of the world, and of his dog. This is more than just the pain of loss. The animal's death has meaning in terms of what it does to the patient's sense of *Self cohesion* and the degree to which it *fragments* his Self.

The therapist monitors her own Self functioning in the consulting room too, and notes any jolts to her *Self equilibrium* caused by the patient. The consulting room constitutes what system theorists would define as an *interpersonal social system*, within which couple dynamics occur. The Self Psychologists regard these dynamics as *intersubjective*. The couple do not simply talk to one another, exchange information, feelings and opinions. The therapist's internal world mingles with the patient's, yielding up much data for analysis by both, though it is devoutly to be hoped that the therapist is further along the path of self-knowledge than her patient. She knows when to speak of her subjective thoughts and feelings and when to keep quiet and bank them as valuable information that helps her play with hypotheses about what is 'really' going on for the patient.

Otto Kernberg and Heinz Kohut

As many readers will be aware, the two giants of Self Psychology are Otto Kernberg and Heinz Kohut. They strongly disagreed over treatment methods for many years and each one's ideas and writings spawned a band of loyal and vocal followers. It is an oversimplification, but it is nonetheless fair to say, Kohut, in his dedication to *accurate empathy*, championed methods that leaned toward the humanistic view (though Carl Rogers was not comfortable with Self Psychology) whilst Kernberg was reluctant to abandon his object relations background and preferred a more interpretive, challenging approach to the patient. Kohut was deliberately supportive of the patient's Self needs whereas Kernberg kept neutral so as to better observe the patient's Self ruptures and point out to him the unprofitable defences he used to counter them.

Accusations were made that Kohut was too 'soft', failed to make personality disordered patients face and take responsibility for the havoc they created; whilst Kernberg was too 'hard', so emotionally distant and preoccupied with the aggressive and libidinal drives that he failed to meet even the basic Self needs of the patient.

The essence of the debate

Kohut assumed that a narcissistic personality suffers from developmental arrest. He is stuck at a very early phase of Self formation when the (usually) maternal environment failed to provide sufficient Selfobject experiences at the right time. As an adult his infantile Self needs are still driving him to make up for the love and attention he lacked from the start. Kernberg felt this ignored the aggressive drives and that excessive narcissism in the adult is a pathological grandiose defence mechanism (acting big to avoid feeling small) rather than the result of a developmental deficit.

Accordingly, Kohutian methods concentrated on making good the shortfall, identifying missed needs and meeting them, so that the patient could grow himself up from a corrected base; whilst Kernberg advocated the educating of the narcissist about the meaning of his defences as they occurred, especially in relation to the therapist, so they could eventually be changed for more mature interpersonal strategies.

Followers on each side pointed out the shortcomings of the other. It was alleged that Kohutians fed the narcissists what they wanted to hear and thus increased the pathology. Kernbergians so offended narcissistic patients with their challenging interpretations that they either elaborated their defences to counter the assault or left treatment.

The Relational Perspective

At last a peacemaker arrived, in the form of Stephen A. Mitchell. His major conceptual contribution to the therapy field was the combining of Kohut's and Kernberg's treatment methods, seeing and evaluating risks and benefits in both. He called his synthesis of formerly opposing ideas *Relational Analysis*.

He helped establish a curriculum in *Relational Psychoanalysis* at New York University. He was also the founding editor of the journal *Psychoanalytic Dialogues*, which invited articles and opinion from analysts of disparate schools. At the turn of the twenty-first century, he helped found the International Association for Relational Psychoanalysis and would have served as its first president but for his untimely death in 2000 in his early fifties.

Although there is a specific Association for Relational Analysis, this reconciliation of opposing theories is taking root in simpler form in many other therapeutic disciplines. Whatever school of thought you belong to as a therapist, and whatever techniques you use, a productive way of working is to identify and selectively meet the patient's current Self needs with one hand, while judiciously challenging his entrenched defences with the other. One might say you are boosting his confidence, thus strengthening his ability to withstand subsequent 'attacks' on his self-esteem, as represented by your necessary interpretations of his behaviour and motives. The idea is to keep the 'hard' and the 'soft' in balance.

Alas, it has to be said that 'relational' therapy has caught on to such a degree that in some circles the term is used simply because it is fashionable. A more benevolent view is that its meaning has been genuinely misconstrued. 'Relational' does not mean kind, patient, respectful and warm, though of course all therapists should possess those traits. To qualify as relational therapy or a relational intervention, it has to spring from the core construct of the *self-maintaining Self* and the subsidiary concepts above, that arose out of Self Psychology and are still being refined.

We have seen how the relational therapist selectively gratifies unmet infantile needs while drawing her patient's attention to them. We have also looked at the importance of defence mechanisms (chapter four) and how these require challenging. There exists a third area he should be shown, but all too often the therapist fails to notice it. This is when the patient unwittingly *re-enacts* with the therapist some unhealthy interplay he once had – indeed may still have – with an important figure. He does not talk about it, just falls into it, a habitual pattern of relating which requires the other Self in the equation to respond in a pre-ordained manner. The therapist obliges – temporarily blind – until hopefully she recognises that which is being *re-enacted*. Here is an example.

Dominic

Dominic's wife, in tears, phoned to ask if I treated sex addicts. Before I could reply she rushed to explain that her husband was twenty-seven, some sort of I.T. whizz kid, and they'd only been married three years. In that time he had slept with at least five other women – old hags, dolly birds, he didn't care – and there must be others she didn't know about. Her best friend was a counsellor who had promptly diagnosed him as a sex addict. She had confronted him with this in a big row last night and he had accepted that it might be true. I asked her to ask him to make an appointment, wondering to myself if this might turn out to be a case for couple work. I'd wait and see.

Dominic was good-looking, beautifully dressed, and well educated, a charming soft-voiced conversationalist. He'd been brought up by two university academics who had travelled a lot for their respective research projects. He had been looked after by one parent or the other, depending upon which one was available, and a series of au pairs. Thereafter he was boarded out at a minor public school. He regarded these arrangements as perfectly ordinary in his social milieu, but was vaguely aware that on the occasions when his parents could actually occupy the family home at the same time, they were absorbed in each other and quite openly "kissy cuddly", which he found embarrassing.

Helen, Dominic's wife, was a successful illustrator of children's books. They had a toddler son they both adored, and apart from his affairs he claimed the marriage was happy. He just could not understand why he was compelled to pursue women, losing interest once they were committed to him. For it was essential that they should become serious about *him*, whereas he had no intention of leaving Helen. He was genuinely puzzled and regretted the pain he caused his wife.

Readers will have already made the obvious connections. Dominic had not enjoyed predictable childcare and had also felt excluded from the parental couple. So he had grown up emotionally hungry and insecure. He had always had to make use of secondary parental figures, the au pairs then, the affairs now, to bolster self-esteem (award him a satisfactory Selfobject experience). How do you feel good about yourself if someone else – and their jobs – have always been preferred over you?

Dominic thought all this through and intellectually appreciated that it was probably true. But so what? It didn't change anything. Therapy slowed down.

I tried to enliven the sessions by asking further about the marriage. Dominic described Helen as a highly creative, introverted, rather nervy woman, the opposite of his confident, independent mother. He loved her for that difference in temperament, and for the fact that no matter how busy she was with her work, she never went away. In fact she was a little agoraphobic. Her studio was a cabin in the back garden where she and their little boy could always be found. Why could he not be content? Why?

It was during this rather stuck phase of therapy that Dominic told me his job had become very busy. He began to cancel the odd session, having deadlines to meet or a conference to attend. In between he started to express half-hearted interest in my outside life and of course I took this up in transference terms. No, he shrugged, it was just that as nothing much was happening in therapy, and his wife's best pal was a counsellor, he'd found himself mildly curious about my profession. I got nowhere.

After another missed session he said he'd been recommended cranial massage for the headaches that his recent long working hours were giving him. He'd had three really good sessions already. A few weeks later he reported the benefits he was gaining from evening yoga classes, so good for the tense muscles.

Each week he did manage to attend I found myself cross and suspicious. Too busy to see me, but he'd found time for other healers, huh! Yet, as little was happening in the sessions – they were almost boring – it was quite a relief to have the odd hour to myself. Then one day he asked if he should defer therapy with me, take a break as the yoga was becoming very time-consuming. The teacher wanted him to attend her workshops, demonstrate for the other students what could be achieved. He'd need to practise…

After all my sincere efforts to help, and my sticking with him even through the dry periods, I felt really mad at him. I felt so provoked by his request to defer that I realised I *was* being provoked. It was time to come clean with him.

I told him (but under total self-control) that I was feeling furious with him whether he deserved it or not, and wondered what was going on between us under the polite exchanges and rather tedious small talk about stress and yoga. I invited him to come clean about his feelings toward me too, so we could sort this out.

It took several sessions but what we both finally understood was that although he was no longer talking about his issues he was *re-enacting* them with me instead. Like his wife who disinvested in him while she was painting, cool and distant, I too (from his point of view) had lost interest in him, wasn't pulling any rabbits out of the therapeutic hat. He turned to other consolations – massage, yoga – where delivery was faster. He simply could not tolerate non-gratification of his need to merge with another, so that his Self could feel safe. And yes, he was mad at me too, for not living up to his idealised image of a therapist who should make people feel good. Like his wife, and his mother, I had failed to see his need and just coasted along as if everything was all right. Like them, I had done nothing wrong, but nothing right! At last he expressed some spontaneous anger at me.

Then he remembered that the weekend before he threatened deferring his therapy, he had seen myself and my partner leaving a restaurant in town. Only now in the session did he suddenly connect that sight with the vision of his parents hugging each other, and his wife hugging their little boy. For a moment he could not speak. He was *feeling* the exclusion, rather than theorising about it.

After this crisis we coolly examined the details of his affairs. They had all occurred when Helen had been working to a deadline, visiting her mother, nursing her son's bad cold, spending too much time with her counsellor friend, or even when her own mood cycle meant she was less erotic than usual, more turned inward, "communing with herself" as he sarcastically called it. He had assumed such normal variation was rejection, whilst she complained of his neediness that sometimes drained her. She admitted once that she was almost glad of his affairs in a strange way, just as I had sometimes been glad of the cancelled sessions, feeling tired and in need of a rest. The sessions had felt empty of content, yet his underlying hungry demands had worn me down.

When the therapist suspects a *re-enactment* is occurring, it is important she try not to *enact* any strong emotion of her own, but rather observe and comment on it, so the therapy couple can discuss it as shared material. No one is perfect, however, and sometimes the therapist has participated in the drama for far too long before she realises what is afoot. If the Alliance is strong it is likely she will be forgiven, providing she is as honest about what happened to her feelings as she expects the patient to be.

Meeting Selfobject Needs

Often, in the early stages of therapy, apparent miracles occur. Where the therapist is skilled enough to set up the real *attunement* that the patient's life currently lacks, he will seize the opportunity, use the therapist as part of his own Self structure, glue himself to her. Having 'borrowed' her Self, his symptoms feel less frightening to him. But nothing has really changed, except that, thanks to that *Selfobject* experience, suicidal impulses, panic attacks or delusional activity have for the moment ceased. The emergency has been contained as police contain an incipient riot; but the troubles from way back that led to the riot are still there.

Basically there are six *Selfobject needs* which I will summarise below. These are: infantile, mirroring, alterego, adversarial, merger (sometimes called idealising) and efficacy needs. Daniel Stern writes cogently about them and in much more detail.

1. **Infantile needs.** These are sometimes referred to in the literature as *archaic*. Very young babies need total care, feeding, washing, billing and cooing every waking hour. They use these interactions with mother to firm up the emerging Self. Under enormous stress we can all regress to these needs but if they are chronically revived in adulthood this denotes pathology. For example, one of my supervisees had a borderline patient who literally camped in her garden for weeks on end during difficult periods of the therapy. She went home for meals and for sleeping but sat in front of her tent all day soaking up benevolent vibrations from the therapist's house.

2. **Mirroring needs.** The meeting of this need reassures you that you are who and what you think you are. You are robust, well-defined. It is a validating response from the environment of things as well as people. You may be at work, writing a poem, making love, when the intrapsychic *Selfobject experience* happens. You are being mirrored and it makes you feel whole, solid.

3. **Alterego needs.** These are associated with a sense of universality: I *belong*. The search for *Selfobject experiences* of this kind underpins the joining of groups, the use of flags and company logos, the deployment of baffling arcane terminology by psychoanalysts! These needs are deeply embedded in the human psyche – people have betrayed family and friends to stay a member of some group. Others have preferred to be executed rather than surrender their ties to a political or religious organisation.

4. **Adversarial needs.** These can be seen in various activities such as competing in the London marathon, joining a protest march, winning the quiz in the local pub, arm-wrestling surrounded by cheering mates. Some of these activities may be noble, others just playful or downright silly. The point is that they are doing great things for the participants. After the activity they feel better, stronger, more self-respecting. They are ready to face the sabre-toothed tiger, or any other foe, and return home triumphant. Their *Selfs* fill with healthy pride.

5. **Merger needs** are about finding a person, place or ideology that allows the tired and battered Self to merge with the calmness, power, wisdom, goodness of that *Selfobject*. For example, I recall vividly a holiday in the Lake District years ago when I stood at the top of Helvellyn in perfect weather with pure visibility. The whole of the Lakes were spread out under me like a carpet. I felt at one, *merged* with Nature, not just an appreciative observer. I was having a *Selfobject merger experience*, and judging from the ache in my limbs and the adrenaline coursing through my blood, it was combined with a meeting of my *adversarial* needs.

6. **Efficacy needs**, when met, award the Self an assurance of mastery and confidence. My I is proud of my Me. Getting a pay rise out of a stingy boss gives more pleasure to the Self than the money involved. A very early example would be the baby's capacity to make the mother come to him when he is wet, cold or hungry. The joy resides not only in his relief from discomfort, but in the proof positive *inside the Self* that he can control his environment, be effective.

Throughout life, on a day to day basis, these essential needs interact with and overlay one another, while the environment of things, places, people and even ideas and philosophies provide or fail to provide opportunities for meeting those needs. A *cohesed* Self is well-equipped to go out there and ensure that the meeting of its needs is maintained, the result being that John Brown changes his depressing job, finds a new woman, goes travelling for the first time. On the other hand a *fragmented* Self has to have its needs met before it can take up opportunities already available in the environment. This is where therapy comes in. The therapist for a time *is* the environment. The patient must find a way to make use of her, just as the infant borrows his mother as a Self strengthener from time to time. The patient in relational treatment has an active role to play. Therapy is done with him, not to him. His needs, present and past, met and unmet, are at the very core of the work. The understanding of and coming to terms with them, *not merely the gratifying of them by the therapist*, is what heals.

Vicarious Introspection and the Inevitable Failure to Meet the Need

In order to appreciate *Selfobject need* as it arises in the session, the therapist must acquire the skill of *vicarious introspection,* following the patient's mood and feelings from inside him, rather than collecting data about him from external observation. It is a process of identification with the patient while retaining the sense of her own identity – not an easy task.

Vicarious introspection, her moment to moment emotional tracking of where the patient is and was, leads to *accurate empathy.* This means she *feels the emotional impact* of his gratifications and deprivations as he felt them then and feels them now; *not* how it would feel for her were she in the same position! However accurate her empathy, it is impossible for her, or anyone, to meet all Selfobject needs. But the communication to the patient of this understanding of his internal experience promotes his working through of her, the therapist's, unintentional failures to detect and meet each of his *Selfobject needs*. Especially significant to the therapeutic enterprise are those needs not met in his infancy. These *inevitable* failures form the growth points for a new and stronger Self. It may be profitable to re-read this paragraph slowly and aloud, if this concept is unfamiliar to you.

Kate

The referral letter informed me that Kate was anxious and depressed, following a mastectomy.

Our therapy in her GP's surgery was conventional, short-term, and apparently successful. There was still mourning to complete but she was well-equipped to do this herself. She had already begun to look forward to a new phase of life where the loss of her breast did not have to mean she was diminished in any way. She had her new special bra, her support group comprised of other women in the same situation, and her quite wonderful husband who I invited for a 'talk', but needn't have bothered. He understood the needs of her feminine Self completely. She and I had looked at her fears about loss of feminine attractiveness, the impact on her marriage and sex life, even the prospect of ageing. She was ready to go.

Or so I wrongly supposed! After all, her childhood had been happy and there was no history of mental or physical illness in the family. She herself developed normally and became a maths teacher content with her job and her marriage. There were two well-adjusted grown-up children.

I was waiting for her to raise the prospect of ending our work together, but she did not. Our sessions became almost friendly chit-chat. She would talk about the news, or the latest doings of her daughter, of whom she was proud, or her husband's hilarious efforts to build a barbecue. Eventually I felt I had to raise the matter, as other patients were waiting and the GP was getting impatient.

She burst into angry tears that left me completely bewildered.

The fury that neither of us understood at first was due to her now seeing me as someone who, just like everyone else in the past and the present, gave up on her as soon as they had delivered the essential care she demanded. Hadn't the hospital dumped her onto me after the operation? Wasn't I now dumping her because she had no more personal tragedies to report? Hadn't her mother always given her the cake but never the icing, while her younger brother was never turned away?

In allowing her (somewhat uneasily) to continue therapy after the symptoms had disappeared, I had, without realising it, been meeting a very deep need in her to merge with me as she had never been permitted to merge with her mother. This time it was going to be different for her: all the icing would be hers – until I spoiled it.

It was my failure to perceive that need over and above the psychological effects of the operation that enabled her to examine her competitive relationship with her brother for the first time. She had not told him of her medical situation, had not seen him for years, but now decided to contact him and try to build some bridges.

Suggested reading:

Bowlby, J. (1953). *Child Care and the Growth of Love.* Harmondsworth: Pelican.

Kernberg, O. (1995). *Borderline Conditions and Pathological Narcissism.* New York: Jason Aronson (The Master Works Series).

Kernberg, O. (2011). *The Inseparable Nature of Love and Aggression: Clinical and Theoretical Perspectives.* Arlington, VA: American Psychiatric Publishing Inc.

Kernberg, O. (2014). *Aggressivity Narcissism and Self Destructiveness in the psychotherapeutic relationship.* New Haven, CT: Yale University Press.

Khan, M. (1997). *Between therapist and Client: The New Relationship.* New York: St. Martin's Press.

Kohut, H. (1971). *The Analysis of the Self: A systematic Approach to the Psychoanalytic Treatment of Narcissistic Personality Disorders.* New York: International Universities Press.

Kohut, H. (1977). *The Restoration of the Self.* New York: International Universities Press.

Kohut, H. (1984). *How does Analysis Cure?* Chicago: University of Chicago Press.

Lomas, P. (2001, New edition). *The Limits of Interpretation.* London: Robinson.

Mitchell, S. A. (1988). *Relational Concepts in psychoanalysis.* Cambridge, MA: Harvard University Press.

Mitchell, S. A. (2004). *Relationality: From Attachment to Intersubjectivity.* London: Routledge.

Siegel, A. M. (1996). *Heinz Kohut and the Psychology of the Self.* London: Routledge (Makers of Modern Psychotherapy).

Stark, M. (2000). *Modes of Therapeutic Action.* New York: Jason Aronson.

Stern, D. (1985). *The Interpersonal World of the Infant.* London: Karnac.

Symington, N. (1993). *Narcissism: A New Theory.* London: Karnac.

CHAPTER SEVEN

THE TRUE OR FALSE PSYCHOTHERAPIST?

The safely daring Mary Smith therapist thoughtfully experiments with contemporary ideas – the still unfolding relational area for instance – whilst occasionally revisiting tried and tested ones from her old days, especially when a particular patient defies all her attempts at making a formulation (a nutshell description of what is unconsciously going on). Surprisingly often these dusty concepts turn out to be as relevant, or even more so, today, as in their heyday.

Such is the case with Donald Winnicott's notion of the true and false self. Winnicott was a British paediatrician concerned primarily with the very early mother and child relationship. Along with others, his penetrating discoveries made way for the emergence of the Self Psychology movement. The Self as described in the last chapter had not yet been elevated to its current distinctive status, so you will be relieved to know that in this chapter you will not find capital letters in odd places; italics will be reduced and the vocabulary will be conventional.

The concept of *mirroring* featured greatly in Winnicott's writings. How does an infant find out who he is? He gazes raptly at mother's face while being held securely in her arms. Her face is radiant with love, her arms sturdy and warm, her breast silky, milky and yielding. If he is looking into a mirror then he must be quite a guy – lovable, desired, beautiful. Of course the infant has no such ideas in his head; he can barely think yet. It is his body – blood, liver, nerves, sinews, skin, full stomach – that registers what he experiences at mother's breast, experiences sent to the brain, there to lodge in the rapidly spreading network of neurones which will later grow into cognitive functioning. Our most ancient image of ourselves resides in our body and if we could peel back the layers of the onion brain to its core, it sits there still – myself as reflected in my mother's face.

Around this primitive structure, over time and stuffed with bodily memories, our so-called mind gradually forms, layer upon layer. I say "so-called", for the mind, whether it turns out to be material or a mere abstraction, is a living and changing organism, not fixed for all time like the colour of your eyes or the shape of your nose. If it were not, therapy would be impossible.

It is not surprising then that many patients born into a damaged family, or to an ill mother, or into an orphanage type of situation, later develop physical symptoms for which no organic cause can be found; or perhaps the patient becomes obsessed with a bodily part that he deems ugly and unacceptable, disproportioned: he believes that people look at him and are repulsed.

Should the newborn fix his gaze upon a blank, exhausted, disgusted face, or a different face each time wearing a different expression, he will see in the mirror a splintered self, a bad, ugly, undeserving self. His brain will carry this archaic image with him despite the many overlays of enhancing responses from his later environment that show him he is indeed worthwhile and wanted. But he will return (regress) to that ancient picture of himself if he is subjected to simultaneous multiple rejections or losses without compensatory relationships or occupations or a faith to reassure him.

If the infant's sense of self is shaky, the mirror giving back unreliable reflections, he will learn as he grows how to solicit a better image. For behind that yearned-for, loving face lies a willingness to engage with him. It denotes interest, a preparedness to exchange messages. Baby signals distress: mother takes in the distress, metabolises it for him, sends it back in a more manageable form. Both then gaze into one another's eyes, contented. This is but the ideal, by definition seldom reached except by the very fortunate. But the infant can at least petition for it. He will oblige, appease, accommodate, bring into being a *false self* that stands a decent chance of being accepted, rewarded occasionally with a smiling if not beatific image. That will be sufficient if it enables him to survive. Indeed anything remotely comparable will do, however false to his true self he must be to acquire it. He will be whatever mother needs him to be, meet all her needs and deny his own, if only she will *see* him. Depending on the quality of the mother-baby exchanges, babies will vary in the degree to which they resort to a false self.

The function of the false self is to protect the true self, which very early on is unable to show itself safely because responsiveness to it is absent. In extreme cases the true self is still embryonic in adulthood and in therapy needs long-term good corrective mothering (mirroring) to give it birth. However, this must be done without seducing the patient into the honey trap of irresolvable dependent transference.

Winnicott says that there are degrees of extremity in the adult personality with a false self organisation. The situation is most serious when the false self sets itself up as real. Observers such as friends, partners, work mates believe this to be the true person at first, but on continued and increasingly intimate acquaintance realise there is something undefinable that is missing. Relationships break down. Tragically, the true self is completely locked away, inaccessible even to its owner.

More hopeful in terms of therapeutic intervention is the person whose false self protects and defends the true self lurking behind the scenes. His true self is acknowledged as a potential and is to some degree allowed a secret life, if only in fantasy, films, books, music, dreams. Further toward health, there is the individual who seeks constantly for an environment which can provide opportunities (be this people, jobs, travel, therapy and so forth) for him to let his real self out of the cage in which it has for so long been imprisoned.

Then there is the person who is frustrated in his attempts to liberate his real self, but refuses to go back into his cage. He may turn to substance abuse, promiscuity, criminal activity for consolation or to express his sense of futility. Eventually his condition deteriorates, resulting in physical or mental symptoms, or breakdowns in relationships. These behaviours or symptoms have meaning. He is trapped in a no man's land between the false and the undiscovered true. Whether aberrant behaviour represents protest, appeal, disappointment or despair, it constitutes an urgent communication to a usually deaf or judgemental world. It behoves us psychotherapists to decode these messages for him.

When the degree of split between the true and false self is not too great in a child, he can live a kind of half-life through imitation of a loved or admired other person, granny perhaps or a loved character in a fairy tale. The child's false self is acting a role, but at least it is *the role of the true self* as it would be if it had existence. In this regard I find patients who are professional actors most interesting.

Finally there is healthy false self organisation, just as there is healthy narcissism, constructive aggression and creative depression. We all put on a show for others, try to be acceptable, likeable, to fit in. Often we are obliged to hide our real views or feelings to avoid causing offence or embarrassment. If we all wore our heart on our sleeve there would be chaos. We cannot attain and maintain our acceptability in society by means of the true self alone.

I hope it will become apparent in this chapter that there is an important parallel between the patient with a false self who hopefully finds his true self in therapy, and the false self psychotherapist who, via her clinical experiences coupled with long and deep introspection, becomes a truer therapist over the years. Let me say at once that I am not here making a simple divide between false (morally bad) and true (morally good) therapists. False self clinicians like false self children are unswervingly dedicated to *getting it right*. They are utterly sincere – not to say unconsciously desperate – in their desire to understand the patient, be *with* him, heal him, whether he be healable by their method or not. For the false therapist, the precise tracking of the patient's interior events feels like a matter of life and death, as does the driving need to give the absolutely correct intervention. Way back when, this terrible need never to make a mistake, to always be attuned and adapted to mother's internal world, was indeed a matter of psychic survival versus disintegration for this earnest practitioner. Her continued existence as an acceptable human being depended on the smile in the mirror. To make that happen, even her true self could be sacrificed.

I shall return to this theme later in the chapter, for there are huge ethical questions here which every therapist should introspectively face and answer. Could we be abusing our patients when we honestly believe we are helping them? Whose needs are paramount here, the patient's or ours?

Illustration of False Self Organisation

The only means I have to authentically demonstrate how it feels to be both a false self child and false self therapist is to look at my own childhood, and my later professional life.

I believe that any worthwhile therapist has had, or will have, at least three trainings. The first is in her pram. The second is on her accredited qualifying therapy course, and the third is that which this book aims to highlight – *the pursuit of the true understanding of her own psychic life*. It is that understanding which binds together all her formal training, reading and practice over the years into the best kind of therapy, whatever ideological school she graduated from.

I shall first relate what happened 'in my pram' and until I went to school.

On the night in 1942 when my mother laboured to bring yet another would-be healer into an unsuspecting world, my father left or was thrown out, depending which version of the family myth one believes. He was to return just before I went to school. The intervening time was spent in paradise – or so I thought at the time and right up to my teenage years. My older brother and sister were at school all day and I had my mum all to myself. What could be better?

I made sure I was everything my mother wanted and needed, without knowing I was doing so of course. I knew she was sad and lonely and sensed it was my sacred duty to entertain and enliven her. Yet I could switch into companionable melancholy when required, slip with her into silent reverie, vigilant for the moment when I could lure her back to tea time or the shopping. Only years later did I appreciate that I had been her amateur psychiatric nurse, an occupation I took up professionally at eighteen. Neither of us in those days knew about or would have understood the concept of depression.

Sometimes in those years we even had fun, her kind not mine. I didn't know what my kind of fun or my preferences were. I stayed in the house all day to be near the creature I adored; friends held no interest for me. She was my queen and I was her court jester. Neither of us were culpable in this, it was just normality, how things were. I thought I was happy, lucky, honoured to have this way of life.

During those years I had a recurring dream that neither pleased nor frightened me. It just lived alongside me like my arms and legs. There was a buttercup meadow full of flowers, bright sunshine and singing birds. At either end of the meadow was a black, oblong open grave. Each night one of us, my mother or myself, would drop into one to temporarily die while the other one stayed alive enjoying the buttercups. The next night it would be the other one's turn to die for a bit. We each had our own grave.

The interdependence, almost symbiosis, is clear. But I like to think that a bit of the true me was yearning toward the light even then, if only in dreams and if only at the cost of temporarily killing off my revered mother. Such a thought and its associated guilt would have been impossible to bear at a conscious level.

I sometimes asked her about her own childhood and her parents. Then she would come alive with happy stories, in which she was always the glowing centre. I could keep her going for hours like this. It never occurred to me to talk about my own childhood, the one I was supposed to be having right now. I banished my tiny true self to a dark cave somewhere. There was no place or use for it here.

I can report that my adolescence was stormy, to say the least. I had no insight then into what was happening to me and why; but my crude, blind untamed, wounded true self came roaring out of its cave to show the world who I was. I argued about everything and rebelled. Oh dear, my poor mum. I am sorry that it was necessary, but it was.

Alas, it was but a token breakout and the false self soon reasserted itself.

I commenced my first analysis at twenty-seven, connected to my work as a therapeutic community sister. I was mainly silent, felt a fraud. I wasn't sick. *I had no right to be here* – the unconscious refrain of youngest children who feel their arrival broke up the family. I felt a desperate need to earn my keep, make myself useful, justify my existence. Yet in the sessions I could find nothing to say for myself until I had cues from my 'mother' analyst to show me how I should please him, keep him happy, keep him interested in me. (And if he also stood for my originally absent, then distant, dad, the same thing applied, as I barely knew him). It never occurred to me to say whatever I liked, present my true self to the analyst, as I had no idea what such a thing could be.

This was the era when analysts were trained to be neutral and mostly silent, blank screens awaiting projection. Frantic at not being able to see or hear any cues (the analyst in those days was invisible, behind the couch) I eventually developed some nasty physical symptoms; my regressed body spoke for me. They miraculously cleared up as soon as the analysis terminated.

Starting out as a therapist I tuned in to my patients as I had with my mum, needing another human being to feel deeply understood by me, so I could lay claim to some right to exist. I was performing a vital function wasn't I? I had earned a bit of positive mirroring. I would have been horrified to see this at the time. I believed my motives were entirely altruistic.

As my various trainings progressed I continued trying to prove my worthiness, locating what was required of me in order to be esteemed and have self-esteem. If I could but master some particular psychoanalytic writers, read the mind and needs of my trainers, show my devotion to the true faith (I went through countless ideologies here and none sufficed), then I would come to know *it*. I would have touched the sacred flame of *allrightness* so long denied me. I would be properly, unassailably qualified, in more ways than one.

My work for a time became my life. What I did not appreciate was that I was pursuing from the establishment a mirroring response that I never had as a child. Its never having been there had to be acknowledged and grieved over, rather than perpetually and fruitlessly chased in my career. I could not turn back the clock. After I saw this, I believe I began the long haul toward becoming a true self therapist rather than a well-meaning phony.

Do all Therapists Act Out of Their False Self?

Like with all other personality attributes, there is the matter of gradation. You can be a little bit false, quite false or very false. Certainly I would say all effective therapists show a ravening need to get inside others that is more than curiosity, and it has to have come from somewhere. Why have they worked so hard to hone their intuition, refine their empathy, focus their attention on others' second to second moods and feelings? This must have resulted from family influences, or lack of them, from birth.

It isn't the influences themselves ("let's blame the parents" – a practice I abhor) that counts here, but how the child makes sense of and adjusts to those influences. Some neglected infants have had just enough mirroring at the start that they fight on to regain what they have lost. They may have to be very canny, alternately appeasing and demanding, fulfilling Mother's needs then requiring fulfilment of their own. They grab at her when she is able to mirror, woo her with precocious empathy when she is not.

Others are forced by unremitting deprivation to live and breathe only through the false self that is permanently at Mother's disposal. Some mothers have been so wounded themselves in early life that they lack the capacity to parent at all, so that from the beginning no embryonic true self in the infant, that might put up a fight, can develop. More hopeful is the situation where true self can find a hiding place until circumstances in later life are more propitious.

Perhaps a budding therapist should be asked: what skills did you feel obliged to learn in order to negotiate your family universe at a time when there was no other universe with which to compare it? And which of your needs did you have to repress in order to be acceptable? For whatever went on around you was construed as normality, and you had to find some way to fit into it.

A false self doesn't know it is false, any more than I knew my mother was depressed and I was mothering her so as to be mothered. This highlights the essential requirement that trainees undertake their own therapeutic treatment.

It is incumbent upon every practitioner to fully investigate this area lest she transfer her own demands to be mirrored to the new environment of the consulting room. She could end up training her patients to gratify her at cost to them, or hating them for not getting well in order to firm up her precarious self-regard.

Demetrios: two false selves

This example shows the false therapist (me) in action. My only excuse is that I was still a trainee in my twenties.

Demetrios was a shy, highly intelligent, artistic Greek student at the university where I worked as a counsellor. He complained of feeling miserable and isolated but didn't have a clue why. My sincere and tireless efforts to get him to talk and share his feelings were eventually rewarded and we became very closely attuned to one another.

Demetrios was immensely physically attractive, slender with a thick mop of dark hair and pale unblemished skin. I looked forward to his session each week, assuring myself I could cope with the protective but highly sexual feelings he aroused in me. Dutifully I took these to supervision to show how aware I was of my counter-transference. Of course the supervisor had no knowledge of my childhood relations with my mother so missed the very important fact that the special rapport I thought I had with Demetrios was my replicating of the spuriously blissful intimacy I believed I had enjoyed with her. No one could possibly have understood my patient or my mother so well as I!

Demetrios too was a false self person. He accommodated me in every way, telling me what I wanted to know, doing things socially and in his family that we had talked over in the session, and reporting back improvements. He took up his neglected studies and developed long-term goals with regard to them. We discussed what being Greek meant to him, what life meant to him, what kind of girl he would want to settle down with. We were always on the same wavelength. I thought we were doing great therapy.

He passed his finals, moved out from home, found a girlfriend and resolved differences with his traditional family. When he left to take up an advanced degree elsewhere I wrote on the notes: "much improved, may need help later."

Seven years later, now a Ph.D. with a successful career, he wrote me an angry letter I have never forgotten. Yet I am so grateful that he sent it. He was in proper therapy now, he wrote. At last he was getting somewhere. In his new therapy he had come to see that he had been appeasing me all along. He admitted we had got on well, so that he looked forward to visiting his only close 'friend' each week. But he'd felt that the only way to keep this special relationship going was to please me, feed my need (demand?) to succeed as a therapist. He'd had to do this all his life with his mum, or she'd think she'd failed and then get depressed. He'd even found a girlfriend to please me (and his mum). Yet all the time, beneath our mutual playing at therapy, he'd been half consciously struggling with whether he was gay or not. If I had been any good at my job, he wrote, then *that* is what I should have identified and worked on, not reinforcing his tendency to placate women.

Demetrios was a client so I could not be sexual with him. I could however make him potent in other areas of his life and he would thank me for it, *smile upon me*. I worked my socks off for him but missed what his true self had all along hungered for, a chance to live and breathe in the consulting room without having to keep me happy. I had reinforced his false self, not helped him wrestle with it.

Case summary

This stinging experience taught me to stop requiring patients to get well for me. Slowly I started allowing them their suffering and the right to learn from it, without having to rescue them as I rescued my mother. If they chose to leave, take pills, leave their husband, run off to India in search of a guru, of course I worked with it; but I didn't *have* to prevent their choices for my own unconscious reasons. It really was their life, not our shared symbiotic one. If they were to consider therapy again at some time in the future, at least they would remember their first therapist as someone who could let them go rather than entrap them.

Martin: a flash of the true self

I had already spotted a false self organisation in Martin's personality. His parenting from day one had been highly disruptive, leading him to propitiate others and deprioritise his own needs.

He was always trying to help and please people, even when they were unkind to him.

To his amazement and everlasting gratitude he had acquired a wife and four children, but felt they deserved better than him. He believed they might suddenly vanish, that he must have dreamed them up. There was nothing he would not do for them. He was plagued by the fear that one day they would discover he was a fraud and leave him.

A senior molecular biologist, he had written many well-received papers, seemed popular with his students but was modest to a self-injurious degree; he never applied for posts for which he was eminently suited.

He looked like the stereotypical professor, long hair, unkempt, glasses stuck together with Sellotape. His clothes were baggy and ill-matched, his briefcase battered and peeling. He was always in a rush, muddled, breathless. He always left behind an unravelling woolly glove or scarf or sticky railway ticket. He was never, but never, on time. Sometimes we only had half a session. I felt fond of him but increasingly irritated by the lateness.

The presenting picture was one of unrelieved physical tension and dreams of being caught up in natural disasters or terrorist attacks. He kept flirting with suicidal plans "just to get a bit of peace, time off the treadmill". His doctor had diagnosed "midlife stress and anxiety".

In the early, exploratory period of our work, he was shocked by my comments concerning others' taking advantage of him, or putting him to the back of the queue when he needed something. What stopped him from standing up for himself? This notion obviously struck him as obscene. Here was a man who thought he had no right to exist, let alone fight for anything. His constant striving to be deserving was threatening him with a heart attack.

Eventually, after many months but without an iota of relief, he saw the false self formulation as almost certainly true. It was only an intellectual understanding however, as nothing changed. For him this was just one more item to add to his list of inadequacies.

I tried to get him to see how his lateness deprived him of the help he so badly wanted, *and which he deserved*, and for which he was giving up his valuable time and money. He saw the point but explained how the phone had rung just as he was leaving, the children needed lunchboxes, he had to finish marking an essay, his proofs had arrived and they wanted them back pronto...

This had gone on for some twenty months. One day I took paper and pen to the consulting room to make out my weekly shopping list, as I knew I would be sitting there for about twenty minutes. To my utter astonishment he arrived dead on time breathing heavily. He flung his briefcase into the corner and practically fell into his chair.

I was so surprised and pleased I could not resist my warmest smile. "You finally made it on time."

But he did not smile back.

I should have shut up, but I encouraged him to feel proud of his achievement. He had finally claimed the full session time for himself, acknowledged there was a true self inside him that had legitimate needs. He'd finally put himself first.

"Legitimate needs be buggered!" he cried, still panting with exertion. "I had three heads of department on my tail this morning all wanting urgent stuff – my prof, my wife and you. *You*, always going on about my being late, always disappointed in me, always seeing me as a failure, a toady, a wet week. Well now I can show you just how wet I am. I haven't got here on time for *me*, you ninny; I got here to please *you*, keep you quiet, stop you nagging. I'm damn well placating more than I ever did! Dear God, I disgust myself!"

His eyes widened and his jaw dropped. "I'm s- s- so sorry..."

Case summary

I was delighted. The angry outburst was the first I had seen, despite detailed scrutiny of the neglect and cruelty in his infancy. It was a glimpse, just a glimpse of his true self. At last he was telling his mother where to go with her impossible demands. He hated me/her for making them, but could not sack us as he needed the attachment to us so badly. It was this irresolvable conflict, escalating week by week, that had momentarily prompted his real self into action.

A Cautionary Note

It pains me to recognise that in the past I have taken many patients into therapy and only long after their departure, or sometimes when they returned, have realised that the work we had done had successfully shored up the false self, made it even better adapted to social reality. At the time both they and I thought they were better. So rooted is the false self sometimes, so capable and practised at running the patient's life, that the therapeutic pair can part with mutual satisfaction without the therapist having once glanced into the condemned cell where her patient's true self still resides.

While the concept and function of the false self appears simple – the false self both starving and protecting the true self – this is a category of patient very hard to treat because the false self so easily passes for the true.

In this book I have made much of the idea of attunement and accurate empathy between therapist and patient and mother and baby. But I think baby and patient are the only two kinds of persons who merit this total selfless attention from a caregiver. The rest of us must mature enough to give out as well as take in, and be grateful for what we do receive.

The false self infant, toddler and even adult is on a mission to discover, via a keen empathy, how to meet others' needs so that his own in turn might be met. For the newborn and the toddler this is an understandable strategy, because survival is at stake. For the adult in ordinary society it leads to the misery of permanent self-abnegation, exhausting himself trying to be what others want.

This raises the question of how much love and attention it is reasonable for a grown-up not only to give, but also to receive. Why *should* another person forgo all their own needs, wishes, preferences, ambitions, just to place their attention, concentration and understanding at your feet for the rest of their and your life? Is not the unspoken demand to be loved unconditionally for yourself (whatever that is!) not the ultimate in narcissistic disturbance? It is certainly the ruin of many a marriage, both parties trying to force the other not into better communication and negotiation, but into absolute accommodation to their inner world, especially with regard to making up for hurts in childhood.

Yes, the true self needs validation, love, companionship, tolerance of its shortcomings. But it accepts that it exists in an imperfect world, is reconciled to the inevitability of intermittent loss, lack of compassion from certain others and upsetting miscommunication that even so need not herald the end of the world. The true self can mourn and celebrate, emotionally fast as well as feed, attach and detach to things and people without too much trauma, and accept the harsh realities of existence without despair or grandiose defence.

Withdrawal of Mirroring and Attunement

Having provided the patient with the special attention he can find nowhere else, what happens when it is withdrawn? No therapist should delude him into believing this happy state of affairs can go on forever, or that it can be replicated in relationships elsewhere. It is the sensitive management of the necessary disillusionment *when the time is right,* by the mother/therapist, which enables the infant/patient to begin the journey to independent selfhood. The loosening of the tie to both mother and therapist brings fear and loss but also freedom and opportunity for growth. The therapist's purpose is not to compensate her patient for what he missed, but to show him the implications of its not having been there on a full-time basis when it was needed. With understanding comes the grieving process, the forerunner of recovery.

When a child is weaned, walks, talks, goes to school, there is no going back, no second chance, ever. No substitute mother, therapist, partner, friend or soulmate can put back time and replace what was lost or absent. Such an attempt by any caregiver would constitute seduction, possession, control, not true healing. The search for the true self is the search for and coming to terms with how it really was, not how in a fairy tale ending it will one day be.

Fathers

Little has been said about the important role of fathers, siblings and grandparents. I am aware of the omission, but where false self and narcissistic pathology is concerned their origins lie mainly with the baby's first relationship before other members of the family have impinged upon its sensibilities. However, it should be borne in mind that a new mother's capacity to mother her infant is critically affected by the kind of support she gains from her partner and her own mother. Their contribution to her care and the care of other family members while she is preoccupied with the new arrival is vital if she is to enjoy the peace and privacy necessary to set up *intersubjectivity* (intimate bonding) with her infant. Mother/child relationships do not transpire in a vacuum.

The Therapist's False Self

The therapist's false self activity is visited on her patient without her being aware. Her true self is tucked away in the recesses of her mind while her false self requires from the patient gratitude, admiration, respect. Most of all he must get well to show her a picture of herself that is worthy, even noble. Of course therapists do not do this on purpose, but those with unresolved narcissistic issues are driven by the false self's hunger for Winnicott's mirroring response. When it fails to put in an appearance the patient may be rapidly referred on, discharged or medicated. In the worst cases the therapist cannot bear the wound to her self-esteem and becomes ill. Her secret inadequacy behind her former success stands revealed. Her body cloaks her shame in illness.

There are a hundred reasons why a patient does not get well or is not at the moment improving. This is a matter for clinical investigation, supervision and consultation. The patient should not be dismissed until the reasons for the lack of progress are understood and a considered judgement is made about what, if anything, to do next.

Sometimes an otherwise competent practitioner is so trapped by the self-imposed *requirement* for results that she simply cannot bear to wait until the patient is ready to move forward. He must adjust to her pace, not she to his. Martin's case above shows just how long it can take before there is a significant shift toward the recognition of a true self, even though both parties are working very hard. Sadly, short-term therapy, however skilled, is not able to address such problems as these. Consideration must be given to this when rationing precious time.

The Swiss analyst Alice Miller became so troubled by what she saw as inevitable exploitation of the patient by the analyst that in 1988 she resigned from the International Psychoanalytical Association. In *The Drama of Being a Child* (1983, p.40) she summarises thus:

> *'The patient satisfies his analyst's narcissistic wish for approval, echo, understanding, and for being taken seriously, when he presents material that fits his analyst's knowledge, concepts and skills, and therefore also his expectations. In this way the analyst exercises the same sort of unconscious manipulation as that to which he [the analyst] was exposed as a child.'*

In other words, she is saying that the false self therapist makes use of a weaker person (the patient) by forcing him to take the unavailable parent's place. She will come to understand him through and through, so he will reciprocate by nurturing her damaged uncohesed Self with his newfound health, which is of course all down to her.

Despite this dark view, I like to think that we should consider the question of degree. If we have no unhealthy false self organisation in our minds at all, how can we help patients dominated by it? How do we know our supposed true self really is true? What if we are deluding ourselves? What if we are still operating under the sway of false self residues? Ought we then to be doing therapy at all?

However, we live and work in an imperfect world of imperfect therapists. Is it enough, perhaps, that we increase our expertise not only in books, CPD and supervision, but also in the pursuit of our own truer selves?

Suggested reading:

Basch, M. F. (1980). *Doing Psychotherapy*. New York: Basic Books.

Broucek, F. J. (1991). *Shame and Self*. New York: Guildford Press.

Coltart, N. (1993). 'Attention' in *Slouching Toward Bethlehem and further Psychoanalytic Explorations*. London: Free Association Books.

Fonagy, P. (2001). *Attachment Theory and Psychoanalysis*. London: Karnac.

Lomas, P. (1973). *True and False Experience*. London: Allen Lane.

Miller, A. (1983). *The drama of being a child*. London: Virago Press.

Miller, A. (1990). *Banished Knowledge: facing Childhood injuries*. London: Virago Press.

Mollon, P. (1993). *The Fragile Self: The Structure of Narcissistic Experience*. London: Whurr Publishers.

Tustin, F. (1981). *Autistic States in Children*. London: Routledge.

Winnicott, D. W. (1965). *The Maturational Processes and the Facilitating Environment: Studies in the Theory of Emotional Development.* London: Hogarth Press and the Institute of Psycho-Analysis (reprint 1976).

CHAPTER EIGHT:

WORKING WITH COUPLES: WHY DO IT?

Many otherwise exemplary therapists roll their eyes in horror at the suggestion they extend their practice into couple work. They think there must be twice as much information to take in, two transferences to disentangle, two sets of notes and, on top of all that, maybe unpleasant quarrels to referee! I hasten to reassure you that this is not the case. For that would mean simply replicating individual therapy for two people at the same time – impossible, I agree.

With some reading and good supervision, a therapist with experience under her belt should be able to help couples with their relationship, whether to firm it up or disengage with minimum fallout. But to 'safely dare' to do this, you must be prepared to adapt considerably your individual therapy orientation, your self-presentation to the couple, and your techniques.

The first bit of comforting news is that you are not out to effect personality change in either partner, so you can relax on that score. Rather, your aim is to open up communicational corridors between the pair that are currently blocked, in order to release and build on any love that remains, however long it has been undermined by marital strife.

Secondly, couple therapy's focus is on the way the pair relate to each other, not to you, and what – unavailable to them at the moment – might be going on underneath when their connection falters, collapses or turns into world war three. Much of the work is actually watching them while they talk, avoid real talk, start rowing and blaming and so forth. For the therapist, it is very like being in the front row at the theatre seeing an intriguing play. They may be arguing about childcare, the in-laws or money. The couple therapist is more interested in their unique mode of handling the topic rather than the subject itself. *The relationship is the patient*, the collecting of double information not the main point. The relevant parts of their two histories will usually surface soon enough, of their own accord. The therapist does not referee or advise: this is not mediation; but aids them to see how and why they are getting nowhere.

Were you to magically heal both partners' life wounds and enable them to fully function, they would no longer choose one another as partners and the relationship would end. It is their unresolved needs and conflicts from childhood that have drawn them together, that form the psychological basis of their mutual attraction. The purpose of therapy is not to take these issues away, but to help both partners understand them. Broadly speaking, your job is to open their eyes to what they deeply (unconsciously), not *superficially*, need and want from each other, and why communication about those needs has broken down. They must each evaluate their own and their partner's demands and learn how to give and receive a reasonable, not perfect, amount of gratification, whilst accepting responsibility for their own pasts which the partner cannot hope to put right in all its aspects.

In this and the next chapter I will pursue the aims and techniques of this way of working, but first a quick scan of some background. Whether couple work is your thing or not, there is no doubt that demand from the public is increasing, and that therapists are more and more seeing single persons who report marital disharmony and virtually bring their partner along with them to the session. Outside of the metropolis there are scarcely any quality services specialising in couple therapy (as opposed to mediation) so that senior individual therapists are badly needed to train themselves up and become the couple work supervisors and trainers of the future.

It goes without saying that mending couples, or assisting in damage-limiting separations, produces massive benefit to families and to society in general, where for the moment the family unit remains the principal transmitter of mental health and good citizenship. It seems to me these facts oblige our profession to fill this gap in our services. Otherwise we will fail to meet the requirements of our increasingly complex culture, continuing to waste time on factionalism between the therapeutic disciplines, or hiding in old ideological certainties. How frequently do I hear: "At least individual work is the therapy I know. I have a Diploma from X Institute to prove it." Further than that they fear to go. Such a pity.

I often wonder if the reluctance to start doing couple therapy is about its lack of bibles with their comforting do's and don'ts, the absence of theoretical giants having a good old fight, inspiring us to take sides, or a stimulating Movement churning out papers by the minute, such as the ones described in earlier chapters. This nervousness in the face of minimal guidance is understandable, but no excuse for our most therapeutically mature colleagues not to 'safely dare'.

Lecture over.

The Basics: What Lies Behind the Quest for a Partner?

Life is full of separations and birth is our first. We suddenly find ourselves face to face with mother rather than curled up inside her, safe and warm. Feeding is the first twosome, the first marriage. How it progresses, stormy or uneventful, will be embedded in our organism and later our sense of self. It will colour all our future attachments to another person.

The second separation, though major, occurs gradually as it dawns on us that Mother is not me. We are not one unit but two. No longer can we just wish and the nipple appears, the bottom is dried, the colic soothed. Good heavens, we are not able to fix these discomforts for ourselves! When we are made to wait, even for a few moments, we start to comprehend that we aren't omnipotent, but rely on something *other* to bring relief and contentment. Insecurity, aloneness, death (or rather the as yet unconceptualised dread of it) looms. A shocking formulation repeats and repeats until it is etched into our growing brain: *someone other, who I may not be able to control, is the dispenser of safety and bliss.*

When the tasks of childhood are complete – coming to terms with Dad, walking and talking, the potty, school, making friends – and the hormones of adolescence start to overwhelm, the hunt is on for a new provider of satisfaction amid all the uncertainty. That person's remit is to return us to paradise lost, to provide a blissful union without us having to do anything at all. Experience will teach us that paradise is lost forever, but there is still much to be gained from a more adult relationship if only we knew how. Sorting out all this longing and disappointment, learning to give up impossible dreams, while deep down our partner is trying to do the same, is where couple therapy comes into its own, whatever the presenting problems.

What Does Couple Therapy Do?

Freud said that most of what we call love is our *resistance* to the prospect of leaving home. Another way of putting this is to say our home, our marriage or couple, is the place in the present where we repeat or try to repair the past. (Our current home and loved ones represent many other things as well – Freud did not say *all* love was resistance). When we fall in love and think of settling down, we fantasise the home we never want to leave, our original family corrected, made whole, which our newfound love is going to magically conjure up for us. We are going to live happily ever after.

I can only say as a couple therapist that over and over again I see couples struggling with just this matter of having ostensibly left home, but still carrying their family inside them. They thought all that was over and done with, nothing to do with their current problems; yet here it is, resurfacing in the consulting room. The fairy tale ending, the attempt to return to a healed home, has turned out to be a big disappointment.

Couples come to therapists because their relationship is making them very unhappy, not because they have an illness to cure, or specific symptoms of mental disorder, or want to change especially. One of the chief objectives in couple work is not to *eradicate* each partner's defences but to help each of them understand and face their own *and* their partner's survival tactics, and why they are so necessary to whichever partner depends on them. Sometimes, where life outside the marriage is adversely affected by extreme defensive strategies, one or both partners may be recommended individual therapy.

As the couple interacts in the consulting room, myself watching and learning from the unfolding drama, I occasionally interrupt, to go up on stage, so to speak. There I shed light on how these two sets of defences are interlocking, reinforcing or competing with one another such that real communication is impossible. Returning to my 'seat in the stalls', the couple try a different, more constructive approach.

I don't mean here that the therapist delivers herself of an intellectual exposition, gives the couple a bit of a lecture; I mean she tries to illuminate the process *as it happens, live in the consulting room*, and, where appropriate, demonstrates the links with their individual pasts that make each participant's behaviour intelligible to themselves and their partner.

Determinants in the past do not excuse cruel behaviour of one spouse to the other, but after the three people in the consulting room have thrashed out the complained-of behaviour and made sense of it, the wounded party, realising the behaviour was much more complex than just pure malice, need not feel so attacked or undermined. And he or she can come to expect the same consideration for *their* past determinants.

The Joneses

Mrs. Jones, a busy and conscientious mum and wife with two kids and a job, spends all Sunday cooking the perfect roast for the family. She makes Yorkshire puds, proper gravy, puts out the best linen and china. Mr. Jones is grumpy. He has been fixing the car all morning and getting nowhere. He comes to the table to discover there is no butter on the sprouts. The butter still sits solidly in the butter dish in the fridge. He blows up. "You *know* I like my butter melted, not in great lumps. You never forget little Johnny likes his potatoes browned at the edges and little Mary has peas instead of sprouts, do you? You can't even remember to take the butter out of the fridge for me – not exactly rocket science is it, just shifting a dish?"

Mrs. Jones goes up the wall. A row ensues and the kids scarper, sensing an escalation. They're used to this. The meal is spoilt.

In therapy, after many a similar incident is reported and argued over, we start to see Mr. Jones as a kid – an accidental pregnancy, last of four, mostly ignored by his older siblings. His mother was too involved with getting back to her career to have much time for him either. His dad worked away from home a lot and a series of local baby minders brought him up. In short, he never starved, but *he never got butter on his greens*. His sense of injustice and deprivation over the sprouts is disproportionate to the current situation, but he has thirty years behind him of deprivation against which he was never able to protest.

What about Mrs. Jones? She was never good enough for her academic parents who both worked all hours, had five children, and an impeccable home. It was impossible to compete with her perfect mother whom father adored and *with whom he constantly compared her*.

We have here two people very sore from the past but totally unaware of it. Mrs. Jones feels criticised despite her heroic efforts in the kitchen, seeing Mr. Jones as her fault-finding father. Mr. Jones sees only a mother yet again preferring the other kids to him and leaving him to get his own dinner.

When Mrs. Jones comes to understand her husband's longing for a special meal tailored to his exact requirements, and when Mr. Jones comes to understand his wife's yearning for approval and praise because of her childhood, they stand of a chance of having more peaceful Sundays. I can't stress too strongly though how the *dovetailing* of these separate sensitivities reinforces both of them, so instead of disagreement or fair complaint they get a blazing row that terrifies or wearies the children.

Secret Reasons for Marrying

Why did this couple marry in the first place, you may wonder as you sit across from them. I shall try to address the unconscious aims of partner choice (the conscious ones everybody knows about), before looking at the aims and techniques of couple therapy itself and where they differ from one-to-one work.

Bear in mind Freud's dictum here: "Most of what we call love is a resistance to the prospect of leaving home." Maturing and becoming autonomous beings actually scares us. A chronically unhappy, mutually destructive marriage may be the devil the couple know, that is preferable to the devil of divorce and independence which they imagine leads to loneliness and/or helplessness, and a sense of failure.

So, think about these statements:

1. We marry to repeat the positive and/or compensate for the negative in childhood. Given both partners have the same unconscious agenda, neither can be satisfied all the time. Disappointment is therefore *inevitable and natural* in marriage, whatever other needs it fulfils. The understanding and acceptance of dual disappointment is a key feature in couple therapy.

2. We marry in the unconscious, but vain hope of getting specifics, i.e. things we missed, like Mr. Jones and his buttered sprouts that symbolised parental care, and like Mrs. Jones who even now never gets the praise she craves because her husband is too busy looking for a mother substitute. When such needs become conscious between the couple in the therapy room, they can begin to offer some degree of what was lacking in each other's childhood, but without feeling they must parent each other all the time. The here and now adult-to-adult good things in their relationship must also be nurtured. If their childhood needs always dominate, how can they bring up their own children healthily?

3. We marry in order to have another go at a first partially failed scenario, to prove we can do better. We say to ourselves our childhood was just a rehearsal. This, our grown-up marriage, is the real performance. And we're going to make a better job of it than did our parents!

4. We marry for familiarity. Even if we were not fulfilled or happy when young, at least we know we are good at being unfulfilled and unhappy. We have a role to occupy. Many men and women cling to their childhood role of nurse, invalid, rebel, victim, problem solver, rescuer etc., even though they complain bitterly about it. They claim that without them doing their role, the marriage would break down completely. They want freedom

from this martyrdom but if that freedom were offered, they would not know how else to behave. They married in order to repeat what they are used to. Of course it may have been their mum or dad who was the nag, the workaholic, the indecisive one in need of propping up, and they have internalised this model. But in some way an old story is being re-enacted because it is reassuring in its familiarity.

5. We marry to have someone whose fault it is. It's not us that get it wrong in the marriage. It's his or her fault, he or she is no better than my father or mother. We can at last fight back, expose the original perpetrators of our dissatisfaction and hurt, and prove ourselves innocent.

6. We marry to avoid the struggle to grow up and work out our own problems from childhood. We lack confidence? So we marry a confident partner behind whom we can hide. We can relax, no need to take the risks involved in cultivating confidence for ourselves. We can't show constructive anger? We marry someone assertive to relieve us of this unpleasant task, someone we can look up to when he's fighting for our twin objectives, but who we can also blame if that convenient anger is inconveniently turned on us. Afraid of emotional intimacy? We find someone so distant themselves that we are never challenged. Alternatively find someone so good at it we think their ability will just rub off on us automatically, make us more like them through some kind of marital osmosis. The point is to, at all costs, evade taking full responsibility for our own hang-ups and to get someone else out there to love us so much they will do the work for us.

All this sounds negative. People join up their lives for a mixture of reasons, many of them laudable and desirable. They enjoy many happy years together complementing one another's characters, trading their psychological and other talents, genuinely learning from each other and helping one another out. But no marriage can be perfect all the time. It is these unconscious intrusions into day to day life, based on the let-down of their underlying expectations, that are the meat of the couple sessions. The couple do need to have the positive aspects of their relationship drawn to their attention from time to time, but they don't need help to do what they are already good at. The purpose of highlighting the good features to the couple is to help flagging spirits, which boosts motivation to study the negatives. Alas, many couple therapists, especially those starting out, rely overmuch on reassurance of the 'count your blessings' variety. These are designed more to comfort themselves while keeping hostilities from erupting, than to help the couple dissect their relationship.

Aims of Couple Therapy: a Summary

In couple therapy I am not aiming to change personalities or turn back time to make the pair fall in love all over again, or to pronounce solutions to specific problems. My aims include:

1. I aim to help suffering persons *understand* through their here and now interactions in the consulting room, through their reports of current strife at home, and family life way back when, how they tick as individuals, and as a couple. In therapy, as they battle out their joint issues, they get to know their own and their partner's psychology better.

2. I aim to promote mutual education in the broadest sense, the couple being enabled to *share* marital disappointment instead of relentlessly blaming the other for it. They need to teach one another about their own needs resulting from emotional nutritional deprivations in childhood, though it can be a hell of a job getting them to recognise those needs or accept them without shame. Then they can each try, to some realistic, attainable degree, to *meet* some of those needs in the other in times of the other's crisis, rather than competing and demanding their own needs be seen as more important.

3. Having realised then shared their locked away need, thus dissolving shame, they now have to *withdraw* unrealisable chronic demands on the other. It is time to take responsibility for their singular problems not caused by the other. Thus they come to accept the other has needs too, maybe different to their own. Both sets of needs can only be met to a limited degree. Psychological maturity

is marked by a capacity to bear an imperfect world while striving to make productive use of what is possible and available. For no partner can roll back time, play parental substitute for the other, denying their own needs entirely. Some try, and this is precisely what brings them into therapy.

4. Once they have the hang of how the unconscious works, how it shows up in everyday life – in their bedroom, in their child rearing, in their work lives, with the in-laws – they can start becoming *therapists for each other*. I do *not* mean forever navel gazing, or scoring points by being the most insightful one, or using their privileged psychological knowledge about each other's sensitive areas as weapons. But when one is in pain, the other, probably more than anyone in the world, is best equipped to help them explore their feelings without the need to deploy defensive manoeuvres. Here, we are of course talking about couple therapy's role in building or rebuilding *deep trust* between the pair.

    The couple learn to feed each other's self-esteem, but also to stand up for their personal rights to respect, honesty and fair dealing. Couples can't always be sugary helpers for each other. If a position of basic trust has been established, then a fight about maltreatment, or a refusal to collude in being bullied, harassed, unfairly criticised or persistently cloyingly clung to, can be borne as part and parcel of married life, even if the incident goes on for days without a clear resolution. A fight does not have to mean the end of the world. Many couples from 'well brought up' families have no idea how to fight, or how to make up. Sadly, they see any sign of impending quarrel as a dire threat to the relationship and so all matters of clarification and negotiation are driven underground. The subsequent deadness is brought into the therapy room in the first session, producing a suffocating atmosphere within minutes that is virtually diagnostic.

5. The couple come to recognise, respect and honour their marriage as a third *joint personality*, as well as seeing themselves as two separate individuals. If the joint personality smothers individuality, or too much self-interest starves the joint personality, the marriage will teeter. Very often I see one party wanting

more separateness, feeling claustrophobic in the relationship, while the other wants more belonging, intertwining. When their respective early family lives are looked at by both, the reason becomes clear. They come to understand that it isn't a case of who is right and who wrong, but how to respect valid differences and to compromise with each other. Constant fighting over perfectly legitimate but different needs, rather than exploring them, damages the union itself. The one who attains temporary domination has won but a hollow victory.

6. The couple's difficulties in distributing *power* between them may be evident from the outset, but often they are hidden as neither party wishes to be exposed as 'the nasty one'. Sometimes, due to events at home, power issues pop up unexpectedly in the sessions. I always try to address these while they are 'hot'.

The Mathews family

The Mathews had a girl of ten who craved her own smartphone. Mum wanted to buy her one so the two of them could always be in touch, face to face in real time. For her the question of safety was paramount. She also appreciated the peer pressure and didn't want her daughter to be left out. Dad on the other hand insisted she was too young. He had been brought up to save, be prudent with money. He wanted to pass on this value to his daughter. He detested the culture of immediate gratification. He was also afraid of her being groomed via the net. So Dad put his foot down and said no. Mum acquiesced then went out and bought the phone anyway, telling the child to keep it out of sight. As one might expect, Dad found it and this led to a huge marital row.

Dad was accused of being a tyrant. Mum was a lying bitch. Eventually both partners saw how they cheated or bullied each other in order to gain or retain power for themselves. They began to examine families of origin, how each had learned as youngsters the most effective way to get what they wanted. Neither forcefully laying down the law, nor tacitly agreeing and then going behind the other one's back, was contributing anything worthwhile to the marriage. These old lessons transplanted into their new family were proving inimical to trust and damaging for their children.

An incident like this can lead to productive inspection by the couple of their marriage's history, how and when the lack of trust developed, how and when power struggles came to fill the gap. This usually occasions much sadness which in turn creates an opportunity for renegotiation, or in some cases a chance to learn how to negotiate for the first time.

7. Couple therapy can help relieve the pressure they put on each other. This aim is to enable the couple to see the interlinking of their leftover agendas from childhood that each are trying to get their partner to address, and that each appears to be bloody-mindedly refusing. To do this I assist them in locating then spelling out the unconscious pact they made when they committed to each other: I will do or be this for you, if you will do or be that for me. Much of their anger and bitterness, constantly expressed over minor bad habits perhaps, like the lid being left off the toothpaste, is due to their belief that the sacred pact has been broken.

The Greens

Mrs. Green endlessly implores Mr. Green to talk to her, chat, be companionable. She asks about his work, his opinion on the news, the weather even. There's no response, a grunt at best. She complains he ignores her for hours, walks out of the room rather than answer a question. She's constantly miserable and it's all his fault. Why won't he share with her? She follows him about the house begging contact but getting angrier by the minute too. She does not see that his refusal to respond, his literally walking away, serves to force her into the begging position that she hates but is willing to endure if only he will communicate with her.

The consequence of his passive-aggressive withholding reassures him he is desperately wanted, despite her rising anger which conveniently proves to him he's right to avoid her. He thinks he is responsibly preventing a dangerous confrontation (he knows 'talking' will lead to her airing endless dissatisfaction) but he also relishes his power. He tells himself she is a clinging nagger and he is merely keeping her under control.

They both need insight into how *equally* needy they are (probably the reason they were so drawn to each other in the first place). They are yet to learn through the same old quarrel – "you stick to me like a limpet" and "you neglect me, starve me" – that each is trying to compel the other into compliance with the contract they set up with each other long ago. It might have gone something like this: Mr. Green agreed to give Mrs. Green all the attention her mother did not, if she would love him unconditionally and not hound him as his father did for his imperfections. Mrs. Green *is* trying to love her husband unconditionally, but she keeps following him about, laying down conditions. As to Mr. Green, beneath his resentment he does love her but she wants him to love her in specific ways and he won't or can't yield to what he experiences as commands.

When they see the pattern and its genesis in their respective families, blame can stop and a new way to handle a *mutual* sense of unfair deprivation can begin.

CHAPTER NINE

WORKING WITH COUPLES: TECHNIQUES AND ANXIETIES

Where are couple therapy and individual therapy techniques similar and where different? I believe too many of the techniques we take for granted doing one-to-one dynamic work have been imported into couple work, to its detriment. Many therapists mistakenly see couple work as merely an add-on, a frill. All the same, there is much from the rigorous discipline of individual work that I believe we should retain if the unconscious interplay between couples is going to be given the chance to emerge naturally in its own time and not be drowned out by fix-it-quick advice, gimmicky exercises or mediation disguised as therapy. (As readers may know, mediation helps couples negotiate over *practical* matters – money, child access, etc., whereas therapy is concerned with coming to a deeper emotional adjustment to and betterment of the pair's *relationship*.)

Once un- or semi-conscious forces do start to suggest themselves they should not be dealt with by a distant, hierarchical therapist fearful of getting 'stuck in'. The consulting room should be a place where the unthinkable is thought and the unsayable said, but within stout boundaries set by an unshockable therapist. Couple therapy is about understanding violent and upsetting emotions, not constraining them within the usual social norms of politeness and self-controlled discourse. Couple therapy works best when the problems are enacted in the room rather than reported weeks after the events. Censorship, however subtle, is counterproductive to the enterprise.

I work to establish an informal rapport with the couple by the way I behave and relate – relaxed, responsive, interested. I want to make it alright for them to let me into their living room, tell me what happens there. In fact I aim to make the therapy room so inhibition-free it actually *becomes* their living room. I hope and trust that due to my ordinariness – no expert airs, no stiff posture – the possibility and even probability that I have had troubles myself is so self-evident it needn't be questioned or fantasised about. They just intuit that their mess will not surprise or frighten me.

In one-to-one work the emphasis tends to be on an investigation of the patient's past so as to demonstrate how it is being re-experienced through transference figures in the present, including the therapist. In couple work the present comes kicking and screaming, or sullen and silent, right into the room. The present has to be attended to before the past can even be considered. Usually the couple have never thought that their previous lives might have any bearing on the way they conduct their present ones. What a barmy idea! This is an emergency; the most important relationship in their lives is under threat. Who cares about the mouldy old past?

The individual practitioner's standing back technique, quietly bringing about an atmosphere conducive to reverie, encouraging the patient to drift back to childhood, is totally inappropriate in couple work, particularly at the start.

The first of my list of ten central techniques, therefore, has more to do with being than doing.

1. **The therapist's way of being.** I allow myself to appear more bodily and facially relaxed than in the one-to-one, very still mode. If the couple in front of me tend to wave their arms about I permit myself to do the same. After all, we are in this together, I am not some high priest come to judge or psychiatrist come to 'shrink' them. I use everyday language and gradually pick up their key phrases and slang. In short I am joining in the marriage's way of operating, rather as a visiting family member might. This is in direct opposition to the traditional tendency of having the patient submit to the conventions of therapy and its

language. I am all the while thinning the filter between myself and my couple so I can get inside the marriage to understand it, rather than observing it from the outside.

Having quickly established my position as non-threatening confidante, I then make simple suggestions that will defuse the immediate crisis that brought the pair for help. I may ask them to suspend any decision about leaving home, seeing a lawyer, moving in with a lover or freezing bank accounts until all three of us have had time to study the problems in a safe neutral place and decide whether some couple sessions on a regular basis could be useful. I explain that this might take a few sessions, but if the marriage is to be properly honoured this assessment phase can't be rushed. We have to know the right questions before we start tackling answers. This isn't going to be just a sticking plaster job. It's amazing how such stabilising arrangements bring clarity and calm so therapy can start without panic dominating the proceedings.

2. **Separate Sessions.** To ensure each partner feels heard at the start by the therapist who is supposed to be helping them (even if they don't feel heard by their other half), and to remove any inhibiting forces exerted on them by the partner, the couple are seen separately at assessment time. Without this procedure one or both parties may succeed in obscuring their true feelings about the current situation in order not to inflame the other, and I miss vital information.

Despite consciously longing for help, couples often arrive with a shared unconscious *resistance* to the therapy. It may be they desire resolution but without all the nasty revelations and confessions the process might involve. Such humiliating exchanges might even make matters worse. This resistance is hard to maintain if I see each member of the pair alone.

My routine, though not written in stone, is to see the couple together, then separately, then together again. On the fourth meeting we all sit round a coffee table and pool our views before deciding on the way forward -- to go on, to defer, to stop, to refer one or both for individual work, to review medication or to request any tests or assessments in the case of physical, neurological or possible psychiatric illness. The example below shows how important these separate sessions can be.

The Browns

Angela and David Brown are having a terrible time over money, work and the children but both say there is no problem in their sex life. In her individual assessment session though, Angela tells me she has not felt erotic for years but goes through with sex or Mr. Brown will get moody with her and ratty with the children. She says sex is very important to him, seems linked to his self-esteem. After a few days of "going without" a big black cloud hangs over the house. She thinks she has lost interest because he dominates her, though in a very subtle way. It certainly isn't verbal or violent. He just makes her feel she's in the wrong all the time. She longs for tenderness, small talk, a bit of light-hearted fun, but he is so serious. She daren't try to explain her discontent to him or he'll say: "I'm not a rapist, a male chauvinist. If you don't like it we won't do it; I will go without." Thereafter his moods would make her life intolerable. But yes, she loves him and doesn't want to part.

This knowledge helps me with my overall assessment of the couple. Angela has tipped me off about the delicate sexual situation which I am sure she would like me to help them address when the time is right.

In the meantime David has told me some of his doubts about being good enough at school, for his father, for his girlfriends and now for his wife. He senses she is not as frisky as she once was and wonders once more if he is not up to scratch in the bedroom, as he fears he is not up to scratch in the boardroom. I can see already that with better communication these two might well make it, if I am not led up a blind alley by the problems they jointly presented at the start.

3. **Interpretation.** Once post assessment therapy is under way I gradually introduce comments that interpret what might be going on between them under the surface of their communication and behaviours, what their body language might mean, what

defensive manoeuvres they keep adopting. These remarks are floated as possibilities rather than certainties, in the hope the couple will discuss and refine them, as well as relate them to events occurring at home. Where apposite I link my observations to one or the other's childhood experiences or relations with original family members. I have accrued this valuable information from the individual sessions at assessment time as well as from their subsequent contributions.

I also *translate* occasionally, speak for each, putting their words into a form the other might more easily hear. "I think what Angela is trying to get across...", "When David does that thing with his shoulders, could he be conveying...?" I *model* confrontation sometimes, when one wants to challenge their partner but fears retaliation. I try to challenge the partner on their behalf, firmly, but stripped of attack, revenge or triumph. I always check with the would-be challenger if I have got it right.

Part of couple work is the retraining of each side to argue profitably, to elicit feedback or understanding from the other, not win points or dominate the other. If one is a bit overwhelmed by the other I may support his desire to stand up for himself, often using just a look of encouragement or a cough rather than words. Of course the one who overwhelms needs to inspect their way of doing this, as well as why they are doing it. For the therapist, remaining non-judgemental can be very hard, but ultimately it is for the couple to realign their communicational habits to suit them, not me.

4. **Pre-therapy containment** is frequently vital, but is rarely discussed in the literature because it consists of ordinary human support and doesn't go by some esoteric term. My phone rings. The voice is frantic. The couple are too stirred up to talk to each other. One has packed their bags; the lover has turned up at their home; one is drunk all the time; Mum has taken the kids to Gran's. I have to stabilise the situation by using good old common sense and friendly advice. "Let the dust settle and take time to regain your composure, then see if she'll accept an invitation to come and talk with a neutral outsider. At least we

know the kids are safe at Gran's." Or: "Why not let him cool off, give him time to think, before demanding he come to therapy as if it were a punishment. You have to choose your moment…"

Some couple workers will not see the pair until lovers are dismissed, questionnaires filled out, little essays written on "what I think our problems are." This may be useful for research purposes but does nothing for a couple who are in crisis. They need to be seen while their problems are at their peak, be this a rowdy business or when, after years of misery, their tether has finally come to an end and they have hit despair. This is when they are more likely to talk openly as there is now nothing to lose, no face to keep up. If they are put on a waiting list, the old collusive cover-ups will return and motivation will slip away. They will let the situation drag on or one party will take impulsive action which may be irredeemable.

5. **Action replay.** This technique is drawn on during the more mature stages of therapy, when the three participants have established a shared language and a resilient Alliance. After a painful scene between the pair in the consulting room, I replay it for them as I saw and understood it, including the latent process (its deeper meanings). I don't interrupt while the altercation is in full swing but let it run its course, the better to trace its development for the couple afterwards. I am not there to stop hostilities breaking out but to make sense of those hostilities for the couple, and aid them to open up better pathways along which to exchange their negative feelings and thoughts. Hopefully these new pathways will be taken home and tried out in other quarrels in the same category.

When the live conflict in the room is being negotiated by stiff silence, sulks, tearful sniffing or long periods of heads in hands, I eventually break the deadlock by using what I know about the couple and the way they are behaving now, to guess aloud what each would say to the other were they able to speak. This usually prompts them to confirm or disconfirm whether I am correct and to what extent. The avoided conflict is thus reclaimed and available for three-way study.

6. **Focussing on the joint personality.** As the couple tussle in the therapy room, each certain they are the one getting the rough end of the stick, they need to see what they are doing to the *relationship itself*, their joint personality. Is that relationship being enhanced or sabotaged by the way they are communicating? A clean fight or even a dirty one, provided it's sorted out afterwards, can enable the couple to progress (and enjoy making up afterwards!). But habitual non-processed fights damage the very fabric of the couple unit they have built together. That twosome is a living organism and needs nurturing as much as the two people it comprises.

Some people can't see the 'us', only the bad 'him' or the bad 'her', the one who is at fault, the one who must change. Others are so bound up in their joint personality that all they can speak of is '*our* problems' or '*our* achievements', as if they had no failures, successes or problems of their own. They have lost all sense of separateness. Helping the blamers to become a couple and to recognise that unit's needs, and aiding the glued-at-the-hip pair to recover their separate identities, forms the very basis of many treatments.

For some, their joint personality is a whinging child they have brought to me for feeding, or at least babysitting, while they go off and indulge their respective interests or careers. Or it is a naughty child who won't shape up and I am the child guidance clinic, the expert who will dictate what is to be done without them having to think about it. Both these couples entertain a fantasy that they can deposit their 'us' with me to be sorted out while they continue with the rest of their life unhampered. They show little distress in the consulting room as I am seen as the one who takes care of all that psychology stuff. Neither do they talk with one another about the sessions during the week. It's as if they have left the joint personality on my carpet to be picked up at the next session, all its problems solved.

This scenario is common with dual career, busy parents, where they only seem to come together for child management, house maintenance, running their business or going to parties. This is not a matter for tut-tutting at them, though the situation is infuriating for the therapist. There are cogent reasons in both their histories that explain why, for them, blending with another in intimate relating would be experienced as dangerous. These antecedents need to be explored with them before the couple can start to take back their 'child' and look after it properly. They have no idea yet that they have been living side by side, not *with* each other.

7. **Introduction of internal parents.** Introducing each partner to their own and each other's internal parents can be difficult, as therapists from many different schools, never mind our patients, battle with this concept. The term does not refer merely to memories of what happened in childhood with regard to parents, but *what the child made of those experiences in his own mind*. It is more often particular *qualities and attitudes* in the mother, father, or parental couple repeatedly directed toward him, and toward one another, that coloured his internal picture of them, rather than specific events or actions.

Children are naturally curious and want to make sense of the world about them. They are daily obliged to absorb parental cuddles, fights, silences, chit-chat and the television and put them all together into some meaningful whole. They make theories, models, stories, grappling to find sense and thereby safety in the mysterious and unexplained adult influences that swirl around them. If they never confide their stories, check them out for accuracy with a trusted adult or sibling, the stories can become very elaborate indeed, perhaps falsely consoling and sometimes very frightening.

Neither do internal parents have much to do with the external, real and now much older ones. *Internal parents* live on in the subject's mind as private images associated with all manner of passions and conflicts from childhood. This is the patient's unique version, his story of his parents, resulting not simply from their actions, but what he *subjectively experienced and then concluded* in response to their way of relating to him. These are the parents that are 'woken up' in later intimate relationships, and frequently projected onto partners. The external elderly parents would barely recognise themselves!

It should be borne in mind, however, that these children's internal portraits, however fantastical, are based on what did occur, and what they did witness, however much they misinterpreted or twisted the raw facts to fit in with their hopes and fears. They have not invented the entire picture from scratch. But it's their own 'take' on their parents as separate and joint personalities that will overlay all their attempts at coupledom when the time comes.

Internal parents and child abuse

A person's self-percept is to a great extent determined by the way he experiences his parents and this view of himself is brought into therapy for examination by both self and partner. How does an abused person see himself?

A therapist sees many patients diagnosed with trauma or abuse, the referral letter hinting at a complicated family history. Beneath the patient's historical account she detects hardened assumptions about himself. "My otherwise nice dad used to beat me so I must have been a disobedient, rebellious kid. I must have driven him to it. *I am now an evil unlovable grown-up.* I hide it, act nice, compliant; but I know I'm just a sham." Or: "My mother played with me in our baths in a sexy way. She said she was 'just rubbing me down to get me clean' and all mummies did this. It frightened but excited me and I masturbated a lot throughout my childhood, feeling dirty and ashamed. *I am now a grubby shameful adult.* I do not deserve love, I would soil it."

As young children, both these patients relied on the defence of splitting. In order to keep the loving side of father and mother whole and 'good' in the child's mind, the 'bad' aspects of the parent were attributed to and internalised by the child's own self and carried into adulthood. "I am wicked and therefore undeserving" the beaten child believed. "I am dirty minded and therefore polluted, unlovable" the abused child concluded. These examples are of course simplifications, but the self-precept resulting from abusive parenting is a very serious matter indeed. The adult victim knows full well that beating or inappropriate sex play is wrong; but he can't afford to lose the parental attachment, the family bond, even now. Many patients go on caring for ageing parents who treated them abominably in childhood. Others separate geographically, may never speak to them again, but they still retain the negative self-image.

At the time of the aberrant behaviours by the offender the child was dependent on that person for affection, a home, an identity, and a predictable, hence safe, environment. Without that relationship the child would not survive. He could not afford to see the perpetrator as wicked and reject him or her. Such people often grow up to be treated badly all over again, or they 'identify with the aggressor' and can only relate to a partner if this time they do the abusing.

The internal parents and marriage

Some spouses have an unconscious wish to destroy or triumph over their internal parents, out of envy of their union, or in revenge for damage they believed was inflicted on them by those parents. It's imperative that their own marriage is seen as a success. They will go to any lengths to demonstrate this, even to the point of making their lives a veritable hell. Any amount of suffering is preferable to letting their internal parents win. They will tolerate appalling treatment, accept any degree of blame, rather than face the fact that the marriage has failed.

Sometimes the internal parents' image is of a sad and broken unit, or a fragile one, and their child grows up with a great desire to heal and unite them through his own marriage. If that marriage breaks down, the reaction is much more disastrous than a separation or divorce for someone with solid internal parents – and that is painful enough!

Doing couple therapy I watch how a pair manage a quarrel. Who is each addressing, their partner or the residues inside them of their parents? Why can't a bullied partner stand up for themselves? Why do they forever pour oil on troubled water, never speaking their mind? How come one of them assumes all will be lost if a fight breaks out, and the other insists a good clearing of the air, even if it means a row, is a healthy thing to be doing? Getting each party to see and understand the other one's internal parental voices that are in great part running the show, can dramatically alter the way they relate.

8. **Facilitating discussion in the therapy room.** Let us move now to a more conscious level of functioning. Ideas and values about what living together means are fashioned not just by books, religion, films, education, class and cultural background and so on, but by what we saw, heard and learned during our day to day interactions with our separate parents and our parents as a couple. We took their relationship to be normal as we had no other examples before us in our earliest years. We imbibed many of their attitudes and beliefs without thinking about it.

When we grow up and marry or cohabit, we bring to the union all kinds of expectations based on those family experiences. We take it for granted that they are ordinary and universal. To our astonishment we find our partner is speaking an alien language, and has completely different notions to ours about living together. Much couple work, especially with younger people, necessitates helping them question their and their partner's upbringing and generate a new shared culture.

During the session, I must at all times be aware of the bulging consulting room. Active in it are Mr. and Mrs. with their personal relationship to each other and each one's relationship to their joint personality. Both partners' relationships to their internal parents as well as their actual parents also affect the therapeutic endeavour, not to mention grandparents who can be central characters sometimes. And I should never forget that I too have internal parents, though the real ones are long dead. I too have had experience of marriage and couple relationships before that, so have my own view on what constitutes a well-functioning couple. Then there are my and the couple's children as real persons but also objects of projection and other defences. Prejudice and viewpoints abound and I often struggle to remain non-partisan.

Facilitating discussion about all these influences on the pair is rather like chairing a busy meeting. I try not to confuse the couple, but make sure none of the 'ghosts' in the room, mentioned above, are left out if pressing to be heard. As therapy reaches its most mature stage I give the couple the floor as much as possible, but occasionally ask the ghosts to join in for a bit.

However, I only do this when there is a puzzled pause in the proceedings and I feel my ghostly observations might expedite the ongoing process. I want the couple to work out their own style of marriage, not the one I think they should have or the one I would want for myself.

9. **Transference.** The most critical difference between individual and couple therapy is probably the way transference is handled. There already exists a massive amount of transference and counter-transference between the couple, as well as projective identification (see chapter two), or they would never have got together in the first place. As the therapist, I stay a real solid person, my own personality characteristics on show. This will, to a great extent, contradict any emerging fantasies they may have about me. The last thing I want is any intrusive transference toward myself, for the job in hand is to promote the couple's insight into what they deposit in *each other* and then complain about; how they see in *each other* aspects of their own or their partner's actual and internal parents; how their *own* defence mechanisms stimulate a predictable defence in the *other*. Although aware of my own 'stuff' that is triggered by their exchanges, these reactions remain my own private property and are hived off for later perusal in self supervision.

Unlike one-to-one work, where transference is not always evident or is weak, or is linked to some other significant person, the transference between the couple is right in the therapist's face; she can't miss it. Almost always it is the persisting transferential distortions on both sides, along with the defence mechanisms used to deal with them, that have brought them into treatment. It isn't their problems that are the problem, but their inability to truly communicate about them.

10. **Developmental phases.** Couples are understandably too mired in their pain in the here and now to wonder about the developmental phases of their relationship and which one they might be living through at the moment. Due to their respective personal histories some of these phases will be easier to pass

through than others. One party may find one marital phase especially troublesome while the other does not, but finds some other phase fraught with obstacles.

Jack and Jill

Jack and Jill married young and their marriage is in the middle of its lifespan. The kids are working or at university. Financial strains are over and both sets of grandparents are settled and happy. Jill is also in midlife, wanting change, new horizons, career development, overseas travel. The marital phase parallels her own individual phase so the two bolster each other and she is raring to go. Meanwhile Jack remains dependent and a loner. A cabinetmaker proud of his traditional workmanship, he has no wish to further his self-employed career, with which he is quite happy. He is not an ambitious man and is content with his marriage and his way of life, despite being a similar age to his discontented wife.

When first married they were very much in love and their different temperaments seemed only to complement one another, making for harmony and happiness. Children came along; the house was extended, mainly by Jack, and everyone seemed busy and content. But now Jill wants to move on whereas Jack remains in his own stage of development irrespective of the fact that the relationship has progressed to midlife. Jill begins to disrespect him, finds him nerdy, withdrawn, clingy. Jack feels he can't keep up with his wife and she might leave him if he doesn't change. But if he's honest he has no desire to change. They consult a therapist.

Toward the end of a complete therapy (rather than the short-term rescue work I am often called upon to do) the pair need to understand this notion of phases, identifying where their relationship is standing now, and preparing for their next phase. What will be its likely stresses and opportunities, given what they now know about themselves as two individuals and as a joint personality? This preventive work is my farewell gift, for soon they will be on their own.

Sometimes there is no need to work with phases, but in cases like Jack and Jill's, a developmental perspective is a vital component of the therapy if they are not to end up just blaming and criticising each other without understanding how time has affected both individuals and the marital unit, without it necessarily being anyone's fault.

A marriage that begins happily can become very stressed as the two partners age and the marriage as a unit also evolves. Often the needs and aspirations of the couple begin to diverge. The reverse is also true, that marriages that begin stormily can grow into mature attachments as time allows for the growth of shared objectives and values. Couples who come to therapy are rarely aware of the effects of time and tend to point the finger at their partner when they can no longer account for the loss of certainty in their marriage. The therapist can defuse much animosity and encourage collaborative investigation by showing which phases each person and the joint personality are currently facing.

This is not simply about chronological age. Both parties may be sensible adults but each will have areas of fixations, that is bits of themselves that are stuck at an earlier time in their lives that they now want desperately to grow away from, or which they feel so comfortable with they have no desire to budge. Jill was her sick mother's carer until she left home and was never entirely happy with looking after Jack and the children when she temporarily gave up her job. Having met all her domestic commitments and now in her forties, she longs to move on. Whereas Jack remembers his happiest time as being a toddler, with Dad teaching him carpentry and taking him everywhere with him: great buddies. Later life was very problematic and his father died when he was only ten. In his marriage he feels he has reconstituted his earlier contentment and has no wish to change anything.

I will briefly discuss the specific stages in the life of the couple in the next chapter, but I want to finalise this one by highlighting some of the anxieties you are bound to face if you are new to this kind of therapy.

Couple Work: Therapist's Anxieties

What is the correct pace? In supervising, I find that many supervisees branching into couple work worry that they are pacing the session too fast or too slow. Over-anxious practitioners tend to keep busy, collect too much history, too many facts for this early stage, in an effort to counter the panicky feeling that they haven't a clue what's going on in front of them and the couple are bound to think they are useless. It's so hard, if you are more familiar with individual work, to bear your ignorance and let them *show* you rather than *tell* you what's wrong. The couple unit's turbulence may have to rule for a while until you start to see a pattern of relating taking shape before your eyes.

Should the couple remain silent at first, waiting for you to ask questions, you might invite them to each give you a quick summary of the problems as they see them, so you have some context. I never say who is to do this first, or how long to take, or whether they may interrupt one another's account. Watching how they negotiate this simple task produces masses of information – not because of what they actually say, but the way they manage the telling between them. You are seeing a miniature model of their communication system right in front of you.

Another tendency is to feel so distressed or overwhelmed by the pain, anger, tears, recriminations and attacks, the sheer decibel level in the room, that you fail to intervene at all and let the pair massacre each other or freeze each other out, just as they do at home. Exhausted by just a re-run of usual hostilities, they fail to return for the next session.

How do I present myself? Clearly you're not going to serve coffee or share your holiday photos, but neither should you appear neutral or mysterious, too much like the traditional analyst. All you would get then is a civilised discussion where everybody behaves themselves out of reverence for the hallowed atmosphere you've created. Precious little access is gained to the marriage itself. Once more they fail to return for the second session.

If your authentic self is not on show another complication might arise. Either or both parties develop a fantasy attachment to you which distracts from the work you are all supposed to be doing. This is a defensive manoeuvre to avoid getting to grips with the couple issue that has brought them. So much nicer to have romantic dreams about the therapist, with yourself in control of the fantasy, rather than face control issues in the marriage. Sometimes the attachment to the therapist is because the wife or husband believes her to be on their side, so it's going to be easy – two against one. Occasionally one partner sees the therapist as hostile or cold and uses this as an excuse to end the proceedings altogether. A friendly but not gushing or over intimate presence is part of couple therapy technique, adopted to avoid the above complications; it's not just the therapist being kind.

What about the honeymoon effect? Yes, the relief of having found a safe place to dump their anguish leads some couples to return home and make love for the first time in years. Their problems have been left with you for safe keeping and this has created a space for the good parts of their relationship to creep back. At first they are overjoyed, but you prepare yourself for facing their dreadful disappointment when the old difficulties flare up again. It is important that they see you're not at all fazed by this symptom return, that you still have faith in the therapy and in them.

What about my personal responses to them? You need at all times to be aware of these, but this is not individual psychotherapy where the counter-transference is woven into the work. You file away your private reactions once you have identified them. If you don't register them, you are in danger of couching any interventions in terms of your own prejudices or preferences. Thus it becomes dangerously easy to fall into a transferential relationship with one partner or with the marital unit itself. Before embarking on couple work it is essential you have a good long think about your own and your parents' couple relationships and face honestly your evaluation of them.

It is especially easy to fall in love or loathing, sympathy or disapproval, when conducting the separate sessions, for the person is understandably trying to win you over to their way of seeing things. I often feel (initially): "She's so selfish, hasn't a clue about his vulnerabilities. *I* would know how to restore his confidence." Or: "What an arrogant prig. *I'd* never stand for it like she does. I could show her how to cut him down a peg or two." Of course it would be totally out of order to use immediate, uncensored feelings in the session, but it's vitally important I am aware of them so I don't fall into the trap of manipulating the work to fit my bias.

Most of us have quite strong opinions about marriage and cohabitation, divorce, the rights and needs of children, open marriage, and infidelity. In supervision I often pick up distaste for or approval of one or other partner in the supervisee's report of her couple session. However fair she is trying to be, her personal views almost always colour her interventions. It is in this area most of all that external supervision can help. But the supervisory couple need to know one another well and conduct themselves as openly and frankly as do the three people in the actual session. For example, I may have to ask a supervisee her honest opinion on gay couples adopting, if that is what she is being faced with in the session. Like couple therapy, couple supervision has to be more interventionist to be effective. However, supervision is not personal therapy, though grey areas exist; so your deeply personal self-examination (self-supervision), often at very short notice, is critical in fast moving couple work.

How is self-supervision better than supervision from someone senior to me? Here is an example from my own experience. If I don't have any kind of reaction to either partner, I worry about my distance, my lack of involvement. What could I be avoiding? Are they really tedious, snooty superficial people or am I perhaps sneakily envious of their achievements, social networks, holidays, their posh home, their money? Is it because they have the kind of uncomplicated, healthy, successful children I always wanted? Could it be deeper, that there is something I want to pull away from, something between them that I suspect was between my mum and dad, or between me and my first husband? Do I shrink from them out of a wish to protect, because if I allowed myself to feel anything it would be poisonous for them? Only when I have answered these questions *for myself*, am I able to work comfortably with the couple.

This illustrates why all the external supervision in the world (for individual, family, and group work as well) can't help you sometimes. No supervisor can know your deepest secrets concerning couples you were or are part of, about your internal as well as your external parents. She may be told the facts, but can't experience the wounds, memories and the coping strategies you have organised to cope with that history. This is where your training and ideology has to be left behind. You are on your own. This is where the mature Mary Smith, safely daring therapist, comes of age. If you know yourself well enough, it is quite possible to fly solo when you have to. Be assured that if you are going to do serious couple work, you have to!

I would advise that you self-supervise fresh from the session, no notes needed, just a bit of peace and quiet. (Notes are a different matter in the early stages when you are attempting to assess patients – see chapter eleven). No time? Make time or you are just scraping the surface of the work. Besides, if you delude yourself that external supervision alone will be enough in an emergency, consider how long it's going to take to fix a mutually convenient emergency appointment, by which time the material has been superseded by even more problematic stuff, or has gone off the boil, leaving supervision redundant. Awaiting rescue from someone senior is not always the most grown-up way to deal with a crisis. If you can do the job yourself, think of the cost and travel you have saved, never mind the added wisdom you have gained.

When I began couple work I changed my schedule so that I left much more than the conventional ten minutes between appointments. I soon got used to it and the quality of the therapy more than justified any extra time taken, because the couples responded faster as I grew in confidence.

Is termination in couple therapy different to termination in individual therapy? Of course. With a couple, as their relationship improves and you become aware of your growing redundancy, you re-experience a painful envy of the now joined-up pair. You have to let your internal parents be together in intercourse while you sit out on the landing unwanted, and you have to bear it. More rarely, you feel able to rejoice at their rediscovered union because it represents freedom from bondage to the internal parents who long ago you had to please, or look after emotionally, or be their go-between. Now you are free of them.

Couple work can feel really lonely toward the end, when you are no longer needed so much. The couple now turn to one another for emotional nourishment and you are soon forgotten. You know this is how it should be, but you long for the sad goodbyes from the solo patient who is grateful, wonders what he'll do without you, who will always keep a little candle burning in his heart for you

With a couple, you have to encourage them to give to each other, *not you*, what was always in them to give, but which you have set free from the mutual strife that first brought them to you. Apart from their polite thanks, any congratulation or celebration of success is an intimate matter between the pair and not for you to steal or feel entitled to. Like a plumber, you have repaired and even strengthened a dodgy boiler that was worn and leaking. You have sealed the pipes after scraping the gunge from their linings: the water flows clean again. Time for the plumber, quite unnoticed, to quit the premises.

Suggested reading:

Bowlby, J. (1969, 1973, 1980). *Attachment and Loss.* Vols.1-3. London: Hogarth Press.

Bramley, W. (1996). *The Supervisory Couple in Broad Spectrum Psychotherapy.* London: Free Association Books.

Bramley, W. (2008). *Bewitched, Bothered and Bewildered: How couples really work.* London: Karnac.

Clulow, C. F. and Mattinson, J. (1989). *Marriage inside out: understanding problems of intimacy.* Harmondsworth: Penguin.

Clulow, C. F. (2001). *Adult Attachment and Couple Psychotherapy.* London: Brunner/Routledge.

Ruszczynski, S. (1993). *Psychotherapy with couples: Theory and Practice at the Tavistock Institute of Marital Studies.* London: Karnac.

Ruszczynski, S. and Fisher, J. (1995). (Eds) *Intrusiveness and intimacy in the couple.* London: Karnac.

Skynner, A. C. R. (1976a). *One Flesh: Separate Persons.* London: Constable.

Skynner, A. C. R. (1976b). *Systems of Family and Marital Psychotherapy.* New York: Brunner/Mazel.

CHAPTER TEN

THE DEVELOPMENTAL PERSPECTIVE

From whichever ideological school of therapy we graduated, and however many years ago, it is a safe bet that we were taught about the human life cycle and the various developmental challenges associated with each phase. In this chapter I will quickly lay out the course of individuals' development, then go on to discuss midlife in more depth, then discuss the developmental phases of the couple.

Different theorists use their own language, but basically we learned that our first major task is to separate out our own identity from the merger with mother that duped us into experiencing ourselves, mother, and the universe as all one. We are weaned from our mothers literally and metaphorically – an incalculable psychic as well as bodily wrench with long-term consequences. Then comes the forced assimilation into our world of third parties – Dad and siblings – necessitating the management of jealousy and competitiveness. At the same time we must master the training of our bodies to be continent. We work hard to eat and speak nicely, totter then walk proudly, all the while earning approval and thus self-regard. Then school presents itself: we have to learn not only academic lessons, but how to survive the playground, make peace or war with our peers and new authority figures outside the family.

Adolescence throws up huge ordeals as we struggle to find our sexual, social and, to some extent, career path, along with becoming independent of the family. Settling down with a partner and maybe having children is the next stage, when self-interest versus putting others first really comes into the foreground. Then follows midlife and old age, having to deal with all manner of endings, and yes, sometimes new beginnings too. But even a new beginning at this time presages the inevitability of death. How are we to come to terms with the life we have led?

All our trainings have no doubt concentrated in-depth on the early stages of life, when the sense of self was forming, the mother–baby relationship laying down a template for future relations with others as well as a firm or shaky precept of ourselves. I am not going to repeat any of that, as the literature is vast. I want to use the so-called midlife crisis, in its early and later stages, as an example and pose the question: What is the use of knowing about human development when doing psychotherapy? *What difference does it make to the treatment?*

What is the Midlife Crisis?

This term, now embedded in every-day discourse, is indisputably useful to sum up many a middle-aged person's dilemmas or seemingly crazy choices. It also lends itself easily to mockery and denial. Many a very serious and rather frightening situation is passed off as "just the midlife crisis" as if it was of little import and, like the common cold, would soon pass.

The term was coined by the analyst Eliot Jacques in 1965 and soon caught the public's imagination. There is now plenty of literature on the subject, though new terms have been invented to return the concept to its erstwhile academic respectability, i.e. "the third passage" or "midlife transition". Those keen to see it as a re-run of adolescent conflicts left unresolved call it "midolescence".

Let's briefly remind ourselves what constitutes this phase of development. In addition to the complicating factor of hormones in women, the biological period of midlife is especially riven with challenges for both sexes, demanding as it does a reckoning with Time and a slowing down of brain and bodily functions. There are also situational factors such as elderly, needy parents, difficult teenage children – or robust, high-achieving children arousing envy as well as pride. Marriages, like careers, are under review as midlifers look to the next forty years or so and ask: Is this it? Is there nowhere else to go? Am I a success or a disappointment to myself and my loved ones past and present? The end of fertility is particularly painful for many women, especially those who have failed to conceive and those whose bringing up of the next generation has been their main purpose in life.

However, the midlife crisis is a stage in the life cycle, not in itself a pathological syndrome or ailment, though its internal and external pressures can precipitate any dormant tendencies into actual mental illness.

The incidence of physical illness, especially cancer and heart disease, is higher at this time. Illness and incapacity have social, financial, occupational and relationship consequences that can often bring a bewildered and frightened relative, or the patient himself, into psychotherapy. Even in healthy folk the normal deteriorations of the body – aching joints, the need for glasses – represent a critical point in the long, erstwhile taken for granted relationship with the self. When body parts droop or bellies swell, when teeth loosen and names and dates occasionally escape you, you have to come to terms with the fact that you are neither beautiful nor immortal, that like all living things you are in the process of decay. How ably you adjust to these changes depends on many factors including your history of managing previous developmental phases. In therapy an investigation of earlier successes and failures, whether and how you embraced or avoided developmental tasks, can shed much light on the current situation.

"Crisis" derives from the Greek "Krisis" and means "decision". One dictionary definition of crisis goes: 'turning point, time of danger or suspense in politics and commerce, etc.' We're interested in 'etc.'! In other words, how this definition applies to persons of forty-ish and over.

What Options Are There to Deal With the crisis?

Look at the simple diagram (fig 2).

FIGURE 2: THE MIDLIFE CRISIS

KRISIS **?**	OPTIONS
	REGRESS (Unconsciously refuse all internal work, instead resort to previous defences and where these fail collapse into illness.)
	GIVE UP (Stagnate: safe but emotionally dead.)
	CONSOLIDATE (Build on achievements, or move sideways. Accept limitations, but don't stagnate.)
	MOURN FIRST, THEN MOVE ON (Learn from the past then let go of it and start again. Take realistic risks.)
	FALL INTO DENIAL (Try to arrest time by being artificially young.)

Option 1: Regress

Our midlifer simply cannot face the situation he is in. As a child, he perhaps withdrew from school bullies and/or from critical parents for whom he felt he could never be good enough. He became a loner. He returns to that strategy now, goes backwards in time, *regresses*. Despite all entreaties from family and friends about various pressures on him to make decisions – mother needs nursing care; young Billy is becoming addicted to alcohol; the wife is possibly having an affair – he feels powerless and bound to fail. As if he were a child again, he chooses the dubious safety of isolation. He stays late at work concentrating on unessential details, solving problems that would solve themselves in time. He insists on new projects he knows he *is* able to control if only he can be left alone to get on with it. He fiddles while Rome burns.

If this position is forcibly challenged, as clearly in the end it must be, he is robbed of his stock defence and may fall into a serious depression. The cause is not the midlife crisis itself, but his emotional paralysis in the face of it.

Option 2: Give up

He stays still, moving neither forward nor back. I envisage him as a World War One soldier in his tin hat safe in his dug-out while all hell breaks loose outside. Safety is his only concern. Such a person's job or health or relationship may be on the line but he can't or won't risk conflict. Others will just have to work round him. Where opportunities to mend fences, rebuild careers and obtain medical or psychological aid are repudiated, sometimes even contemptuously scoffed at, many a marriage or career has wavered then irretrievably broken down.

Option 3: Consolidate

Maybe our midlifer is not one of those reach-for-the-sky, ambitious types. Maybe he has made his money, achieved a professional station in life with which he is content, is relatively happy in his marriage, and his children are doing alright, if not exactly setting the world alight. He knows he has many years left to live and fears letting things slide. Ought he to be chivvying up his children to perform better at university? Should he be reinvigorating his marriage somehow; it's getting rather boring to be honest.

He has been advised to start a new business, stand for parliament, take up circuit training, surprise his wife with a second honeymoon in Tahiti. All this horrifies him, far too adventurous, but he knows something needs to be done if he is not to end up a couch potato. Let's surmise that he visits a life coach and sorts out some pleasant, not too frightening goals, before talking to his wife about his plans. Shocked by his admission of rumbling discontent, she begins to identify her own midlife issues. Together they begin designing future projects built on top of, rather than instead of, what they have already achieved.

Another mid-lifer might consider a sideways move. Within his work, hobby or relationship network he can try doing different things with different people but related to what and who he knows already, so there is little threat to his self-assurance. He gains plenty of stimulation and a widening social circle, so he won't vegetate.

He may take on a mentoring role, passing on his experience and knowledge to younger people. Or he may enjoy widening his existing skill base by doing an advanced computer or statistics course, learning first aid and ferrying folk to hospital appointments, refereeing football at local schools, getting embroiled in conservation projects. It doesn't matter, so long as it brings him growth, interest and esteem rather than stagnation.

Option 4: Mourn first, then move on

By middle age there are bound to be disappointments. There may be divorce, failed business enterprises, bad financial investments, alienation from offspring, irreconcilable hostilities with parents, or all of these rolled together with recurrent illness. Which of these were self-wrought and which ill luck? Such a backlog of disasters can cripple any faith in a better future, particularly if self-regard has always been pretty battered by early negative experiences in the family. Fatalistic thinking is hard to dislodge, but often tracing its source with professional help can be a start.

Beginning afresh is daunting, but not impossible if disillusionments can be examined and faced honestly, mistakes learned from, and new realistic plans made. This is more than just a rational matter, like drawing up a balance sheet. The chronic history of failure may disguise a long festering wound incurred in infancy and reinforced by self-defeating defence mechanisms ever since. Once the pattern behind the failures – the beliefs, behaviours and coping strategies that in part contributed to them – are understood, then bad luck and personal responsibility can be separated out. The defeats, however caused, need to be mourned before they can be let go. A period of quiet and sad reflection should be allowed for this process, before the patient is ready to try his hand once more.

Completed mourning can pave the way to a second chance, a total change of direction in life, be this personal or professional, or both. There is some truth in the old saying: *Life begins at forty*.

Option 5: Fall into denial

Some people react to midlife's vicissitudes by refusing to take up any of the above options. They may appear to be racing ahead with their lives, but are manically retreating from the reality of the ageing process. We all know the signs – the face lifts and the toupees, the new partner half his or her age, the second time round wild parties, the competitions to look 'cooler' (or is it 'hotter' these days?) than sons and daughters. When age can be staved off no longer and despair sets in, such a person has reached the later stage of the midlife crisis and perhaps seeks solace in drink and drugs or more hopefully seeks professional help.

Therapists do not treat the midlife crisis as such. It is not a pathological entity. It does not have to lead to treatment at all. It is the manner in which people address this time of life that dictates whether or not they could benefit from our work.

So what are the tasks associated with the crisis?

The midlife crisis is not all bad news. It represents a fresh opportunity to get things right, or at least better, this time. It can be a great motivator. If life is a soccer match, the referee, a skeletal figure with a black cloak and a scythe, has blown the whistle for halftime.

Midlife is a time when most people find themselves making an inventory of their lives so far, wondering if they should change any part of it. Should I settle for a comfortable marriage, or ought I to jazz it up a bit? Huh, sounds a bit tame. Would I rather recapture lost youth in an affair while I still have my looks? Perhaps that wouldn't be so wicked. Look at all the compromises I've made for the sake of the family and kids. Surely I'm entitled to a bit of untrammelled pleasure?

What about my unfulfilled ambitions, my creative side for instance? Ought I to recommence my painting, do it seriously this time instead of that amateur dabbling? Or maybe I should finish that novel I've been putting off for years. I have the necessary life experience now. Artists should travel, get inspiration. The kids don't need me any more really, and I'm at the top of my professional tree. Why don't I retire early and do all that globetrotting I promised myself years ago? Hmm, I suppose the right thing to do is to 'give back to the community', but do I really want to?

Then there are the internal questions. It's taken me so long to admit my weak spots, is it too late to change? Have I treated people badly on my way to the top? Or, conversely, should I stop shying away from people when I ought to challenge them? Have I let others fight my battles for me? Have I played manipulative games to force my nearest and dearest to meet my needs? Have I done enough to meet theirs? Have I been selfish, too inward looking (or too outward looking)? Do I *need* to change and do I want to? I have never felt really confident in social situations. Is it too late to develop this, and why bother if I haven't done too badly in my life so far?

A bereaved person knows the fact of his bereavement and feels awful, but is unaware of the deep mourning currents through which he is passing. Similarly, in midlife the need for decision making may float in and out of a person's consciousness, but underneath there is great turmoil as the mind turns over past successes and failures whilst assessing whether future hopes are realisable or just pipe dreams. To progress, regress, stay still, consolidate or manically deny the march of time? Discontent in the present but fear of the future, the extent of which the person may not fully appreciate, often accounts for the moodiness, restlessness, sleeplessness, and even depression that seems inexplicable to family and friends.

At this time parents are ageing, sometimes mellowing and sometimes instead intensifying old characteristics. They could be living it up on a world cruise, but they could also be losing independence and needing professional care. Thus the middle-aged person is confronted with the prospect of his own demise: his will be the next generation to age and die. The real biological parents may cause stress and worry, but his attending to them in the external world must remind him of his internal parents, the ones he has been carrying inside for four or five decades. It is they, not the ones for whom he is arranging residential or medical care, who have so coloured his relationships and his view of himself all these years. Could this be an opportunity to acquire a more balanced view of how it was for them when he was little, and whether his picture of them then might have been distorted by his own needs and his own pain? Do the elderly external parents accurately reflect the internal young ones? If not, why not?

Both confirming one's internal portrait and greatly altering it as a result of bringing the real and the imagined together can make for a firmer basis on which to build the second half of life.

The weight of conflicting feelings about parents can be lifted now that there is clarity.

For the midlife therapy patient, accumulated feelings toward the internal parents – perhaps both rage and gratitude, love and hate – can be re-worked so that he may now make a proper reunion with his family in the real world, should they still be alive. If they have died, a true if belated farewell can be made, without having to continue living with ghosts. If he decides the coldness, cruelty, ignorance, negligence in live or recently deceased parents is, or was, identical to what he remembers in the *past*, then the impossibility of any reconciliation or satisfactory farewell is accepted. He can mourn for a relationship that never was, and now will never be, then go free.

Sadly, such people have often tortured themselves for years, guilty at hating what was hateful, doing mental penance when they have committed no sin, trying still to elicit from Mum or Dad at seventy or eighty what they are simply unable to give. A slave to false hope, they disavow their rightful anger and sacrifice their own family's enjoyment in the service of the declining parents. Duty and loyalty to the aged is one thing, perpetuating emotional dependency that brings no reward is quite another.

Benedict

Now forty-seven, Benedict was the son of a devout Anglican minister whom he felt he had disappointed, for he'd never been able to believe in God, though he'd tried very hard. He was always fascinated by what made us human however, and he grew up to be a successful research neurologist. He was close to his mother in whom he confided and who acted as a go-between for Benedict and his high-minded father. The somewhat timid Benedict married a 'decent local girl' at the age of twenty-one, hoping to please his father and at the same time avoid all the sexual and social strains of being a young man about town. (I wondered too if he was avoiding temptations that would further alienate him from his revered father.)

Benedict's twenty-one-year-old happily married daughter was seven months pregnant when he first consulted me. He was both thrilled and shocked at the prospect of becoming a grandfather.

Benedict gave off a rather intellectual otherworldly air, but was astonishingly good-looking, slim, with thick fair hair and penetrating blue eyes, their effect exaggerated by his glasses. He said he was crippled by guilt, but the truth was he wanted to leave his wife. She had done nothing wrong, was a sweet lady and a dedicated housewife. She loved her garden and her dogs and occasionally trekked on horseback with girlfriends. But she was without ambition, never read a book. The world of ideas and any kind of science was totally foreign to her. They never quarrelled, but it felt as if they were just two people amicably sharing a house.

Last year, just after his daughter announced her pregnancy, Benedict was presenting an important paper in Philadelphia. There he met a journalist writing up the conference. She asked for an interview with him and they met at his hotel for coffee. She called him later to have him check what she had written before publishing, and he found himself "madly infatuated".

The relationship continued over the remaining two weeks, culminating in an attempt at intercourse that failed due to his guilt and too many martinis he'd drunk "to get my courage up". The woman was very understanding and said if he did decide to leave his wife, she would love to make a go of their relationship. She was coming to London in a few months' time, for a whole year. But no way was she going to be held responsible for breaking up a marriage. He must understand that.

He came to see me at his doctor's surgery four weeks before she was due to arrive. They were Skype-ing regularly and she had laid down the ultimatum once again.

It was not my job to make the decision for him, but to enable him to see his midlife position. Whenever a person feels stuck at a crossroads in life it's important to look at previous crossroads. Often he is still standing there, as bewildered and conflicted as he is today.

Benedict was stuck in midlife because he was still mired (*fixated* as Freud would have said) in adolescence. Then and now he admired and feared his father, longed for his approval. He'd taken A-level topics as near to God as he could get, but it wasn't enough. He'd courted the right girl who eventually became his wife, sowed no wild oats, forced himself to join his parents on dreary walking holidays and attended church at Christmas and Easter, all to please his father, and was doing so still.

In therapy he saw how his father was the only model of successful manhood to which he had so far subscribed. Were there other models? His mother too had been closely allied with him in keeping Father happy, rather than encouraging him to find a path of his own. Now, in midlife, the journalist had woken in him the desire to shape his own life. As he had never explored this territory before, had instead retreated to a rather ivory towered academic existence, he was absolutely terrified of "going solo", as he put it. Even now he consulted his mother and daughter about what he should do. His father, of course, was kept in the dark about this scandalous development.

By the time he saw me, Benedict had confessed to his wife, assuring her that nothing physical had occurred with the journalist and that he had no complaints about her as a wife. After tearful scenes she announced she was prepared to forgive him if he never saw the woman again. But he must decide now, at once. Her own life at forty-six would be utterly ruined if he left now. His daughter, mother and remaining grandmother supported her side in all this. Benedict felt his whole family were lined up against him and he was once again letting them down. Could this ghastly pull and push to make a decision just be a "silly midlife crisis"? Ought he to pull himself together and do right by his blameless wife? What did I think?

My interventions were aimed first at helping him see how this genuine (not silly) midlife crisis had thrown him back to adolescence and that he needed to do the work now he had been too afraid to do then. My second aim was to resist his transference to me. He fully expected me to tell him what to do and why. He could no longer count on his mother's support unless he took the decision she wanted him to take, so it fell to me to be her substitute. My third aim was to get him to take his own decision and not then wait to be rescued. If he left his marriage there would be fallout, and it was his responsibility, not the journalist's or mine, to deal with it. If he stayed with his wife, it was no good complaining later that he had wasted his life. What was he going to do when the next developmental stage of retirement hit? So far his work had seemed the only source of satisfaction in his life.

There were fourteen days left before the journalist arrived. I remained firm and neutral with him, though I understood the painful nature of his conflict and his desire to not hurt anybody, especially his father who seemed to me more important to him than his wife. Why, I asked him, was everyone, including him, protecting his father from knowing what was happening to his son?

In the last session before his new lady turned up, he finally confronted his father's rigidity during his childhood, and his mother's collusion which had been for the benefit of her marriage, not for Benedict. Even so, he grudgingly admitted his hope that his mother, despite her disapproval over his situation, might intercede for him, for he could not imagine facing his father himself. Against all the evidence he still procrastinated, hoping for some impossible solution to appear. I asked him gently, but firmly, how dithering and delaying was going to bring round his family, and especially his father. He needed to face facts, however unpleasant, and take the decision or risk losing both his marriage and the journalist, never mind his self-respect. He hadn't thought of this. "What kind of a man am I really?" he intoned, over and over.

My answer was to review and reinforce our meetings so far. We had seen how he was complicit but blameless in the family dynamics because, until now, he had been unaware of them. So he could stop beating himself up on that basis. But now he did understand the way his family had always functioned he could elect to be consciously complicit or change the way he related to them once and for all. The decision was his alone. This was the central issue, not the desire for and guilt over the journalist. She was but the catalyst for an underlying long-term and avoided issue.

I did not enjoy the role of non-partisan outsider presenting him with facts he was assiduously running from, but at least I felt I left him with just enough independent thinking capacity to make his choice.

He left his wife and began a relationship with the journalist. I never heard how it all worked out.

Later Midlife

As the midlife phase progresses to the fifties and sixties, middle-agers find themselves increasingly *identifying* with their own parents, rather than continuing to hold grievances from childhood against them. If they themselves have alienated offspring they may 'try again', having grown in wisdom, able to now see where they could have done their child-rearing better. They may have attempted reconciliation before, but now they are not so proud or defensive; they know time is short. They recall their own parents, perhaps dead by now, and wish they could make things up with them too, now that they know the pain of being rejected by their own children. There is a 'last chance', somewhat melancholy feel, to this stage of life.

Many late midlife parents who come to therapy dig deep into themselves and their memories, and discover how much the way they themselves were parented (and their parents were parented) affected the way they handled their own children. They long to make amends. Family culture, good and bad, easily passes down through generations unnoticed, and so rewards investigation. It can lead to significant changes in current parenting – and grandparenting – habits.

Due to the acute awareness of the ageing processes at this time, it is not surprising to find the big questions – me, God, the universe, what does it all mean if anything? – arising as surely as they do in the adolescent, though this time backed by lots of life experience and knowledge. The sensitive adolescent is finding the right questions to ask. The mid-lifer feels pressed to locate some answers, unless of course he still lingers in denial and finds busy ways to dodge these matters.

Retirement looms. Will this be a deserved rest and a chance to pursue neglected or new projects, or a loss of all that defined him as a person? For some people work is their chief relationship with the world and all else is secondary. Loss of professional reputation and status can mean loss of identity. No longer is he invited to social and professional events that before held him in a reassuring network of like-minded people. Such loneliness can be exacerbated by widowhood or loss of parents.

A healthy conclusion to the midlife period is achieved when one's deepest and most private relations with one's inner and outer family, one's own love of one's body and one's talents, one's attitude to death and desire, so long put off because one was too busy *living*, are sifted and sorted. Only then are we really prepared enough to take the external decisions about how to live out our remaining years in the most fulfilling manner.

When working with the elderly, therapists are often tempted to see only frailty and impending decay. Perhaps they are seeing in them their own ageing loved ones and want to coddle and reassure. Yes, we should be empathic and containing, measuring carefully how much confrontation with himself the patient can safely take; but when the time and ambience is right, he will find that honest exploration is more rewarding, if less comfortable, than just befriending. No matter how old, he has come for therapy, not a hot water bottle. He has the same right as any other patient to be empowered to take his own decisions and face the consequences of them with some confidence. We should not rob him of his suffering (or his joy) as he pores over his life then, and life now, and comes face to face with disappointment, grief, fury, remorse. He can't put back the clock and we can't promise him everything will come out in the wash and be all right. It is the working together, the doing what is possible in the circumstances, the *relationship* itself that contributes to the quality of his elderly life, however limited the therapeutic results.

Mick

Mick was fifty-five, around my own age, when he first came to see me privately, joking about his midlife crisis. He was married to a woman he loved but he "could not resist" attractive, intelligent women and so had enjoyed numerous short affairs. The chairman of a London borough council, he knew how to be discreet and how to leave the ladies without bitterness but "just happy memories". He was sociable to a degree, popular and powerful, the life and soul of any party. Portly but handsome, he entertained and impressed me with stories of his "deals", his connections to celebrities, his honorary position at the university, his travels, his Aston Martin. At the same time he portrayed himself as a champion of the working class, a fighter for better services for the poor and disadvantaged.

You had to keep that sort of thing under wraps of course, try to carry on your fight while pretending to be one of the boys, out to line their own pockets or make a political career. He was, he boasted, a veritable Trojan horse.

His problem was that he was suffering from horrific dreams about being shown up in public. He regularly woke in panic. He was drinking too much and knew this was to quell something inside that kept niggling him. Trying to extract this sort of information from him was like getting blood from a stone. He much preferred witty chit chat. I sensed he wanted to show his pain but felt shamed by so doing. "Telling me this stuff must feel like your dream, except you are awake," I said. This observation relaxed him enough to start talking more directly. He admitted that he had come to the realisation that he was a fraud, a total fraud. His origins were humble. He hadn't even gone to university because he was so thick at school. The glamorous lifestyle (he'd offered me free tickets for an opera box) was a cover for sheer inadequacy.

I saw him weekly for a year. He came to understand himself quite deeply, and to not blame himself so much, but could not remotely give up the public façade. He put on weight and continued drinking alone at the end of the day. The affairs were less but he still could not resist the thrill and risk, which he knew very well represented but temporary reassurance of his desirability. At this point we agreed that group therapy might help bring the public and private person together and he transferred to my private group where he remained for a further three years.

As expected, he became the most popular member of the group. He was a model for the twenty-one year old aspiring executive, a father to the fatherless, husbandless, single mother, and a knight in shining armour to the recent divorcee who, though beautiful and clever, had lost all self-esteem. As for me, I was therapist in chief and he adopted the role of my assistant. His previous individual therapy made him really good at the job. It was a pity I had to comment on this and gently discourage him. Fortunately the group eventually recognised how he had been disguising his true self and demanded in a friendly way to know what was under the surface.

Revealing his secret was agony for him, but he was brave. Finding his 'fraudulent' side accepted by the group – and moreover being allowed to continue with his extravert mask when needful – was a massive relief. His treatment went from strength to strength. Throughout I was conscious of my great affection and respect for him. Had we met under different circumstances we would have become great friends.

About four years after his therapy ended, Mick ("Michael Jason Burton, call me Mick") phoned me to make a one-off appointment. He was slimmer, seemed dignified and composed. He told me he wanted me to know he had been diagnosed with a rare blood disease for which there was no cure. He had a few months at most to live. He didn't want therapy; he knew how to manage his affairs and how to make his goodbyes. He just, well, wanted me to know.

Of course I was shocked and dismayed. Just being in the room with him brought back so many memories of our work together, especially in the group, to which he brought much jollity and optimism along with his serious and insightful observations. The group had sometimes felt like my and Mick's family. It had been a lovely feeling, watching the children doing so well under our parenting. Of course I used these counter-transference feelings to gradually wean Mick from his therapist role, so that he could take his place as a proper group member and receive its rewards. But I regretted having to do it as we were such a good team.

We made our sad farewells and I said to call me for a session at any time.

A few weeks later he made another appointment. This time I was profoundly shaken by his appearance. He was thin as a rake, his face sunken and yellow. Yet he remained self-possessed. Surely he must be terrified underneath. He was certainly sad, wistful, but not at all agitated. I didn't know what to make of it.

He said he had but a few weeks left, and had one last request of me. He knew I was a stickler for boundaries but, given the rather unusual circumstances, would I allow him to take me to dinner? "You're quite safe," he quipped sadly, "I'm in no fit state to seduce anybody, and I can't sue you for taking advantage of me because I'll not be here." What he said he wanted was adult conversation and friendliness with an intelligent woman. Definitely no therapy. His family were fussing and worrying and being ultra-supportive, but he just longed for one normal, pleasant, unfussy evening before the end.

I was in no doubt of his sincerity; he wasn't playing games. I confess I was thrown into confusion. How would I ever get through dinner with tears in my eyes? What would we talk about? How on earth could such an occasion be 'normal'?

I sensed Mick was being valiantly 'normal' with his relatives, trying not to upset them. The last thing I wanted was for him to have to do the same with me, and in a public place to boot. This thought brought me to my senses (I hope). I appreciated the honour, I said, but I felt the best thing I should do for him was to remain his therapist to the last. All sorts of fears must lurk beneath his coping exterior and there is no one out there he would want to witness them. He has any fear under control now, but who knows what is to come? My room is the place to come if control breaks down, if there are any….well, last things. "I will be here for you, at any time," I reiterated. He soberly accepted this but assured me there was no way he was going to lose control. No, no further appointment, thanks. A bit late for therapy now eh?

Should I have granted a dying man's wish? Such are the dilemmas of working with mid and late life patients. He never contacted me again and I read his obituary in the newspaper just a few short weeks later.

Developmental Phases in the Couple

Birth. As previously discussed, a couple is born when two people clinch an unconscious deal with one another. Where attempts at deals fail, the couple aborts. There is a joint fantasy that the successful deal will meet all previously frustrated individual needs and that the couple unit will be all-inclusive and self-sufficient.

At first the couple relationship resembles the mother–infant one. New lovers, like new mums, are left alone for a honeymoon period. It's understood they need time together to learn the meaning of each other's cues, develop commensurate responses, create an intimate language of their own. Once this bonding is established they will return to friends and family as a recognised unit of two.

Weaning. As with milk-to-solids and other infant accomplishments, *necessary disillusion* soon sets in. To learn something new and valuable, something has to be let go of, lost. Lovers have their first quarrels, test reality and find their partners are just fallible humans like them. There remains enough love, hopefully, to keep the non-disappointing aspects of the relationship as a secure, if no longer complete, base from which to relate to the world. Family and friends, once deemed superfluous upon the arrival of the beloved, are restored to favour as supporters and comforters when the ideal of blissful union falters. If they are to survive as a bonded pair, then sooner or later the couple must turn their gaze outward as well as at each other.

Unsuccessful couple weaning is evidenced by those pairs who stay home most evenings, never cease texting each other while at work, stick to one another like glue, cannot function without reference to the other. At the other extreme are the frantically busy pair so obsessed with their own career, business, hobby or cause, that their underlying fear of intimacy is successfully averted. This couple felt too threatened to even fulfil the task linked to the first phase (the *establishment* of intimacy). It's the deal, not any common emotional language that holds them together. Part of the deal was: "I will not force you into closeness if you don't force me."

Latency. This was Freud's term for the period between school and puberty. Sexual and familial tensions subside as the child discovers hobbies, sports, special interests, special friends. It's the acquisition of social and academic skills that excite him now, make him feel confident, proud of himself. In the same way couples turn outward, wanting to be seen as a successful twosome. They establish their credentials, so to speak, going to dinner parties with other likeminded couples. There they can talk about 'our' garden, 'our' house renovation, 'our' cooking projects, 'our' exercise routines, revelling in their confirmed status as a bonded pair.

Adolescence. After a time, conjoint cosiness can wear thin. Each partner may start to feel a loss of individuality; they are just half of the Joneses or the Smiths. They may feel claustrophobic or bored. They pick up old hobbies perhaps, contact single friends they'd neglected once they had achieved coupledom. If the couple's deal is getting a bit ragged at the edges there's always the fantasy that someone else might make a better one. If the urge to rebel is never talked about and resolved, such temptations increase. Along with it, internal pressure grows to reclaim the long-lost benefits of personal freedom, rather than settling for the diminishing glow of joint identity.

By this time children may have arrived on the scene, and/or careers are dramatically altering, for the better or the worse. The in-laws might be a help or a hindrance. Such factors disrupt the formerly smooth running relationship of the latency period. There are many competing expectations and demands. Who is to look after the children? Whose career is to be put on hold? Who is doing well and who failing? Whose fault is the failure? Who is or is not pulling their weight around the house or earning the money? Why is there never down time? What happened to our sex life? Such ordinary but powerful tensions can quickly lead to impulsive adolescent action – affairs, stubborn refusals to compromise, running home to mum, drinking or drugs to blunt or evade the stress. Assertions of independence from the other's claim on them are common: "I am a person in my own right." What a difference from the earlier phases when merging was all that mattered!

Whatever the presenting problem in such a marriage, it is important the therapist makes the couple aware of the phase their relationship has reached, and the normality of this. The time has come to rebalance legitimate objectives – the need for separate individual growth versus the need of the pair-bond (the joint personality) to be refreshed and nurtured, given all the pressures that have been exerted upon it. Both the joint and separate personalities have rights, responsibilities and needs. The couple in the consulting room might be enabled to understand this, so that they can co-operate in negotiating that rebalance, rather than fighting over who gets what, who has been most 'put upon' and wants redress, who has contributed most so is now entitled to more freedom.

The adult stage. This occurs after the storms of adolescence, when, if the couple are still together, peace descends. A gradual but significant shift in viewpoint takes place, to which the pair are oblivious although an external observer would notice some new attitudes and behaviours, particularly towards any children.

The couple begin to identify with their parents, instead of rebelling against or criticising them from the child's viewpoint. It slowly dawns on them that their parenting stresses with each other and with their children are similar to those their parents went through with them. They become more tolerant people – but not so identified and so tolerant as they will be in their fifties and sixties.

This is also a time of consolidation. The pair are now quite experienced at coupledom, have hopefully learned from mistakes, so are sufficiently confident to structure the way they propose to live for the foreseeable future. The house extension, the degree of contact with in-laws, the children's schools and activities, their circle of friends, their work–life balance, their sex life, all fall into a comfortable and predictable pattern.

Nowadays second marriages frequently require the blending of two lots of children and co-operation between the exes and the new partners. Understandably this complex process can somewhat defer the successful adaptation to the adult stage. Once attained, perhaps we should call it the super adult phase, in recognition of the maturity required of the couple of couples to triumph over almost insurmountable difficulties.

It should be remembered that all these stages are but models. Progress in real life rarely replicates the phases precisely or in tidy sequence.

Midlife. In a long established marriage, particularly after children have left home, unresolved issues from earlier stages – and sometimes an accumulation of them – tend to rumble once again. They refuse to stay repressed as the parties grow increasingly aware that the relationship is ageing and perhaps deteriorating. Sadness and disappointment that dreams have not come true reawaken bitter memories of historic hurts. Better late than never, these need to be aired and healed lest they fester, causing chronic mutual dissatisfaction, withdrawal or even separation.

Confronted with what feels like a crumbling marriage, one or both parties will try to enliven it, resign themselves to it, or find excitement and hope elsewhere. This does not necessarily mean affairs, but unaddressed discontents often lead to the couple pursuing quite separate paths, be this hobbies, travel, emotional investment in grandchildren or family of origin, such that they risk almost living separate lives. Careers may have taken diverse routes, or one career has shot ahead. How does this affect domestic roles? None of these situations have to constitute serious difficulty unless they are never discussed. The therapist's consulting room provides a safe environment for such honest but sensitive exchanges to occur.

Familiarity over many years means communication itself has become somewhat lazy by now, could perhaps do with an overhaul. Whatever the chronological age of the pair, in their marriage's midlife stage they still have human needs for affirmation, affection, respect, security, stimulation. How can these be given and received without making the effort to say or do something? The biggest danger to an otherwise comfortable midlife marriage is when partners take each other too much for granted.

Old age. Looking back, how to balance the books? Has the partnership on the whole been cause for mourning or celebration? Have shared and separate losses and let-downs been tidied up or do resentments still linger? Can regrets be faced together or does a denial pact keep these at bay but impoverish the quality of the couple's last years? Is it yet possible to take back lifelong projections, withdraw blame? Or will recriminations be taken to the grave? Is there still room and time for gratitude and forgiveness?

Marion and Ned

This couple, in their seventies, came complaining that they were always bickering. Anything could set them off, a towel left on the wrong part of the rail, the dishwasher never emptied, finger marks on the white wall. Yet they claimed to love each other and neither could bear to think of living alone. As you might expect, fears about dying, illness, being put in a home were all explored and dealt with satisfactorily.

Two other historical topics arose which surprised them. Each had thought these were lost in the mists of time. Ned had lost interest in sex before Marion and this had been a source of great sadness for her. She hadn't wanted to be seen as "one of them nymphos" at sixty so had kept quiet. But whenever Ned wanted a little favour these days, his favourite food, an ironed shirt or a little cuddle, she would feel the old resentment and hurt, way out of proportion to the perfectly reasonable request. "I have to meet his wants these days, but he never met mine then, not in that department anyway. And he never asked me if I minded; that was the worst thing." She always acquiesced to current requests but found other minor sins to complain about later, like his leaving the top off the marmalade jar or not wiping his feet. Ned had never had a clue about any of this.

The other unresolved subject was that of their daughter Jennifer, who had Down's Syndrome and had died at fifteen of heart failure. Thirty years had gone by since her death but Ned still resented that Marion had never understood his grief. (His own sister had died at just thirteen.) He claimed Marion had been heartless, half relieved by their daughter's death. He still held it against her and it came out in little criticisms over the smallest thing: he wanted, needed, to keep her in the wrong. Marion protested about all the nursing care and dashes to hospital she had had to endure. She had watched the child's terrible suffering while he was at work or down the pub with the lads. So yes, it was a relief in a way, though she felt very guilty about that, had never been able to talk about it.

Both these issues were ventilated and quarrelled over at length but were finally laid to rest, leaving the couple to enjoy their last years more peaceably. Both wished they had 'buried the hatchet' years ago.

Discussion

An old marriage does not automatically mean geriatric partners. A relationship of, say, thirty-five years may have reached this stage, but the couple may still be in their fifties. A second marriage may still be in its infancy when the parties are sixty.

Working with individuals or couples, the developmental lens opens up an extra dimension for the therapist to use. Many patients, mystified by their symptoms and complicated relationships, find them so much easier to comprehend when enabled to see them within the context of their own and any partner's developmental phase, as well as that reached by the marriage itself.

I am conscious that this chapter's summary of human development is somewhat limited. I have assumed most readers will be familiar with the theory aspects, though these may be rather dusty and neglected. Accordingly I have just tried to reinvigorate them a little, before attempting to illustrate their use in therapeutic practice. For a fuller and most accessible account I recommend Hugh Crago's recently published paperback (2017): *The Stages of Life: Personalities and Patterns in Human Emotional Development*, most informative and interesting. You can read for example about the midlife crisis in famous people, from Amadeus Mozart to Elvis Presley.

I will conclude this chapter with Mari and Georgia's story, showing how I used the developmental lens.

Mari and Georgia

My list was full. The GP to whose surgery I was attached part-time asked me if I could squeeze in half a dozen sessions to sort out "a row about having a baby".

Mari was African, very thin but athletic. She appeared rather jumpy, her eyes darting to and from Georgia, her civil partner, every few seconds. She was tiny, wearing a rainbow-striped, skinny jumper and cut-off jeans. There were two red stripes in her closely cropped hair and she had two studs in her nose. I learned she was thirty-three but she looked like a lean, fit teenager.

Georgia was English, a buxom fifty-two, with a big grin and thick salt-and-pepper hair in a figure of eight lopsided bun that threatened to come unloose whenever she got emotional. She wore voluminous prints and sandals.

It became quickly apparent that they expected me to be judge and jury, to decide whose case was the most deserving. If I couldn't manage that, I was to advise them on criteria so they could take "the big decision" themselves. Disabused of this idea, they both looked crestfallen, but somewhat sulkily agreed to give me more background.

Georgia was a self-qualified pub chef. She came from a family of travellers, having left at sixteen to wander across Europe on her own. She loved being independent, never found it hard to get a job, and indulged her love of cooking in several countries. She had had many short-lived encounters with her own sex, but she never considered settling down. Until, that is, she was cooking for the summer in a Cotswold pub where Mari was pulling the pints.

"This great brute of a bloke started swearing and pushing people around," Georgia told me. "The owner asked him to leave and the bloke grabbed him by the lapels and headbutted him. Mari shot round the counter and delivered a karate chop across his neck, leaving him humped on the floor blubbering. Everybody cheered. And me, I was in love!"

At this point the couple exchanged melting glances. They were still very much in love after seven or so years. Until "the big decision" reared its head, they had been enjoying a very stable life together.

Mari said she too liked to change jobs regularly but her real passion was martial arts, in which she had achieved a very high standard. Every day she did circuit training and some gymnastics too. Georgia interrupted to tell me about Mari's early years, "as she doesn't like to talk about it". Mari visibly shrank into her chair, looking mutinous, as Georgia explained that both Mari's parents had been shot in a terrorist raid on their African village when she was four. She and her younger sister were the only survivors. A charity brought them to England where they were adopted by kind parents to whom they owed everything.

Mari sat up straight. "Can we get on with it now? Look, Wyn, we had a great life for seven years. Neither of us wanted kids. We were that happy. Now she goes and gets all broody and nags me to death to have a baby. I can't, I can't, I just *can't*. She doesn't believe me."

A long argument ensued, angry, but mutually pleading too. Both felt the injured party. Georgia couldn't get pregnant, she was already menopausal. She reluctantly accepted Mari didn't want kids, but she could surely loan her body for a mere nine months to please her partner? She, Georgia, would do all the mothering. Mari wouldn't have to do anything.

At first Mari argued that her training and her body were the most central part of her life, apart from their relationship; nine months plus getting back into shape seemed an eternity. Eventually, in later sessions, it became clear her worst horror was having a man's sperm inside her. She gagged on telling us this; I really thought she might vomit. In a yet later session she revealed her mother had been raped before being shot. Georgia was aghast. Why hadn't she been told? There was much discussion about secrecy and shame,

Georgia at last appreciating the depth of Mari's revulsion. They never talked like this at home. As Georgia said, "we're not touchy feely types; we just get on with things."

Adoption was mooted by Georgia but she admitted it was a very poor second best. Mari shot back: "What about the kid? Only one parent, the other not interested, black and gay as well. The brat wouldn't stand a chance."

There was wisdom in this, I thought, but I detected panic beneath her protest. I suspected it was largely a rationalisation. It became clear to me, as she talked on, that Mari was very possessive indeed of Georgia and was not going to share her with anyone. Any child would be a rival and a threat. On finding a new family in England, Mari had still felt displaced. It was her younger sister, just a baby at that time, who received all the attention while she stood to one side and looked on. Georgia's eyes widened with surprise and tenderness as she watched tough, resilient Mari weep for the potential loss of their exclusivity.

During these sessions, at carefully selected moments, I inserted the odd developmental observation. By the end of our contact I wanted Mari to understand the powerful pull exerted on Georgia by her midlife crisis. Georgia wasn't restlessly longing for pastures new, as in the stereotypical scenario. She had done all that. Her huge change for the second half of life, now she had found a permanent partner, was to do what most did in the first half – settle down, raise a family, join the ranks of ordinary folk. It was that now-or-never feeling on reaching her fifties that made her so insistent on having her own way, not to mention the menopause forcing her to face the loss of her fertility. Mari's fertility was her only hope.

Then they were off again. Georgia raised the possibility of using Mari's sister as a surrogate. Mari was outraged. "Why should she do that when she knows I am perfectly able to bear a brat myself?" "Then why don't you? It might cure all that daft shame stuff and make you proud." "I can't. It isn't won't; it's *can't*." Both were terrified of breaking up, but neither could give way. Each claimed the other would sacrifice a bit of self-interest and come to an agreement if they had enough love. Clearly they hadn't. Both felt betrayed.

I wanted Georgia to gain some insight into Mari's developmental stage, at which she was well and truly fixated.

Georgia was Mari's mother virtually returned from the dead. Mari's relationship with her adopted parents had been one of respect and gratitude, not the love she believed had been there for her in Africa, although she could hardly recall any of her first four years. A child now would be a devastating intrusion into her sense of safety. Although fully grown up in many ways, part of her remained a traumatised four-year-old.

Similarly, Georgia was a successful healthy adult, normally easy-going and accommodating, but gripped by the demands of time, she could not afford to abandon the one thing that would complete her life. Which of them had more capacity to weather the non-fulfilment of her hopes? Which might fall into short or long-term melancholy? Whose developmental stage, if unattended to, was riskier to the maintenance of their relationship, which I had no doubt was permanent, whatever they decided.

Last but by no means least, what about any child that did come along? How would he or she fare with these two as parents?

Case summary

I had my own answer to these questions, but held my peace. It was for them to work out their own answers, now they were possessed of more psychological understanding. The sessions taught them to stop quarrelling and to start thinking about one another's developmentally determined needs.

It took some time and repetition for Georgia to fully understand Mari's relationship to her body, how a pregnancy would leave her utterly vulnerable. The martial arts and her dedication to fitness insured her womanly self, her internal idolised mother, and her own baby self against being taken over and abused by others. Without this literal and metaphorical defence she would feel powerless and out of control. Furthermore, a pregnancy (and by implication a man) would mean the enemy she had so carefully trained herself to keep out was now securely rooted inside her, the worst of all possible fates. She was desperate, not bloody minded, when she kept saying "I just *can't!*"

Love of each other was reasserted as they tuned in to one another's sadness and regrets, rather than their indignation and blame. For the first time in seven years they began to see the psychological import of their respective pasts and resolved to pursue this together after the sessions were over.

The therapist's own life phase feeds into the work too. What if her stage is very different to, or the same as, her patient's? What effect will that have on her attitude and technique?

Suggested reading:

Blythe, R. (1979). *The View in Winter: Reflections on Old Age.* London: Allen Lane.

Crago, H. (2017). *The Stages of Life: Personalities and Patterns in Human Emotional Development.* London: Routledge (Lifespan Development).

Fonagy, P. (2003, new edition). *Affect Regulation, Mentalization, and the Development of the Self.* London: Karnac.

Hollis, J. (1993). *The Middle Passage; From Misery to Meaning in Midlife.* Toronto: Inner City Books.

Jacques, E. (1965). 'Death and the Midlife Crisis' in *International Journal of Psychiatry*, 46, 502-13.

Levinson, D. (1991). *The Seasons of a Man's Life.* New York: Ballentine Books.

Sharpe, S. A. (2004). *The Ways we Love: A Developmental Approach to Treating Couples.* New York: Guildford.

Sheehy, G. (1976). *Passages: Predictable Crisees of Adult Life.* New York: Ballantine Books.

CHAPTER ELEVEN

ASSESSING THE PATIENT
(especially but not exclusively in the NHS, education, and other time-limited services)

If you work in the public sector and are growing impatient with my predilection for therapists burrowing about inside themselves, I sympathise. Nothing is more irritating, nay damaging, to the healing enterprise than a self-obsessed practitioner. Anyway, where does this paragon of self-knowledge find the blinking *time*?

However, my purpose in writing this book was to redress a balance. I believe that as a profession we are becoming too intellectual, too theoretically oriented, intent on gaining more credentials as if we still need to prove our professionalism in a world that values only academic qualifications. Sadly, there remains insufficient emphasis on the quality and depth of the student's own self-exploration and treatment whilst in training – and afterwards too, whenever the need becomes apparent. It is just as important to become acquainted with your latest Self state as to read the latest theory. What a pity insight into one's own mind can't be quantified and carry weight on a CV.

Secondly, I feel that the qualified senior workers to whom this book is addressed may well have missed out on much of contemporary thinking about counter-transference and the impact of the Self Psychologists, who place so much weight on the therapist's internal world. Their old training may not have included this, and they may have followed a different ideological stream to psychodynamics in their CPD choices. I have no wish to turn competent therapists from their existing school of thought, but I do believe that without incorporating an understanding of the unconscious mind, in whatever language that is expressed, no therapy can be fully effective. As previously stated, we can ignore unconscious processes between therapist and client but they won't cease affecting the therapeutic process. As they are present and active in every encounter it behoves us to come to grips with them. I have therefore selected material that might stimulate therapists from all schools to use their training and ideological background as a launching pad. They might dare to leap from it right into their interior world, there to discover its fertility and inescapable value as a therapeutic resource, before returning to a hugely enhanced base.

All the same, I can understand that hard-pressed counsellors and therapists trying to cope with short-term work in busy surgeries might find all this introspective stuff a luxury they can't afford. They have more pressing things to think about. Why has their counselling room been changed for the third time that month? Why do they have to counsel a bereaved person with a life-size model of a pregnant woman's pelvis on the table in front of them? Why must they pay for their own supervision? Why do their terms and conditions of employment keep changing, such that they can't plan more than a few months ahead: what the hell is going on 'upstairs'? Why can't their patient, poised at a critical moment in their therapy, be awarded more sessions? Why so many forms and questionnaires interrupting the work? And so it goes on, harried week after harried week.

All I can say is that if you want to avoid burnout and pay the mortgage too, you may, like me, have to sacrifice a few socialist principles and do some private work alongside your NHS commitments. I am seriously worried about our counsellors in the public sector who undergo enormous stress. This is not just about seeing too many distressed patients with little time in between to clear the mind ready for the next one, but about the inadequate facilities they often have to put up with, and the huge pressures laid on the therapist to get the patient well fast. She must then fill out all the forms and tick all the boxes to prove it. She has to squeeze her patients in to six or ten sessions, whatever their actual need, and if she can't fit a litre into a pint pot the failure reflects on her.

It is there in black and white for all to see. She stands condemned by bald statistics. Is it any wonder many of these valiant counsellors become exhausted, disillusioned and cynical, despite their long-time dedication to the NHS's *raison d'être*?

Some rewarding private work over which the therapist has complete control can slow down or compensate for the threat of professional burnout. It also develops her repertoire, as she can now branch into medium and long-term, calm and thorough work, without the fire-fighting atmosphere of the NHS surgery.

In this chapter and the next I will try to demonstrate how a state of self-awareness can combine with a very practical scheme to bring about optimal conditions for a good short-term therapy outcome.

Stages in Assessment

The stages of assessment are Tightening up, Loosening up, Interview Proper, Contracting (already discussed under 'Mistaken Alliance' in chapter one) and Self-Supervision. The latter includes my suggestion for economical but in-depth note-taking. I will pursue this in the next chapter, transposing a case to the proposed assessment chart. This chart is but a prototype; you may wish to amend it somewhat, to fit your particular needs.

Stage 1 -Tightening up

This first stage refers to brief but critical preparation by the therapist or counsellor, before setting eyes on the patient. Depending on the amount and quality of information on the table, the therapist can often make an educated guess concerning the future work focus. All she has to do in the first few minutes of contact with the patient is firm it up. This makes for more time in the few sessions available for therapy proper, rather than floundering about in search of the central underlying issue – which may not be directly related to the symptoms or self-diagnosis that the patient presents. She should be ready to be contradicted by subsequent events, however. A guess, no matter how educated, is still a guess.

Precious minutes are often wasted as the first session opens, while the therapist recovers from whatever went before (traffic, disrupted school run, incoming phone calls or whatever). The patient may be too upset to notice, or the therapist is a great actress, but her *attention* is not fully present. How the patient walks in, sits, opens his narrative, is vital. The body speaks volumes. We know this from basic training but as we get more experienced and adept at hiding our *in*attention, we get worse at being truly available at the start of the session. Even now I have to struggle with this; it takes real self-discipline, which, like self-supervision, is these days much neglected. We become lazy, leaving our personal and domestic tasks till the last minute, no time to spare for emptying the mind, striving toward stillness, receptivity. In short-term work especially, getting to the session early and sitting silently in your therapist's chair for a minute or two can mean all the difference between missing and harvesting crucial data about the patient. Even if the therapist habitually arrives on time, should her mind be on other things while she settles in the therapy as a whole can be significantly delayed without her even being aware of it. In short-term work every moment counts.

Even prior to getting into the right frame of mind there are other matters to mull over. Who referred this person to you? What is your relationship with that person – long-standing or recent, trusting or suspicious, rivalrous or dependent? Is he more or less skilled than you, higher or lower in the hierarchy? Is this an appropriate referral or do you need to block it until you've had further discussions? Do you feel dumped on because the referrer just doesn't know what else to do? Are you being begged for rescue as he's got himself into some kind of pickle with the patient? Are you being set up to fail so you, not the referrer, can be criticised later? Are you being idealised? Are miracles expected of you in a few sessions with someone clearly requiring long-term treatment? Or, heavens above, could this just be a straightforward, apt referral because the referrer trusts and respects you?

What about the referrer? Is he hyper anxious, always referring too soon, or does he leave referring until there's a crisis that you are expected to sort out? Does he overmedicate or refuse to medicate? Does he understand what therapy means so you can have reasonable discussions with him, or does he wash his hands of people once they are referred? Has he a concept of team management or does he expect you do it all? Do you share the same values with regard to confidentiality? And do *you* properly understand the work *he* does, or do you expect him to be as psychologically aware as yourself? Is there contempt on either side, or magical expectations? Are there authority/status issues?

The referral letter, scribbled note, phone call or chat in the corridor ought to be read sub-textually in all the ways above. Processing the referral in the light of your reactions to it, rather than just absorbing the facts, is another time saver. It can also alert you to possible hitches or supports in the patient's forthcoming treatment.

As you read, take note of your heart lifting or sinking. Ask yourself why. Are you responding already, positively or negatively, to this particular kind of patient problem? Is this therefore a transference issue for you, or are you picking up clues from the referral material about the effect the patient has already had on the referrer and possibly other professionals? How long and/or serious are the patient's difficulties? Does he have family support, or friends he can rely on so you can work at maximum speed knowing there is a safety net out there? Does he seem mature enough to withstand rapid self-scrutiny? In other words, would the hidden developmental age beneath his chronological one be able to cope? Is he likely to bolt, to miss sessions, to develop a fantasy relationship with you? Is it realistic, even risky, to restrict him to only a few sessions? Or is he simply the ideal candidate? If you have suspicions, would looking at his fuller notes be a help?

Stage 2 - Loosening up

In an NHS setting with limited resources you can't treat everything that ails your patient. You have to find a focus and not wander off. You have already narrowed the field a little, so what comes next?

Having thoroughly digested everything you know, guess, dread, and hope about the patient, the time has come to resolutely shove all that to the back of your mind, along with any miscellaneous data supplied by the patient in the opening session which you feel isn't pertinent to the key area for study. This leaves the front of your mind spacious, unbiased, and receptive for him. However, you will need a conduit between the front and the back so that your thoughts, hunches, ideas, and feelings can flow both ways. If too much data from the back runs forward too often you will not be truly listening to the patient; you will be rushing to premature conclusions hinted at but far from confirmed by your preparatory work plus bits and pieces of the patient's narrative. But if any present or future stored information is *prevented* from flowing forward when new material from the patient connects with it in some way, then you are not working dynamically. Keeping open channels and tributaries linking the front with the back, along which major and minor hypotheses shared with the patient can flow and recede, is the therapist's primary function in time-limited work.

The material you stored in advance is of course very sketchy. As the patient tells you his overall story much of that too is sent to the back of your mind, perhaps seen as just elaboration or avoidance of getting down to things, while you retain at the front those features that seem salient to the complaint that brought him for help. As you listen, tightening up or discarding hunches and assumptions about his central concern, you may find yourself needing to recall bits of material relegated to the back of your mind that after all turned out to be relevant. There needs always to be a foreground and background in your mind or you will become confused through data overload. But you need to be able to rapidly switch foreground and background content when the material proffered by the patient suggests you may have given prominence to the wrong thing. Here is an example.

Glenda

I learned from the referral letter that Glenda, aged 43, "might be bipolar" but that she had never been in hospital or officially diagnosed as such. For the past ten years she had seen her GP on and off for "blue moods" when she could see no reason to live but didn't want to die. Medication had not helped and now she wanted some talking therapy. She had been on the waiting list for months.

She bounced into my room at the surgery and immediately broke into cheery apology. She was fine now, but didn't want to waste the appointment she had waited so long for, so could we just have a one-off chat? "Well, let's see how we get on," I said, friendly, but deliberately vague.

She was small and a little chubby, with bright eyes and a big smile. She wore little coloured brooches all over a bright red cardigan and grips supporting her ponytail shaped like butterflies. Her clothes made her seem younger than forty-three but her creased and puffy skin made her look older.

She told me she ran a bakery with a shop out front and employed several young girls in the kitchens who were lovely "but a right handful". She was married and had been to Relate with her husband in one of her "blue periods". She laughed, saying the lady counsellor had counselled him while she just sat there and listened, but he treated her nicer for a while afterwards. Then she talked about her business and all the problems with the staff who, it seemed to me, rather took advantage of her good nature. Then all of a sudden she was telling me about her best friend who had borrowed money to set up her own business but had never repaid the loan. "But that's what friends are for, eh? She's been good to me over the years."

Conscious of our limited time, I asked her to say more about the blue moods but she was acutely embarrassed and claimed she was over them now. Would I ask her something else, anything; she really wanted to help. I commented with a smile that I was supposed to be helping *her*, but the point was lost on her.

Feeling a bit desperate, I invited her to talk about her family of origin. She rattled off the facts as if they might be too boring to interest me. I watched her fidgeting hands and flushed face which revealed far more feeling than her words. Her mother died a few days after giving birth to her. Her father took to drinking heavily and by the time she was six he was alternately at AA or relapsing, taking to his bed for weeks at a time. His two sisters helped out with Glenda's basic needs but resented having to, so she tried not to give them any trouble. As she got older Dad became quite mentally unfit and one sister had to move in. In his maudlin cups he would curse Glenda for killing his wife and for spoiling his chances of a new life in Canada.

Now we are getting somewhere, I thought, and dispatched all Glenda's former chatter to the back of my mind. However, she had no intention of feeling sorry for herself. She assured me her dad was at peace now and couldn't curse her any more. Yes, it had been a bit lonely, but look at those poor refugees, and those dying with cancer, and the starving kids in Africa that you see on the news all the time. She'd had it good compared to them. And you can't harp on about the past, can you?

To my dismay, she went back to what I'd judged to be rambling anecdote and could not be persuaded to talk further about her childhood.

I did a quick think: we had six sessions scheduled and if I didn't get something serious across to her very soon she would not return. I hauled forward everything I had pushed into the background and re-ran it in my head as she breezily continued some tale about giving one of her girls the day off to be with her new puppy. I realised it would take more than six sessions to put her in touch with the pain of her tragic childhood – there was a great barrier there – so with great reluctance I let that subside into the backwaters of my mind. Having switched the flow, I began to concentrate on the chatter. What did all the stories have in common? Was there something there I had missed, due to not knowing earlier in the session about her ghastly formative years?

It would take too many pages to relate her breezy yarns in detail, but what I divined from her constant entertaining of me was this. She had never been given any familial love and coped by being grateful for whatever else she did manage to scrape together. She'd learned to keep smiling, smiling, smiling, so as not to be rejected for being miserable, the way everyone moaned at her despised curmudgeonly father. As an adult she was now pouring out non-stop attention on others, metaphorically as well as literally baking them cakes. She gave to them what she so desired for herself, in the hope she might get some faint echo of it back, even though she had no right to it. Hadn't she killed her own mother?

Glenda saw the good in everyone, refused to stand up to them, kept the peace at all times. Her husband and best friend exploited this, not wilfully I think, but rather because she seemed to be asking for it, so it couldn't hurt, could it? One of her giggling tales about school was how she stole money from her aunt's purse, penny by penny, over weeks. When she had enough she bought cigarettes to give to her school pals. Always she had to buy popularity; it never occurred to her that she was intrinsically lovable or even worth noticing.

Swiftly reviewing her chatty productions I was now seeing clearly her jolly defences against massive grief. Those defences, and especially that smile, must have been exhausting to keep up. No doubt when they eventually failed her the blue moods followed.

In the end I held my hand up like a policeman to stop her talking, and asked her if I could tell her what I was thinking. She eagerly assented. I put a simple formulation to her, missing out the obvious link with her father and the aunts' negligence because, despite her wish to please me, I knew her philosophy (defence) of every cloud having a silver lining would prevent her from acknowledging what had been done to her. Maybe this would come later. For now, I had to offer her something she just might accept. She gasped in shocked recognition when I said she believed she had no right to exist. The notion that she might be intrinsically worthy of love, and have no need to work so hard for it, left her speechless.

That was the end of our first session. She did return.

Stage 3 – Contracting

See chapter one under "Mistaken Alliance". There is further discussion on this in the next chapter too.

Stage 4 - Conducting the First Session (Interview Proper)

The short-term patient may feel heard, understood and temporarily relieved of distress even when you fail to make links to deeper matters in his story. But is that enough? With luck, your link-less wanderings might stumble upon the specific matter in need of treatment as well as compassion, but by then there aren't enough sessions left to follow it through. There's no time to draw up for him a new way of seeing his problems, a reformulation he can continue working on alone.

Glenda was not ready to make major links, but she understood lesser observations about the way she related to others and her unconscious assumptions about herself. This made her curious enough to want to come back and we still had several sessions left to see how much further we might safely go.

You will already be comfortable about the way you conduct the first interview or two. You've done it hundreds of times. You will have refined your personal and technical approach over the years, supported by colleagues and your training institute. If its psychodynamic input was minimal though, could you integrate additional attitudes and techniques discussed in these pages, adapted of course to your own professional language and clinical style, without too much disruption of tried and tested methods? You would be creating your personal blend of therapy, not following any orthodoxy. After all, you are no longer a student and can think for yourself.

We should not forget though that the patient does not give a fig for the niceties of assessment techniques, yours or mine – he just wants relief from unhappiness. He sees a long awaited opportunity to offload lots of troubling emotions and have someone be nice to him while making some kind of sense of his dilemmas. You may be striving toward an Alliance, a dynamic formulation, a central conflict or a transference manifestation to someone in his life, or to you; but he may just want pain relief, preferably by yesterday.

When supervising, I find that the more sophisticated therapists are so keen to get on to the advanced work that they tend to skate over the basics. These differing perceptions and priorities between the patient and his therapist may be self-evident, but it's crucial they are monitored. Your behaviour, questions (or scary silence), your whole attitude and demeanour, may seem quite barmy or insensitive to the troubled patient sitting opposite you. Whilst retaining your own need to handle the time carefully and quickly, and to find a focus for joint work (I say 'joint' because short-term therapy has to be collaborative for it to work), you must also find your way into the patient's subjective experience of you. If you have no idea how he is perceiving you, how do you hope to ever share the same wavelength?

By listening, deploying open questions, hunches, trial interpretations, demonstrations of patience and empathy, careful management of silence such that both can ponder and mutually consult, you build a tentative dynamic formulation. Your school of therapy may have some other term for it, but I think most of us therapists are out to clarify the main issue *beneath* the patient's presentation along with his characteristic and maybe self-defeating manner of addressing it. This spelling out of the underlying material in need of exploration is usually initiated by you, then corroborated by your patient or amended by both. From then on you are both working under the same banner.

Making Use of the Patient

In the best short-term work you are using your patient as an unpaid colleague, an ally in acquiring and understanding the meaning of his symptoms or complaint. Any recovery, plus the instillation of self-worth (without which there can be no healing), comes from the experiential training he has with you of being an unofficial co-therapist. This is the very opposite of the earlier, more traditional assumption in long-term work that the patient should be enabled to regress (go back to an earlier, more helpless, stage of development) in order to mend. With only a few sessions to hand, you can't afford this even were it desirable. You study and tease out the agreed formulation together (without needing to refer to it as such: this is not a tutorial). You look at how it runs through work and marriage perhaps, or social life, or how it impacts the kids. You work on *why* and *how* he became like he is, has the attitudes he has, makes the same mistakes he does, why and how these various events and relationships 'now' fit a pattern that is all about 'then'.

He will not change overnight. Neither can treatment promise easy solutions or a panacea for pain. Nonetheless, having been helped to see his unconscious motivations, self-precepts and defences for himself, he is now hopeful that future problems, stresses and relationships can be faced differently. He now knows how to look inside without fear, how to make links and how to challenge his defences without being overly critical of himself. He remains an imperfect mortal like the rest of us, but now possesses the personal insight that makes for wider options as to what to do and how to be. In common parlance he has 'got the hang of' therapy thanks to your joint work; the rest is up to him.

If the therapy has been productive, he will do well within his own limitations and capabilities. Short-term work is too daunting to even attempt if the medical model of disease and cure is not given up. Therapy should not be applied like a dressing, with the aim of restoring the wounded part to its former healthy state. Psychotherapy is not applied, *done to* a person; neither is restoration to his former state its aim. The patient actively contributes not only to his own healing but also to his growth, his progression toward a new and different state.

Transference

Transference is a big part of short-term work, particularly in GP practices where the team constitutes a ready-made field in which the patient can reproduce his family dynamics. For instance, the counsellor – his very special person – and his doctor can be experienced as parents; the receptionist in charge of his access to the parents a bossy older sibling. If any 'off key' reactions to you or to any of the team, or to them as a group, show up persistently, you will speedily enquire about them with your patient in a non-threatening way. You will model for him the unbiased spirit of enquiry you stand for, while simultaneously discovering more about how he ticks.

If his transference is very negative you will have to make a boundary about his actual behaviour and language to the staff, yet somehow convey to him that, rather than judging him, you are seeing his inappropriateness as part of the problem which you and he both are going to help with. Does he upset other significant people in his life and how do they respond? Could his picture of them be distorted? You have already plunged into the work!

You do not need to *cultivate* transference to yourself in a short-term contract but it would be a shame to waste it if it is right in front of you, clamouring for investigation. However, under more usual circumstances it might be better to stick with being a neutral helpful figure, so a relationship of sensible grown-up to sensible grown-up can prevail. Then both parties can quickly get down to looking at relations with other central figures in the patient's life 'now' and how they might make sense when put in the context of 'then'. This co-operative relationship is hard to engineer when the patient is consumed by transference to you. In this case you are mostly working alone.

Sometimes transference suddenly pops up in the session ("you sounded just like my English teacher when you said that") and of course it shouldn't be ignored. Unless it leads to focus-related matters though, it can be left to fade naturally. There is no time for side-tracking, however tempting. It is the transference distortions *currently* impinging on his life – with regard to his wife, boss, children and so forth – that should be given priority.

Stage 5 - Termination of Short-Term Therapy

It is common knowledge amongst seasoned therapists that, on occasion, closure of treatment can produce more emotionally laden material than the rest of the work put together (see forthcoming example). In a busy surgery, already anticipating the next patient who will fill this one's place, we can forget this important fact and tie up loose ends too fast. Aware that this is our last chance, perhaps we over advise about what he should do in the future, or we are tempted to refer him on – anywhere, so long as we don't have to experience the guilt of 'throwing him out'. Perhaps we re-iterate to him the main points of the treatment, so he won't forget and we don't have to feel the guilt at having given him so little time. Maybe we recommend him books to read, or explain the rules about how and when he can return for a second set of sessions. Once again we are feeling bad about sending him out into the cold.

In soothing our guilt this way, we risk losing the opportunity to work on whatever the termination has triggered in him. Endings often unexpectedly release powerful feelings and memories long locked away.

We should take responsibility for our own reactions to the separation. Are we relieved he is going? Worried about his future prospects? Wishing we could have had more time? Or will we simply miss him as he did so well, reflecting our professional ability? Such reactions are neither good nor bad in themselves, but if we are not conscious of them we may resort to doing well-meaning hasty things in the last session that nonetheless prevent more important feelings and needs on the patient's side from emerging.

This is especially so with the patient who has a history of multiple loss, abandonment, and/or a broken family which the impending separation from you replicates, be it ever so minor a loss by comparison. Aware of the past and present link, the therapist allows time for a companionable silence in which whatever needs to surface and be expressed by the patient can do so.

Anticipating such an ending (and noting it!) right at the beginning – there may be clues in the referral letter or in his presenting story – helps prevent the therapist's evasion of last minute sadness or reawakened grief. She should be able to fully acknowledge the re-emergence of such feeling in the patient while managing her own reactions to the ending, however painful and whatever memories of separation are rising in her; this is her private business. If the last session is feeling awfully busy, she should ask herself if she could be making it so. Are her own emotions, or threatened emotions, overshadowing her patient's?

The return of symptoms is common in the last session, especially with very anxious people. This is usually a panic reaction to the imminent loss of the supporting environment and will soon fade. Providing this is a correct reading of the situation, reassurance can be given that the patient's learning is not going to disappear along with the sessions. The surgery and the GP will still be here in the case of any emergency. Where appointments are rationed and there is a long waiting list the counsellor must be fully aware of the consequences of extending current sessions where they are not absolutely needed. Is she taking care of her patient or does she have a problem about saying no?

Another difficulty I observe while supervising counsellors in GP practice, is how hard they find it to accept thanks. This is no time for false modesty. Giving thanks for having received quality attention, having been understood, is an important last step for the patient. We may underestimate what he feels, mistaking real gratitude for common courtesy, a polite gesture. We should never brush away his thanks to save our own embarrassment. He may have never received that intensity and unconditional quality of attention in his whole life. Therefore he has never undergone that warm emotion we call gratitude with its correlate of deep connectedness to another. He must not be robbed of that feeling. We must ensure he takes the opportunity to fully inhabit this emotion, so he leaves therapy with a sense of closure, but with the positive experience of it thoroughly lodged inside him. The worst thing you can say, should gratitude be forced upon you, is the dismissive and minimising: "I was only doing my job."

What's wrong (providing it's true) with: "I'll miss you", or "we've been through a lot together, haven't we?" or "you know I wish you well for the future"? Many a time it's just two smiling faces, two lumps in two throats, and a murmured "goodbye".

When the work has not gone well, an opening should be made in the last session for the patient to say so. He should be permitted to air his disappointment and have it discussed frankly. Did he think this was the wrong setting for him or were you the wrong therapist? Did he find the contact too short? Was it the language you used that he objected to, or your nosing around in his past? Did he think another type of therapy might have suited him better? Does he know what other kind of treatments are on offer? What would he have preferred to happen in the meetings? He may give you valuable feedback that can help the surgery better manage their counselling service. He may give you feedback that you need to take to your supervisor, and/or think about privately. He may be someone who would complain whoever tried to treat him. He may be a pain in the neck and you have not been able to find out why. No matter; he has a right to speak his mind. The practitioner should *make* space for his grumbles, and not in fear and trepidation pad the last session with meaningless noise or the filling in of questionnaires. All that does is reinforce his negative feelings.

We should remind ourselves that we are not the only therapists in the world. Should this patient go on to find another, it is important we have at the very least left him with the memory of a respectful experience that did not strip him of all hope.

Here is a case where the last session was the most important. It belies what many assert, that there's no point in opening up new work when the therapy is ending.

Larry

Larry was a thirty-two-year-old drummer in a rock band. He came from a wealthy Surrey family who had given him and his two older brothers "everything our hearts desired – we were spoilt rotten." He'd dropped out of university in his second year to go professional with his band. They all lived a fast and furious life, using drugs and alcohol to excess, having sex with countless women, experimenting with new music until the small hours and sleeping until teatime. He relished touring, here today and gone tomorrow, girls galore in every town. He said he loved the life, was grateful to the cool parents who had made it all financially possible.

The trouble was that every few months, especially in midsummer when all the festivals were on and he should be feeling really high, he would unaccountably sink into a kind of ennui. Nothing interested him. He lay on the sofa not even wanting a beer, uninterested in sex, indifferent to his drums and the need to practise. He forced himself to perform at the gigs but his standard dropped and in the end a substitute had to found. His mates in the band insisted he see someone about these moods. First he went to the GP surgery where I was working. Blood tests showed his drug-taking had nothing to do with these bouts of what the doctor could only suppose was depression. He was fit as a fiddle. Larry denied he felt depressed, said it was more inertia, boredom, emptiness. He was then referred to me for six sessions of counselling.

My first job with Larry was to get him to slow down his verbal delivery and use plain English rather than rock-speak. He understood my difficulty at once and we both laughed about this. Clearly his mood had lifted while he languished on the waiting list. (Despite his wealth he had very strong beliefs about equality and had refused to consider private treatment). He insisted he wasn't ill. Others were much more entitled to this service. His was more an existential problem. Those other poor sods who came for counselling would give anything to have his life. For a moment he appeared positively guilt-ridden, then shrugged it off.

In that first session I commented on how two-sided he seemed, sort of hellraising and pensive at the same time. Was the ennui the other face of his frantic drumming? His eyes lit up. He began to talk seriously about the state of the world, free will, artificial intelligence, stopping occasionally to muse about his mates, what they would think if they could hear him spouting all this philosophical stuff.

This very attractive rich young man had never had to struggle. His school record was excellent and I suspected it was boredom with the insufficiently demanding course at university that prompted him to leave as much as the lure of his band. Fame meant nothing to him; it was the constant stimulation the life and music awarded him that mattered. He said life could never go fast enough to satisfy him and that was why he had chosen to learn the drums. He could drum himself into a state of frenzy, yet return to sanity as soon as he stopped. He assured me he was not into self-destruction. He wasn't that stupid.

We wondered what he might be running from, rather than what he was running to, but got nowhere with this. We looked hard at that 'other side' of him, what he might have done with his life had the music not intervened. He might have become a left wing lawyer, he said grandly, defending the rights of the common man. Or a writer-journalist, like his well-known father. Maybe a brave war photographer recording the unspeakable. Or he might have made small budget political films that revolutionised the way all those complacent bastards thought. Under the self-mockery, I thought he was quite serious.

His childhood seemed idyllic, so we used the later sessions to talk about how he might realistically plan his future, reconciling his opposite temperaments. In his low periods he knew what he didn't want but had little idea about what he did. Now we were beginning to find out. We really enjoyed being together and the sessions flew.

At our last meeting the atmosphere was subdued. We were going to miss each other. In addition I had a nagging feeling that, despite a good outcome, I had missed something. Larry had made a five year plan involving further study and drumming part time. He was thinking about women differently and was wondering if he should settle down. He was optimistic. So what more did I want?

In my mind I had categorised this piece of work as 'developmental'. I had been facilitating a young man's passage from a somewhat delayed adolescence into maturity, rather than undoing some pathology rooted in his upbringing. As we talked about his immediate post therapy plans, he casually mentioned a visit to his Surrey home "as it's June again". I must have looked puzzled, for he said, "Oh, didn't I tell you? I'm an identical twin. I lived. My baby sister died. I usually visit my parents on the anniversary. We don't talk about it or anything. But I like to be there for them."

I was flabbergasted. Larry hadn't the faintest idea about the significance of his twin. I had thirty minutes left to show him. In the sessions he had told me about his addiction to living fast. Was he trying to live enough for two people? Or was he running away from his guilt at surviving? And what about the episodes when he retired to his sofa? Was it denied sadness (like that of his parents) catching up with him? His wish to do good works, study, help people – is this how he thought his twin might have wanted to live her life? He had intermittently criticised his wild life as pointless and self-indulgent: is this what she might have thought had she been allowed to live? Could it be that his noble aspirations, once achieved, might go some way to atoning for her death? On the sofa, without energy, his mind empty – was he joining her in death, or in the womb before they were born? Was it some kind of mental paralysis, stuck between wanting to contact her, bring her to life in his mind, and wanting equally to be free of her, to accept she was dead and gone so he could get on with his life in peace? There were so many possibilities with so little time to look at them.

A very thoughtful Larry left the surgery. He knew now he had repressed all his responses to his sister's death, and he had much work to do before the midsummer hauntings would cease.

Stage 6 - Self-Supervision

External supervision is vital of course, providing you find someone further along your particular journey who can constructively criticise your work. She can throw more light onto your clinical reports, model different techniques for you, share her advanced experience and maybe recommend some further reading. But she can't know you in the way you know yourself – or should, if you have been in receipt of effective therapy during training. This is why I advise the qualified practitioner to do more self-supervision and a bit less external supervision as she matures. It's easy to get lazy, depend on the external supervisor, and not discipline yourself to examining yourself with all that private knowledge you possess. External supervision, though very important, can never be complete supervision.

I would recommend combining a full self-supervision session with careful note-taking at the outset, as the one influences and improves the other and provides a solid base for the work to come. Thereafter a short spell of looking inward after each session should suffice unless the patient is especially problematic. These short self-supervisions ought to prepare you for, and increase the value of, your external supervision. I will go into further detail about self-supervision and writing notes in the next chapter.

Now an admission. I have been using the terms 'focus' and 'dynamic formulation' rather loosely and sometimes interchangeably. What is the difference between them? The formulation is a nutshell conceptualisation of what is really 'up' with the patient, something that can be written down in a few sentences. Were you to leave the job or get ill and another practitioner had to take over, the formulation would tell her all she needed to know. It would contain information about what unconscious forces are at work and how these are linked to which important figures in the patient's life, 'now' and 'then'.

The focus, on the other hand, refers to the restricted *area* on which the time limited therapist is going to concentrate in order to achieve maximum benefit. *It is the area in which the dynamic formulation, if accurate, should reveal itself in vivo for further elucidation.* For example, the formulation may guide her toward the study of early family relations and how they are being repeated or compensated for, or taken revenge on in the patient's current family, to the consternation of his wife and children. Or she may have seen that authority clashes are regularly drawing the patient into troublesome conflict, so she elects to trace those throughout his history, ignoring lesser concerns. Perhaps the formulation describes a man whose well-meaning attempts to parent his teenage children are being sabotaged by unconscious conflicts. The therapist therefore decides to focus on his own adolescence, and will no doubt find unresolved problems there.

In short, the *formulation* at which the therapist arrives steers her to the best *focus* for investigation.

A Note on Private Practice

Self-employed practitioners working from home or hired rooms also need to have assessment procedures, in order to protect both parties. Private practice is seldom so easy and relaxed as it may appear. True, the therapist enjoys the luxury of doing long-term open-ended work. Yet inadequate or no assessment can leave her with a patient that in retrospect she may have preferred not to take on, and she is stuck with him for years. Unlike the GP counsellor or therapist, she doesn't have a doctor next door who can make speedy hospital or social work contact in emergency. The private therapist always takes details of the patient's GP for emergency purposes, but he can't be summonsed quickly and may know very little about the patient's background. Employed by a surgery, the therapist can swiftly acquire prescriptions for those patients who intermittently succumb to a mental illness, but who can use therapy perfectly well in times of remission. Many people with medically controlled schizophrenia or bipolar disorder want help with problems totally unrelated to their illness and are entitled to be seen independently of their chronic label. What does the private practitioner do though, when the schizophrenic sufferer, normally perfectly reasonable, stops taking his medication (as such folk are wont to do) and turns up to his session jabbering nonsense about cosmic plots to kill him?

Readers experienced in private practice will know all this. But the NHS therapist, however senior, who is considering setting up privately, needs to be keenly aware of what support she is losing and select her new private patients accordingly.

Psychiatry

In both public and private sectors psychiatric diagnoses are ignored at the therapist's peril. The medical and therapeutic model of treatment should work complementarily. They are not antithetical: us (good) therapists being warm and understanding; them (bad) psychiatrists being cold and labelling. Abuse occurs when these professions are split off from each other by these antediluvian attitudes. I have seen ideologically bound therapists battling to keep their patients off drugs when they desperately need them as part of an overall treatment strategy with several inputs including counselling. And I have seen psychiatrists investing total faith in medication and letting bipolar patients in their down phase wander about with no family, job, or friends to support them. Then they wonder why there is no improvement. There are good and bad practitioners in both the therapeutic and psychiatric camps.

Sadly, most training courses I have come across teach no psychiatry. This is a serious omission and seems to be based on ideological prejudice. I hope the mature therapy reader will dare to leave her comfort zone and learn something of mental illness. The necessity for being able to spot the signs can then be passed on to her supervisees and trainees, eventually counteracting the psychiatry-avoidant culture that still reigns in many places.

Ask yourself the following questions. Whatever setting you work in, can you sense when a diagnosed bipolar person is veering toward a crisis necessitating medical intervention? Can you tell the difference between chronic suspicion and incipient paranoia? Can you tell a dreamer from someone with schizophrenia? Do you understand the different types of schizophrenia? Can you tell a chronically repressed person from a high functioning autistic one? At what weight do you think it is safe to embark on therapy with an eating-disordered person and would you be prepared to do it without backup? Do you know enough about alcoholism to assess if someone really is 'dry'? In longer term work do you have a built-in assessment period that the patient knows about? (Should you identify a pronounced personality disorder you feel insufficiently experienced to treat, you can suggest some treatment facility more appropriate for his needs). You will increasingly meet with patients who are caring for relatives or spouses with dementia, or age related disabilities. How much do you know about these, such that you can be truly empathic? How much do you know about psychotropic drugs and their side effects? Loss of orgasmic or erectile function, for example, can play havoc with the relationships you are trying to help.

How often do you have to decline taking on someone because you don't understand or are afraid of their psychiatric background?

I don't propose that therapists become amateur psychiatrists but there is a grey area between therapy and medicine where practitioners can teach and learn from one another if old ideological barriers can be pulled down. Can the senior therapists to whom this book is addressed lead the way? It should be remembered always that this is not a binary matter in which either someone is mentally ill or they are not. People slide in and out of illness and wellness. Some become a little unwell mentally or a lot, depending on lots of other factors, many of which are unpredictable. Some recover fast and others become chronic sufferers. Some people have a lifelong illness but with extensive spells of remission. Many rehabilitated substance abusers return to their addiction in times of crisis and may need emergency medical or psychiatric intervention. No diagnosis is ever one hundred per cent conclusive and all-encompassing. The point is that the more the medical, psychiatric, and therapeutic professions can work harmoniously together, the better and more holistic overall treatments will become.

CHAPTER TWELVE

SELF-SUPERVISION / NOTE TAKING

Unless there's an explanatory counselling leaflet, an informal contract is agreed with the patient toward the end of the first session, so he knows exactly what is and is not available to him. The counsellor then needs to take some time to review and record the essence of the session while it is still fresh. Afterwards, self-supervision is repeated according to need as therapy proper unfolds. There are no rules. You trust your experience to guide you.

It has to be said that some patients are more difficult than others and some counsellors more experienced than others, so that on occasion in time-limited work the dynamic formulation is not arrived at until the end of the sessions. This is not necessarily a disaster. The saddest outcome is no formulation at all or one based on wild guesses. The formulation, however cumbersomely couched (pure poetry not required), should result from insight, not intellectualism. If it does not feel like a lightbulb going on, or at least a flicker from a candle, it isn't a true formulation.

Without a shared idea of what the focus of the work is going to be, the patient may still feel heard, but the cosy glow of attention soon wears off. If he only comes to understand the formulation and the focus to which it points in the last session, then at least he has something precious to take home and deeply think about. Due to lack of resources the finding of the formulation often *is* the therapy.

In my book *The Broad Spectrum Psychotherapist* there is a dedicated section on the finding and refining of the dynamic formulation. It contains illustrative clinical material and examples of how to compose written formulations you may wish to use for presentation in seminars or in clinical reports.

Usually it's the therapist who alights on a formulation first, though it may be a bit rough and ragged at the start. The patient provides the associations, memories and feelings that assist them both in honing it into a clear statement about those influences, until now hidden from him, that have contributed to his troubles. Some patients 'cotton on' quicker than others; some find it very hard to think psychologically at all, even if they are most advanced in other fields. Brains are not all wired in the same way. This will of course affect the speed at which a formulation can come together.

Even when the dynamic formulation is clear to the therapist, communicating it to her patient can be problematic. This is not necessarily her fault, though many clinicians have become skilled at translating the formulation into metaphors and analogies that the patient can understand. They do this by borrowing the patient's own phraseology, or ideas he can relate to, such as those linked to his job.

Jock

Jock was a P.E. teacher and part-time fireman, very proud of the work he and his mates did for the community. He came to the surgery fed up after a week of taking Valium for his agitation, worried about becoming addicted or too dopey to do his part-time job properly.

He was married to a warm, home-loving wife who enjoyed soaps on the telly and making wonderful food after watching all the cookery programmes. He loved her to bits, he said, but he still wasn't happy. As for her, she constantly complained about his restlessness, his never sitting down for more than five minutes. Even in sleep he woke her up with his tossing and turning, not to mention his keep fit exercises at five in the morning.

Jock's father hit his mother and sisters frequently but never him or his brother. "He had it in for women," he told me. His mother always tried to fight back or put herself physically in front of Jock's sisters to shield them from the blows. Jock tried to protect his family and so watched the build-up to his father's tempers from second to second, becoming expert at getting his siblings and mother out of the way at the last moment before his dad lashed out.

Jock had married a quiet and obliging woman who would never provoke or fight back but then felt ashamed at how dull he found her. I put it to him that he'd married for peace after the terrible wars of childhood, but had not found out yet how to enjoy peace, having had no experience of it. *All he felt any good at was firefighting – indeed he'd made a career out of his childhood role of rescuer.* The position of relaxed and cherished partner was foreign to him. He hated his father's idea of being a husband but lacked any other role model to imitate.

He was quiet for a bit then said, "You mean there's no fires in my marriage so I can't cope, don't know what to do, get all fidgety and have to go looking for someone to save – is that it? Because I'm never agitated at the station you know, or at a practise or a real fire. Cool as a cucumber."

He pondered a bit more, then added, "Blimey, no wonder I don't know what to do with her. I'm secretly wanting her to do something that gives me the chance to save her and she doesn't need saving. I'm ruddy well redundant! They say you get restless when you've been laid off, don't they?"

We were on our way. His marriage and the link to his parents' marriage was to be the focus, no need to further spell out my rough and ready formulation that pointed to it. He'd well and truly got there himself.

If the patient's subsequent material firms up the formulation, your job in the remaining sessions is to bring him round to seeing what you can see, inviting him all the while to embellish or otherwise adjust your hypothesis. If you can at least come to a shared appreciation of what the patient's pain *means*, it is a new start for him. Ideally you want further sessions to look at present and past settings in which his pain declares itself, and how he perhaps unwittingly perpetuates it, or tries to avoid it, which only leads to other problems. You are hoping that you might also identify the individual or family interactions that originally set him off on his unhappy trajectory.

It has to be noted too, that not everybody requires a formulation, or even psychotherapy for that matter. Some come to confess, to grieve, to be angry at their lot, to express doubts about their convictions, to just be listened to while they gather up their dwindling emotional resources. Some of these leave before the six sessions are up, having gone as far as they are willing or able to go. That is their legitimate choice.

Now, on to my self-supervision chart. Oh heavens, I hear you cry, not another set of boxes to tick! But wait, this is not for anyone's eyes but yours. It should help you keep up to date with a fully rounded view of your patient's progress, rather than just being a historical linear account of his life and symptoms, plus what you said and did. A chart, once you are familiar with it, is in any case quicker than an essay. Many supervisees bring copious notes to the session then find themselves frowning at what they have written, unable to bring the reported therapy session back to life. Spare a thought for the poor external supervisor, trying to make sense out of their supervisee's fog.

The chart I'm suggesting is but a prototype. It demonstrates an alternative recording method to the traditional pages of notes. It takes a bit of getting used to, but gets easier with practice. Another of its advantages is that the act of filling it in is also an *act of self-supervision*. You will be forced to *think*, not just faithfully reproduce what was said by whom, as if you were tackling a set of minutes.

You can peruse the empty chart (fig 3a) on the following pages. I will explain it more fully in a moment, before sharing Beth's case. After that I will lay out for you how the completed chart looked after our third session (fig 3b).

Figure 3a

Self-Supervision Chart

Patient:	Clinical Picture	Formulation	Previous Personality
What I know / still need to know	1	2	3
What I can / can't offer		8	9
What the patient can / can't offer			
What the practice can / can't offer			

SELF-SUPERVISION / NOTE TAKING | 211

Risk	Future Outlook	History	My Notes
4			

Can I just digress a moment to issue a warning about notes to any NHS therapists planning to move into private practice? Make sure you have excellent insurance which *includes legal representation* should you require it. Write only essential factual information on any formal case notes that a court might demand to see. I may sound paranoid, but I have witnessed several sad cases of private practitioners having complaints made against them to their professional bodies by their patients. Some of these bodies fall over backwards to be fair to both parties and worry greatly about Joe Public's opinion. Their own reputation is at stake after all. Lacking any solid evidence – it was one person's word against the other – they failed to offer the expected support to their therapist member, leaving her alone, frightened or self-doubting, and at emotional breaking point. Such organisations ought to work out their priorities. Many professional members pay hefty fees expecting to be represented and defended if a case is lodged. So who then would defend the complainant? The qualifying body cannot properly do both.

It is essential to censor what you may long to write in your formal notes, in order to avoid incriminating yourself. This strictly personal chart is not required by any employer or agency and should be shredded as soon as it becomes redundant. By the time a court asks for any records it has long since ceased to exist. It functions solely as a temporary mnemonic.

It has to be owned that some complaints lodged are the result of inexperienced therapists saying or doing impulsive things in the tension of the moment that are then understandably misconstrued by the patient. There is a huge difference between punishable, unethical behaviour and clumsy technique. I would hope the chart, if consulted before a difficult session, might aid the therapist to prevent such errors of judgement because they have already been anticipated in black and white.

I will take you through boxes 1 and 2 to start with, providing examples of the type of entries you might make, depending on your particular patient. I will suggest a few more later in this chapter. It would be far too tedious for you were I to wade through every single box here, so I have laid out many of the other possible entries not described in this chapter, on a copy of the chart (fig 3c). It comes after the chart I have completed for Beth (fig 3b).

Box 1

You need to write here *in your own, not official, language* what you know but still need to know, with regard to the clinical picture – what the patient presents to you as his reason for coming. It might be just a description of the complaint – boyfriend trouble, parenting teenagers, stress at work. I use the term 'clinical picture' here in its informal sense, referring to your personal perceptions, not some psychiatric term, unless of course they coincide. For instance, both you and a psychiatrist might agree this person is depressed, obsessional, confused, phobic, eating disordered; so this is what you write down. It will be of help to you later if you can also squeeze into the tiny space whether this seems a serious or minor, acute or chronic presenting picture, and whether the patient is actually ill, not able to run his daily life adequately. Maybe you are not sure. Fine: write that down in your own shorthand as something you 'still need to know'. If he *is* ill, additional services are likely to be needed rather than just half a dozen sessions of counselling in the surgery.

Box 2

You will have observed that *Box 1* cross references 'what I know / still need to know' with 'clinical picture' along the top of the page. *Box 2* to the right is 'what I know / still need to know about the formulation', second along the top of the page. 'Formulation' includes your attribution of *meaning* to the presenting picture. (See the dynamic formulation in *Box 2* of Beth's chart in fig 3b). When you fill in any box it should be with reference to two titles, one along the top of the chart and one down the side. Thought needs to be given before scribbling spontaneously. You can cut verbs, sub clauses and lengthy adjectives; you can use all the slang and personal shorthand you like – no one is ever going to see it. But you must *think*. Does what you are about to write refer to both headings, the vertical and the horizontal? If it doesn't, your data gathering is no different to note-taking by conventional means.

There are no right and wrong entries, only truthful ones reflecting what you are thinking at the time. Sometimes you are unable to fill one square, or can make only tentative guesses. You may just write down '?' in *Box 2*, or 'still half baked' if you have a rough idea but are still puzzled about the formulation. You can't always achieve it in the first session, especially with a morose, agitated or hyper anxious patient. All entries are for your information only, and for comparison with future charts, so there is no need to gloss over a difficult session and your imagined inadequacies. This is not an exam or any kind of self-evaluation unless you make it so, in which case you have some important questions to ask yourself! This chart is designed to help you, not judge you.

Contracting

After completing the chart, then chewing over the results in front of you, you may realise the second session has to be used for further assessment of the patient's condition and to find out whether, consequent upon clarification of that, you are going to continue with him. It may be wiser to return him with your recommendations to his GP or other person who sent him to you, or refer him on to a different kind of service more congruent with his needs.

If he is to remain with you, then a contract, however informal, needs to be agreed, in order to motivate both therapist and patient to exploit the maximum potential of the brief time they are going to share. Contracting may only take five minutes, but it is five minutes that can save much anguish and possibly a messy or disappointing ending for the patient. He has a right to know precisely how many sessions he can have, whether there is any chance of an extension, and under what conditions. What will happen if he misses a meeting? Is it replaceable? How do you send messages to each other concerning emergencies or absences? Should he inform you of any changes in his medication, or how he is using them? Should he tell you if he is also seeing someone else about his problems? His and your clear understanding of what can be fairly offered, given tight resources, helps you both to pace the work, whilst entertaining realistic hopes of what might be achieved. It takes pressure off you both.

Reviewing

Toward the end of the sessions it is also important to build in a review for the patient's benefit, or at least keep one in mind, even if for good reasons it never comes to pass. As an adult, the patient is entitled to the benefit of your professional feedback after you have worked intensively with him for several weeks. Reviewing is something best done together, but you are more educated than he in psychological matters so it is fair that you answer if he asks directly for your angle on how things have gone. You give him your frank opinion as might a kindly lawyer, financial advisor or the citizen's advice bureau. Sometimes, of course, there is no need for opinion and advice because a shared view is already established about the way forward after this contract is concluded. I shudder at the thought of doing short therapy by formula. If a step is superfluous, cut it out and use the time for better things.

In other time-limited treatments the patient still wants feedback from his therapist, but it just comes up naturally as part of the conversation between them. Working out if this is a legitimate adult request deserving of a straight and honest answer, or something in need of closer examination because of what may be lurking behind it, can be a tricky business. Generally speaking I would hope the patient can have his query answered by the end, but if he is a dependent kind of chap, constantly asking you to tell him what to do, then clearly it is his inability or unwillingness to make decisions or take responsibility that needs addressing first. As ever in therapy, there are no rigid rules but many clues in the patient's history and in the current session material to guide you.

Another temptation, as mentioned earlier, is to so crowd the last session with advice and opinion that all emotional content is safely censored and a proper goodbye is never said or experienced.

All I am saying is *in principle* the patient has a right to know what you honestly professionally think, adult to adult, once the brief work is over.

Back to the Chart: A Few More Entry Examples
Box 3
Here you ask yourself the question: what do I know but still need to know, about the patient's underlying personality? Its robustness or otherwise indicates to some degree the likelihood of maintaining any improvement when the counselling support ends. Will he be able

to manage on his own? You may not yet be sure about this; it will depend on what material he has so far volunteered. You may have to be patient and await developments. Each chart entry just shows how far along this road you have so far travelled and reminds you to keep alert for further evidence.

The strength or shakiness of the patient's normal personality also helps you determine the speed and depth at which to work, how much insight he can stand, which defences to challenge and which to leave alone or approach delicately to test if he's ready to face them.

You may find yourself writing "not known", "suspect OK", or "wait / watch" on the chart, or "always been unstable". The next week's chart entries might be much more definite. Consecutive sheets depict the progress and direction of – along with corrections and adjustments to – your evaluation of his personality to date. Lingering uncertainty evidenced by an unchanging chart entry could indicate a need for external supervision.

What might you 'still need to know' about his well personality? Say this patient's mother died when he was young but he got on well with his stepmother – how relevant then is his mother's death? Is it more or less critical than other life events you'd be well advised to look at? As yet you are ignorant. You might write in *Box 3* "Mother trauma" which is your shorthand version of this question. It alerts you to watch out for future material relating to the two mothers to help you decide the extent to which his relationship with them has affected his character and temperament. He may have adjusted very well, or he may have been devastated and this is reflected in his moody and vulnerable personality.

Box 4

This is about what the assessor knows and still needs to know (down the side of chart) about risk (along the top of the chart). Under what conditions is the patient likely to become a danger to himself or others? There's no need to panic if the patient is sometimes aggressive, or threatens his partner, or if a mother is so low her children may not be looked after properly. The point is whether or not the surgery and all its back-up facilities could cope with your assessed risk, should your worst fears be realised.

Can you rely on them rescuing you? Do you need to prepare them in advance? What if the patient lodged an unjustifiable complaint? Would they support you? Would they deal promptly enough with police or section the patient if necessary? Would they blame you if there was a suicide attempt?

Perhaps you write down, with a question mark while you are not sure: "hits his child". What you still need to know is the procedure and timing for the reporting of abuse and whose is the responsibility for actually doing it and drawing up reports. Space in the box is short, so all you need to write is: "legal obligations".

Box 8 and Box 9

I draw your attention to these two boxes because they encroach upon the assessor's interior world. Bearing in mind this is a private, soon to be shredded document, resolute self-scrutiny is required of you if this patient is to be treated in the *intersubjective* manner advocated by this book, integrated with whatever other outlook you espouse. Otherwise the chart is just one more form-filling exercise. Each box is designed to promote your own careful post examination of the session, including the investigation of yourself. It will take time, peace and quiet, and concentration, just the same as external supervision.

Box 8 poses the implicit question: if the patient's dynamic formulation is similar to your own, even if your issues are resolved or are not so entrenched, can you still keep the right therapeutic distance? Might it be an advantage even? Or do you feel averse to working with him? And, if so, will that aversion affect your capacity to help? If worried, would some external supervision or a one-off consultation with your ex-therapist be useful? If the answer is no, should you decline to see this patient altogether?

Similarly in *Box 9*: what are the implications of the patient's underlying personality being very close to your own? You probably feel comfortable in your professional role, are confident about the way you present yourself to patients and colleagues, but underneath you know there is another you, susceptible to certain influences and situations that can leave you anything but self-assured. Naturally you will have accrued all manner of (hopefully appropriate and measured) defences to cope. What to do if meeting your new patient for the first time is like looking into a mirror? Again, is this a help or a hindrance to effective work? At least the question of 'what you can / can't offer' cross referenced with 'underlying personality' is out in the open for you to mull over. The chart will not let you hide from it.

There is also the question of how a patient's dynamic formulation or his underlying personality affects you if either or both of these are utterly foreign to your personal experience. Does their strangeness limit your ability to empathise or make an Alliance?

Twenty-four boxes are a lot to take in. You may care to finish this chapter first, and return to the final complex chart (fig 3c) later on, when you can study it in more detail and at your leisure. I have tried to fill all the boxes with examples of the most common entries I would anticipate seeing, should I look over your shoulder as you write.

I will now tell you Beth's story. The chart I drew up for her appears as fig 3b.

Beth

Beth, thirty-seven, returned from the Isle of Skye four months ago. Two weeks ago she came to see the GP at whose surgery I worked part-time. Alarmed by her mental state, he prescribed a high dose of anti-depressants and referred her to me. He had been her GP as a child when she had endured several complicated operations on her hare lip. When she grew up, she moved away to make a career in London, but had now re-registered with the practice. All he told me was that she was "in a state" and although it was a long time ago he remembered her mother as "a drama queen".

She came into my room flustered, visibly shaking, dabbing at her eyes, and gazing about her as if wondering where to sit or what to do.

She talked fast, frequently not finishing her sentences. She flitted from topic to topic – childhood (her operations), adulthood (her successful publishing career) and her wrecked marriage, her husband still on Skye winding up their business. It was after three more sessions that I had the story in the proper order. I spent most of the early time containing the agitation (praying the medication would kick in soon). She would hunch herself up as she poured out self-recrimination, or jolt upright, crying out that she had lost everything, messed up her life, and there was never going to be any way back. The catharsis seemed to calm her though, and each time she left feeling "more of a piece". I sensed she was coming to depend on myself and the doctor already; she appeared to have no one else.

Weaving together the various strands of her muddled, half-finished accounts, I worked out this sequence of events. As an only child of a lady-of-the-manor type of mother, her hare lip made her feel self-conscious and ugly. But much, much worse, was the way her mother "stole the limelight", as she put it. Whenever the operations went wrong Mother would play damsel in distress and have all the doctors and nurses fussing over *her*. When the operations went right her mother would demand all manner of add-ons, begging them to turn her ugly duckling into a beautiful swan. She said her mother loved the hospitals, dressed up to the nines for them, was always glad to accompany her there so she could grab lots of attention. She felt the hare lip was her own tragedy, not Beth's, and that people should sympathise with her maternal grief, which they generally did. She completely ignored Beth's school record, which was remarkable given the necessary absences for surgery. All she wanted was a daughter as beautiful and socially connected as herself – in fact an extension of herself.

Beth did well at university and went into publishing, rapidly progressing to deputy director. She never applied for top jobs, was always the reliable, charming, self-effacing but deadly efficient second-in-command. She was a great cook and warm hostess, but would always be found at the end of the evening clearing up in the kitchen. Privately she longed for marriage and children but felt no one would want her. She resigned herself to being single forever and dedicated herself to her rewarding job.

At thirty-one she met her husband-to-be at a conference and decided to leave her job and throw in her lot (including savings) with him. They set up an antique furniture restoring business on Skye, with Beth doing all the administration, accounts and phone contacts. Her husband Tyrone 'networked', contriving invitations to all the affluent residences, dining out with clients while she, as ever, made herself the backbone of the business.

Tyrone was very creative but not good with customers, especially those who did not share his exquisite taste. He angered easily, would stay out late then drag Beth from her bed at 3am to go through business records he felt she'd done incorrectly, costing the business as a result. She knew her records were correct but calmed him by investing more of her own savings to subsidise new ambitious projects that she knew would fail. But she would do anything to keep him happy and her marriage alive. Tyrone got angrier and angrier, blaming her for the business deteriorating. "I worked like a dog but it was never enough for him," she wept. He started staying away for days at a time, when she suspected he was drinking. Finally he hit her. Even then she told herself all would be well if she could just rescue the business. She worked harder still and invested the last of her savings.

When their business collapsed completely after only two years he sent her back to England, ostensibly to her mother who had never approved the match and whom Beth hated. Instead, she returned to her childhood GP practice, of which she had fond memories. By now her mother, in her seventies, had retired to the coast.

Beth had lost contact with her old publishing colleagues in London, and in any case could not let them see her like this. She was house-sitting in a big draughty farmhouse while the owners were on sabbatical, never seeing anybody and grieving over the loss of her marriage. Her money was gone and it was clear she was totally unemployable. She could no longer face a computer and her tax affairs were in a mess. She was sleeping in the day, had put on lots of weight, and felt as ugly as she had as a child. Her luggage from Skye remained unpacked and stacked in the hall.

I felt we were making a bit of headway though when in a sudden outburst, loud and clear, she wished her mother, husband, and herself dead. Her rage was at last about to erupt. I was very conscious of the risk level and reminded her she could contact the surgery at any time.

To return to the first session: I spoke with the doctor afterwards and said I couldn't help her unless he permitted me to offer three lots of six sessions from the very beginning. After that we would almost certainly need to line up the CPN for further support. In the meantime was there any unit to which she could be temporarily admitted? She needed proper diet, nursing care, exercise. She was acutely ill.

I felt it was too soon for therapy unless she could visit me from the safety of a protective environment, but she refused to go into a psychiatric unit (understandably she was phobic about hospitals of any sort!) and couldn't afford a private nursing home. She wanted to continue with myself and the GP, who, for the moment, she was clearly seeing as dependable parental figures. The GP had been her rock in childhood and she wanted the same help now. I was concerned about her regression, but how could I refuse to see her, given the circumstances?

She remained sweating, breathless and hand-wringing throughout the sessions but we did accomplish some work around the mother, my chosen focus. She came to see that her husband was just another version of her mother, which increased her loathing of them both. He was supposed to have been her saviour, not a replica. Her disappointment was turning to fury.

In her publishing career she had turned her meekness and passivity into something valuable for, and appreciated by, the bosses she supported. She had been happy and healthy for a time. Her marriage had thrown her straight back into childhood. In trying to be indispensable as a wife, she had found not praise and respect, but exploitation. She began to see these links but was far too demoralised to muster her old professional talent. If only we could retrieve that earlier pride and confidence she had once enjoyed, but it seemed a very distant prospect.

Just as I thought she was settling down a little, she missed a session and I had to write to her as her phone had been cut off. Just before her next session I received a letter from her saying the taxman was threatening court action and there were lawyers' letters about debts incurred by the Skye business. She had no more money and nowhere to live as the academics whose house and cats she had been caring for had returned early from their sabbatical. The only thing left was to go home to Mother. She wrote that she hoped she could stand up to her this time, but for the moment she needed a place to hide and rest. She thanked me for my help and said she would keep safe what she had learned.

I hoped for further news from her, but many years have passed and there has been nothing.

My ideal but unrealisable recommendation for Beth's management would have been first and foremost a comfortable nursing home where she could break down in peace. The treatment package would include gentle, holistic nursing care, with twice a week therapy once medication had lifted her mood to a level where she could make use of it. Someone in the surgery or nursing home would take charge of the debt situation, getting the authorities to hold off until she was able to cope. Visits to her trusted GP, ostensibly for monitoring medication, would be a valuable part of her recovery. Unfortunately we could not provide such a programme.

I was deeply saddened by the premature return to Mother.

Note on Figures 3a, 3b and 3c

Figure 3a on pages 210 and 211 shows the self-supervision chart before it is filled in. Examples of how to use the boxes can be found in the following pages, corresponding to the numbers in boxes 1-4 and 8-9 on the diagram.

Figure 3b on pages 224 and 225 demonstrates a completed chart using Beth's story.

Figure 3c on pages 226 to 229 shows many different examples of the type of entries readers may find themselves making, and so do not represent any specific case.

The empty chart (Figure 3a) in its entirety is designed to fit on A4 paper, but due to the configuration of this book it is not possible to illustrate this in an A4 landscape format. However, if you use either Microsoft Word or Excel you will be easily able to adapt the chart to an A4 landscape format for your own use.

Readers who do supervision/training may also find the chart a useful teaching aid, especially for those supervisees/ trainees who find difficulty in coherently reporting their counselling/therapy sessions.

Figure 3b

Self-Supervision Chart

Patient: BETH	Clinical Picture	Formulation	Previous Personality
What I know / still need to know	Agitated, depressed. Very ill. Will she cope? No pals.	Uses pseudo collaboration / victim role to avoid fighting back, which would spoil chances of *potential* maternal love. This defence failed in marriage but not work. Lost both worlds along with all self-esteem. Need more info re mother. Dad?	Gregarious, resourceful, professional success. Craves status. Lots of denied aggression that needs freeing up. *Chronic* low self-image makes her vulnerable when lacking external validation. Can she get back to work?
What I can / can't offer	Permission to extend sessions if need be. Can do needed CBT attitude stuff as well as dynamic. Can't give her home or friends.	Help her study her major defence in present / past when current symptoms allow. Release the pent up rage. Can't use any of my own identification with Dynamic Formulation – am not identified.	Reaffirm positives. Help her with *future* by using / building on past successes. Can't offer chances in present to practise her talents.
What the patient can / can't offer	Receptive to soothing, explanation, advice and empathy. Can't take too much dynamic work – too chaotic.	Understands at intellectual level, but does not yet appreciate full impact of mother / operations, etc. She will work very hard / excitedly as she *does* realise. Can't be rushed.	Longs to return to normal but lost faith that she can. Can't promise anything.
What the practice can / can't offer	Medication, excellent GP relations. MH team referral. Can't do nursing home / social contacts.	Team *not* interested, trust me to 'get on' with it.	Practice has no data on this.

Risk	Future Outlook	History	My Notes
50 / 50 now, outlook cautiously good if we / she can find better environment. Needs max sessions. Will she make it with less than ideal helping conditions?	Good with adequate time therapy followed by CPN support. ? Employment to regain status. ? Divorce trauma – how long to recover? How long before ready for employment?	That mother! Good experiences with father. Facial reconstruction – huge effect on self-image. Hatred of mother not then expressed. Which will win, regressed need for a mum, or new job?	Beware idealisation / termination problems. Use of CPN later? Agreed to look up dietician / gym later. Not talked re sexuality so far. Important, or not? Under all, still longing for Mum's love??
Access to doc 24/7. Extra sessions. Discuss suicide. Risk should diminish with alliance-making as *Prozac* kicks-in. I can't offer enough!	Help her see recovery likely in longer term. Worst bit is now. Suspect has capacity, but she first needs to completely break down. No facilities, refuses hospital.	She never looked at her history before, just 'bore' hatred and unconditional longing for Mum. Help her own her history. 2 sessions weekly not available.	
Has made agreement to talk re it, but not do it. She is ++ relieved by talk. Can't guarantee anything but will try.	She very doubtful (depression), but longing to hope! Too low to seek out old friends.	Eager to talk and courageous enough to look. But despair and tears break in to disrupt 'flow'. Can't get over marriage enough to stay calm and think.	
Emergency call service. Doc chats. Adjust medication. Can't find residential patient will agree to.	? Extra sessions but tight resources. Surgery an anchor in future. Patient already has good attachment to surgery.	Keep good notes for future use. (GP due to retire). Old notes lost.	

Figure 3c

Self-Supervision Chart

Patient:	Clinical Picture	Formulation	Previous Personality
What I know / still need to know	Developmental crisis. Personal crisis – not ill. Diagnosis firm / tentative, e.g. – Neurotic illness. Psychotic illness. Personality disorder. Organic /neurological. Substance abuse. Gender issue. Other / Mixture. ? More assessment, 2nd opinion.	This is the Dynamic Formulation……. Half-baked. Concerns shame / violence. No Dynamic Formulation (me puzzled). Need more time + info.	Robust (when well). Strong positive / negative attitude to his problems / illness. Always been vulnerable. OK if there is constant external support. OK so long as work / home role successful. Unclear as yet.
What I can / can't offer	Am I informed / experienced enough? Supervision good enough? My counter-transference, + fatigue level OK? What vacancies / holidays / availability? Can I be flexible ideologically if other techniques needed? Can't offer certainty.	Further work on the Dynamic Formulation. If Dynamic Formulation near my own: OK or not? Do I wait or grab supervision / personal therapy input now? Safe to leave other patient stuff alone / not safe? Can't know yet.	Strong Alliance likely. Too like / unlike me for comfort. Will need much support / education. Can only take a bit at a time. Ripe for therapy. Always had trouble thinking straight. Can't firm up patient's OK self in time available.

Clinical Picture/Formulation/Previous Personality
Continues on page 228

SELF-SUPERVISION / NOTE TAKING | 227

Risk	Future Outlook	History	My Notes
Functional breakdown. Suicide. Homicide. Child abuse (law). Domestic violence. Psychosis risk. Separation-sensitive. Regression. Hospitalisation. Refusal of medication. Return to addictions. How likely?	Good with short-term. Short work no good! OK with intermittent short-term. Fair with *team* involvement, but without? Poor with anyone, so do what we can. Unpredictable, may bolt / deteriorate in therapy. ? Likely to get worse before better.	None. Chronic but no treatment. Lots – routine and successful treatment. Lots – different practitioners, varied results. Problems, at life-phases only (marriage, motherhood, retirement). Patient's memories retrievable / denied?	*Alerts: GP treats patient's mum. Nurse dating patient's brother. Extreme religious beliefs, cults. Extreme diets. Family traits / culture.* *Omissions: Dead siblings, twinships, deaths. Shameful secrets. No mention of key figures. Information I have from case notes, or other sources, but not given by the patient.* *Counter-transference: Patient intimidates me with their IQ. I feel 'chosen'. I feel 'in the wrong'. I want to defend myself. Goose pimples.* *Literature: Do I need to mug up?* *Supervision: Any special queries?*
Access to psychiatrist, beds via GP. Legal obligations in conflict with treatment. My holidays at risk. Needs help to manage medication + self care. Preventive / management-of-illness advice: me or other team member to do? Case conferences. Can't guarantee safety.	Define level of realistic achievement for us both. Signpost other services for the future. Patient suitable for short versus intensive work – let's go! Can't give long-term that is needed. Private therapy not affordable.	Make sense of his history. Better management of old triggers + identify defences. Can do much if patient already self-aware. Can help him come to terms with tough life events not his fault. Much trauma, can't work miracles.	

Risk/Future Outlook/History/My Notes
Continues on page 229

Continued from page 226

Patient:	Clinical Picture	Formulation	Previous Personality
What the patient can / can't offer	Good / poor previous self-management. Panic / terror *pro tem*. Long / short / new experience of this clinical picture. Resistance / avoidance / hostility to symptoms. Can't collaborate in describing more of picture?	Capacity to 'get' Dynamic Formulation? Capacity to obtain relief from working on it / elaborating it. Toleration of pain – how much / often? Link-making capacity? Rage / regret at not seeing before. Likely reaction to Dynamic Formulation?	Tough, may be too defended. Slow pace only. Too much intellectualism or too much mood swing. Too concrete. Risk of crack up (borderline)? Stable concentration will come, once calmed.
What the practice can / can't offer	Standard of psychiatric knowledge / care among doctors. Medication ideology? Standard + availability of other resources. Quality of backup for therapist. Referring on.	Do other staff understand? Do they need to? Do they need to be 'tipped off'? Notes: what to put in e.g. childhood abuse, criminal record.	In chronic cases or frank illness, team backup needed. Standard good enough for this patient, or not?

Continued from page 227

Risk	Future Outlook	History	My Notes
Got relatives / partner support? Awareness / lack of, of risk. Capacity to take responsibility and seek help – enough hope? Honesty versus secrecy. Contract-making ability. Can give reliable feedback, or not on inner state?	Patient's expectations realistic or not re outcome? Needs underlying stuff tackled later / left alone – can / can't accept this. Too dependent / aversive to make solid Alliance. Should recover +/- permanently, but will always be susceptible to X or Y.	Insightful or not re history? Too scared to face past trauma – needs longer therapy. Longing to get past out of cupboard. Identification of recurrent illness onset – can patient read own signs? Can / can't see meaning in symptoms.	
Consultation with therapist when needed – fast enough? (State of waiting list). Emergency services for patient – holiday locums, home visits, CMHT.	Team expect too much or too little from therapy, are / are not prepared to act if asked. Re Personality disorders / team asset / liability? Can they share?	Notes plus word of mouth: family history often resides in team staff. Case conferencing easy / difficult?	

Suggested reading:

Bramley, W. (1996a). *The Broad Spectrum Psychotherapist* (especially chapter 5 – Dynamic Formulation). London: Free Association Books.

Bramley, W. (1996b). *The Supervisory Couple in Broad Spectrum Psychotherapy*. London: Free Association Books.

Coughlin, P. and Malan, D. (2007). *Lives Transformed*. London: Karnac.

Davanloo, H. (ed), (1980). *Short-term Dynamic Therapy*. New York: Jason Aronson.

Jesette, T. H-D. L, and Neborsky, R. M. (2012). *Road Map of the Unconscious: Mastering Intensive Short-term Dynamic Therapy*. London: Karnac.

Malan, D. H. (1979). *The Individual and the Science of Psychodynamics*. Oxford: Butterworth-Heinemann.

Molnos, A. (1995). *A Question of Time: Essentials of Brief Dynamic Psychotherapy*. London: Karnac.

Yalom, I. D. (1989). *Love's Executioner and other Tales of Psychotherapy*. Harmondsworth: Penguin.

TO THE READER

This book has been addressed to you, my fellow psychotherapists, whose career, whatever your own chronological age, is in midlife. What next? To rest on laurels, walk away from the stress and responsibility, do some life coaching or mentoring, take up private practice, apply for a sabbatical? Of course you could choose to leap forward, become a safely daring Mary Smith therapist!

But before any leaping goes on, time is needed to look back, take stock of your working life so far, including that private part of yourself that *is* the work. Has it evolved in parallel to your CPD activities, reading, and any further training? Do you need a further spell in therapy without the training course dictating who, how long and what type? Are you anywhere near prepared enough to let go of the apron strings of your original ideology? Can you autonomously appraise the new gurus on the scene or the latest theories from America, incorporating or rejecting particular aspects of them according to what enhances your personal brand of therapy? This is not to refute any of those innovations; but maturity and independence permit you to pick and choose, select from all that presents itself to you, without having to fall back on old 'family' traditions that could inhibit your judgement and restrict your development. No school of therapy has a monopoly on the right way to do things.

Neither is there any need to drop those doughty old concepts that seem as true to you today as they did when you were a student. The context will have changed as new ideas, literature and prophets emerge; but what you have personally learned and valued over the years – what works for you and your patients – should never been downgraded or embarrassedly put aside in favour of the latest trend. You are a free agent. And, as has often been observed, there is nothing so scary or so exciting as freedom!

Even well-established practitioners with a high reputation for good work sometimes doubt themselves, wonder whether therapy really works, or whether they are just peddling hope? Are they masquerading as healers when what they offer in truth is little more than a sympathetic ear dressed up in a lot of theoretical gobbledegook? Are their motives suspect? Do they use their patients as guinea pigs, stealing insights gained from them to secretly apply to themselves? Why did they take up this rewarding but difficult career in the first place? Why expose their most private self (if they are working Self Psychologically) to pain and suffering all day if there is nothing in it for them?

To address such doubts it's important to make a time and place to review your therapy career as a whole, both subjectively (close up) and dispassionately (from a distance). Has it been worth the effort, the training, the expense, the inroads it has made on family and partners? How far have you progressed or do you just 'get by' and hope no one notices the shortcomings? Have you kept up on the inside (personal growth) and the outside (updating knowledge) or just muddled through? When all is said and done, are you any good at this job? Not everyone's personality is suited to this work, however sincere their motives and however hard and long they have trained. Have you gone as far as you are able in this field and it's time for a career change? Could you be exhausted and too proud to take the rest your system badly needs?

To obtain a less ruminative, self-devaluing view, I suggest you might locate in reality or in recall an artefact of some kind that symbolises the course of your career, then stand back and look at it, see what it can tell you. Time, I know, is at a premium, but I am going to invite you to do a 'meditative' exercise – just the once – before proceeding with any decision about making changes to, giving up on, or moving forward in, your profession.

A few years ago this exercise fell into my lap and I found it extraordinarily useful. In fact it helped reverse my decision to retire. In Self Psychology terms, my efficacy needs were fully met and I found myself wanting to carry on. Until I wrote the (amended) article I am about to reproduce here, I had no idea just how far I had come in my interior life as it related to my work. I had also not taken full account of the vast distance the therapy movement has covered in half a century. This gives me hope for its future.

At that time, the editors of the Oxford Psychotherapy Society journal approached myself and another couple of senior society members to write an article for them. The remit was this: *What three things / events / people inspired you to become a therapist?* They said it might be paintings, landscapes, music, teachers, films or books – anything we liked. I racked my brains. There were so many interacting factors. I needed three bold specifics though, if the piece was not to be too woolly or navel gazing. In the end I returned to my professional roots and then it was easy.

You may not enjoy writing. To switch off and make contact with your truest self, you may paint or sculpt, or take long walks, or luxuriate in deep scented baths. Whatever your preference, I suggest you find a private space and time, switch off all electronic gadgets, and have a thorough 'floating' (as opposed to scientific) examination of this question of why and how you came to be a psychotherapist. Pick three specific items / persons / moments / material objects that set you on the therapy road, even though you may not have realised it at the time. Contemplate each of them with an open, quiet mind. Let them take you into your interior world of memories and associations, one thought or feeling linking effortlessly to another. Through the meditative concentration on these three items, meet again your old self, *be* your old self. Let your past speak to you across the chasm of years, remind you of who you were before you trained. So consuming is this profession, it is easy to forget!

When you return to the hustle and bustle of your current life, ask yourself what happened to that person in the intervening years, to bring her to where she is now. I hope this might help you understand what needs to be done about your future therapeutic career.

Meanwhile, let me introduce you to...

Three Muses Who Made Me a Therapist

Essex, England, 1960. I'm eighteen, green as grass, and just down from Lancashire. Having always been curious about how folk tick, I'm taking up my first ever job as a student mental nurse.

I have anticipated a thoroughly modern immersion in applied psychology: what I get is a living museum of early twentieth century psychiatry, most of it botched. The hospital is a big, self-contained village in blackened Victorian stone. The ever smoking incinerator tower soars above the mortuary, the steam-puffing boiler rooms, the never sleeping laundry and kitchens, and the maintenance workshops. Fanning out from this huddle are the endless echoing corridors, all painted in the same army surplus green and cream, connecting up the long narrow wards shooting off from them – 'Ones' for neurotic admissions, 'Twos' for acute psychotics, 'Threes' the ECT central recovery clinic with enough gleaming metal beds in regimented rows to cater for all the wards in need. There are many tucked away 'back wards' each housing forty or so burnt-out schizophrenics, manic depressives, lobotomised epileptics, tertiary syphilitics, alcoholic dements, and sundry chronic, also lobotomised, personality disorders / sociopaths / drug addicts. Most of these patients are ambulant but robotic, dressed in faded 1940s hospital issue clothes. There are wards especially for the mentally deficient, and several geriatric wards, plus wards for the deteriorated bedridden – diagnosis no longer relevant; and for those over-enthusiastically lobotomised people unable to care for themselves. Many have been admitted twenty or thirty years ago.

Mental nurses plus the rarely, sometimes never, seen psychiatrists, plus the odd occupational therapist, are the only carers. The term 'counsellor' has yet to be invented and no one in my circle has ever heard of psychotherapy, though we are dimly aware that a few weird people calling themselves psychoanalysts hang about Harley Street London – another planet entirely.

After the initial shock, I adjust quickly, enjoying the all-too-rare days in training school with keen young tutors eager for Change. The chronic ambulants shuffling, dribbling, head-banging, hair-sucking, chatting-to-their-voices, masturbating or swearing next to me in the tuckshop where I buy my Mars bars soon lose their strangeness.

Indeed, I feel more relaxed in the miles of corridors always populated with wandering, muttering, pacing or shouting patients, than I do in the world outside. I suspect we nurses unconsciously conspire to make ourselves as institutionalised as our patients in order to normalise and thus make easier our working environment. We can make hardly any of the patients 'normal' like us – only admissions ('Ones') boasts a success rate; but we sure as hell can become like them, by refusing to notice their bizarreness and sharing their inmate status. After all, our uniform, our food, our social club, and our bedrooms are all supplied by the hospital, which we rarely leave.

Still in my teens, I have no worldly ambitions yet; I just want to know how human beings *work*. Years later, as a sister at the Cassel Hospital, one of Britain's earliest and most fundamentalist Therapeutic Communities, I will come to comprehend the importance of unconscious individual and group forces and the curative impact of good interpersonal communication. Thus my career direction will become clear (though I will have to challenge the prevailing culture, where only doctors are allowed to train in psychotherapy. Damned if I'll let that put me off).

But until then I continue with my mental nurse training. Only in retrospect will I realise that three patients in particular are already shaping my attitudes, values, and beliefs such that a training in therapy becomes inevitable. In this article I want to honour these three long-dead women whose real names I shall use because they were real to me, and never 'case studies'.

KITTY

Kitty is twenty-nine, an ex-professional runner, a murderer and a psychopath. Six foot two, of athletic but feminine build, dark and sultry in an early Liz Taylor kind of way, she silently dominates the long straight aisle with side rooms and kitchen off, that constitutes 'Twos'. This is the locked ward for the acutely disturbed or legally detained. All day she sits, by negotiated agreement with staff, on the threshold of her side room, chain smoking and brooding. Her room is the last one, furthest away from the double-locked doors at the opposite end of the ward. No patient, however manic, deluded, paranoid or aggressive, ever goes near her room. We nurses approach in tandem at mealtimes. If Kitty wishes to eat she is obliged to withdraw to her bed whilst we deposit her tray outside the door on the floor. I think: "as if she was a dog!"

On my first ever night duty stint, 'Barty' the senior nurse (middle aged, heart of gold, built like a rugby player) warns me not to talk to Kitty as many young nurses have been seduced by her into doing all manner of 'errands' out of pity, and then got themselves into serious trouble. Terrified yet fascinated, I take my turn at leaving her supper by the door. Sometimes, through the haze of smoke, I detect a dark hump on the bed. She is facing the wall, lights off, in blatant contempt for me. At other times she whispers to me from the shadows: "What's the weather like in the real world?" or: "What do you do with your weekends as a free person?" "What's the boyfriend like?" Gradually our exchanges become longer, and each time she inches nearer the door.

I know from Barty what psychopaths are like but aren't they human too? No one knew who or why she murdered – it could have been a crime of passion. What future has this intelligent and beautiful woman, legally confined indefinitely for 'treatment' consisting only of enough of the newly discovered Largactil to fell an elephant throughout the day, and barbiturates at night. I watch with aching heart when, as her night pills start taking effect, she sways, eyes hooded, mouth agape, words slurred, down to the lavatories, elbow gripped by a soothing, cooing Barty. This is Kitty's only exercise.

One night after supper the three of us on duty are finishing our cocoa in the kitchen before the last medicine round, and routine side room checks through their peepholes. Suddenly there is a loud yell followed by repeated slamming of doors, as all patients remaining in the social area of the aisle run to their rooms. "She's out! She's out!"

Some large heavy object whizzes past the open kitchen door, and a moment later there's a loud splintering as whatever it is crashes to the floor. I dash toward the door, thinking to calm Kitty as I have seen Barty do (and to show I wasn't a coward, though my knees have turned to water). Haven't I developed some kind of unspoken understanding with her, I tell myself over and over. Might I not now show her that I see the real woman beneath the drugs, the brooding bored days, the despair and frustration she must feel?

It all happens so fast. Barty *assaults* me! In one swift tackle she pulls me to the floor while the other nurse cowers in the corner. "Get in here you silly bitch!" Barty orders as my nose collides with the brown lino and my body is unceremoniously slid, belly down, back into the kitchen. Then she locks the kitchen door *from the inside*. I can't believe it. She, the most famous and respected night nurse in the whole hospital, is locking us *in*! Appalled, struggling to rise from the floor, I protest: "Aren't we supposed to do something? Aren't we in charge? Aren't we supposed to help?"

Barty glares at me as a wooden lampstand flies past the peephole: "Shut up Jonesy (my maiden name). Watch and learn!" She turns to my fellow nurse, pats her arm, and says: "It'll be all right. She'll burn out. Sit down, have a fag."

We all sit down round the Formica table, smoking and listening to the destruction going on outside – ripping and tearing and dragging of furniture. "Yep," says Barty, "that'll be her bed she's pulling into the middle of the ward. And that... (enormous thud)... is that lovely old sideboard I always fancied. Probably ruined."

After a quarter of an hour and three fags each there falls an eerie silence. Barty cautiously unlocks and peeps out. A huge oak table, four legs in the air, lies against the ward's heavy locked doors, presumably Kitty's target. Her strength must be superhuman. All over the floor at that end of the aisle are strewn curtains, pictures, lamps, smashed shelves, books, crockery, chairs, broken vases and spilled sour water, Scrabble boards, crayons, even her mattress. And in the centre of the ward stands her stripped bed, turned upside down. And amid the carnage lies Kitty, sprawled like a rag doll, limp, utterly defeated. Barty hauls her up and practically carries her into her side room before locking the door. She tells me to fetch the medicine keys and be quick about it, and to get that other nurse to put the kettle on and find the spare packs of Woodbines (secreted in the bread bin for just such emergencies as this).

I know from training school that you can't cure psychopaths, but there has to be something better than this dehumanising permanent incarceration, surely? Though frightening at the time, I find Kitty's rampage entirely understandable. Her chemical straitjacket is no improvement on, or any more civilised than, the calico version we still have gathering dust in the linen cupboard.

(Though the 1959 Mental Health Act banned them, you never know when you might need one for a bit, especially on 'Twos'. Who's to know?)…

Thanks for setting me on the road, Kitty, the road to humane treatment communities rather than locked wards. My training in psycho social nursing at the Cassel assuaged some of the helplessness and anger I underwent, witnessing your decline. Now, along with expert colleagues, I would know – even in a secure prison – how to bring together difficult patients to talk with and learn from each other, rather than being condemned to permanent isolation, impotent rage, and chemical stupor.

HATTIE

Hattie on 'Elevens' (geriatrics) is ninety-two. All the ladies are bed-ridden, doubly incontinent, and some have bedsores the size of dinner plates, catheterisation having been abandoned due to the high incidence of kidney infection. The combined smells of ulcerating flesh, stale pee, disinfectant, and the sour odour of chloral hydrate, the colourless liquid-sedative to which all are addicted, is a reek I shall take to my grave. Though we try valiantly, we can never in one shift wash, toilet, change and feed everybody and then dress those sores. So some ladies are obliged to lie helpless in their sodden beds until the next shift comes on.

For Hattie, this awful ante room to death could be the Ritz. Possessed of one waggly yellow tooth, top row dead centre, she sits erect in her bed waving frantically at us as we come on duty as though we were returning heroes from some foreign war. We wash her and tie up her few strands of hair into a wobbly topknot and then she gazes at herself in a little oval gilt mirror, her sole possession, as if she's in a West End beauty salon and she's all of seventeen again. Her voice is high pitched, loud and squawky, exactly like the Monty Python chaps when they try to imitate women. She never stops chatting to us no matter where we are in the ward, a running account of the latest gossip with wicked chortles at the naughty bits. Though it's impossible to fit the broken up memories together into any kind of narrative, it's plain she's living in the past and for her we represent different people each day, or each hour. (One day I am Winston Churchill, kissed, then congratulated on singlehandedly winning World War Two!)

Hattie is unfailingly merry, grabs her chloral and throws it back with a "chin-chin" and sticking-out little finger, clearly believing it to be gin and tonic. At mealtimes she opens her slack but cavernous mouth as wide as it will go and with vigorous nods encourages us to spoon in more of the brown sludge of mince and vegetables that's sent daily from the kitchens. "What's on the menu today?" she crows hungrily, eyes rolling in anticipation. "A nice lamb chop with mint sauce," we tell her, or "a bit of pork and crackling with apple sauce." She groans with delight. Clearly she hallucinates whatever imaginary dish we put before her.

Because she eats so much but can't exercise, she suffers terribly from constipation, despite the water and aperients we constantly give her. Every week or so we have to perch her on the old-fashioned, high backed carved commode she calls her throne (it would fetch a fortune at Christies these days), and leave her, prattling away, to produce something, while we tend the next few beds. On our return it is always the same – nothing doing! She is so deluded she doesn't realise where she is or what's required.

By now we're getting really worried. Her stomach is swollen, hard as rock, and, unusually for her, she complains of pain. Then she adds wickedly: "D'you think Harry's knocked me up again? Got another bun in me oven?" At this my fellow nurse and I exchange glances: we have both had the same idea. My colleague yells (for Hattie's hearing is shot to pieces; it's why she squawks so loud, so she can hear herself) that yes, she is indeed pregnant, about to deliver in fact. But the baby is stuck so she'll have to push really hard. Hattie chortles and begins to bear down with every phantom contraction. Her old face puce with effort, she nonetheless keeps up a running commentary. "My Charlie, my first, he was just like this one, a right bugger, never wanted to come out and face the world. I 'ad to be cut right open for 'im, I did." Then: "Oh lor, the agony!" and she pushes like mad.

But it's no use. My eyes meet my fellow nurse's. There's nothing for it if we are to relieve Hattie's physical and mental anguish. "Hattie love," I hear myself shouting, "we're going to have to get baby out manually and it could hurt a bit. We'll lift you on the bed, and tip you on your side, okay?"

We roll her skinny gnarled frame (despite all the food) onto its side, and don plastic aprons over our starched white ones. We put on gloves and masks and take out a jar of lubricant that we keep in her locker with her mirror. We proceed with the extraction. Between oohs and aahs of pain she chatters on: "Can you see the head yet? Will he go blue like Charlie? Oh, oh, he's a-coming! Is he all right? Is he all *right*?"

The smell is unspeakable, the heap of hard accumulated faecal matter greater than any carthorse could produce. Hattie is jubilant and swears to name the baby after us wonderful "doctors".

We wash her again, change her linen, and tuck her up with a rolled up towel for the baby. We leave her propped up against high pillows, cradling and crooning over 'Wyn Margaret Blank' (for no one knows Hattie's last name, least of all Hattie.) Time for us to move on to the next bed.

Recalling how yet again we have taken Hattie to her fool's paradise, I lie awake at night, guilty and sad. We trick her, collude with and reinforce her delusions. We love the old girl, but is making her into a ward clown the most respectful way to treat her? Who abandoned her to this place all those years ago and why? (No one here ever has visitors). Even I can see that it is too late *now*; but *then*? Couldn't someone have sat with her in a familiar room as her mind started to fade, play her music from her past, show her photos, help her write notes to herself, take her round her old haunts to preserve what little functioning was left to her?

This question of how to humanely deal with the dementias has never been more relevant than now. Cutting edge pharmacology, neuroscience, stem cell research: yes to them all; but specialist counselling for sufferers and relatives is going to be essential in the coming years if our old people are to enjoy better lives than Hattie's. Rest in peace, dear Hattie, and may your successors get a better deal than we were able to give you.

OLIVIA

Olivia is a tiny, young-looking forty, with big expressive brown eyes and a long black plait down her back to her waist. Her face is a smooth, waxy white as if it has not seen the sun for years – it hasn't.

The only non-bed-ridden patient in a ward similar to Hattie's, she whizzes or skulks, depending on her mood, down the long aisle between the closely packed beds, sunk deep in an enormous NHS wheelchair circa 1930. She hand washes her pearly-pink silk dressing gown each night and under it wears a clean split-at-the-back NHS nightie. Over her knees are piled an unnecessary plethora of plaid rugs, for the ward roasts beneath an over-effective and clanking Victorian heating system.

As a result of my usual pestering, I discover from her yellowed notes that she is a grand hysteric, with multiple sclerosis. Whatever the diagnosis, she is totally sane, so why confine her to a geriatric ward, I ask indignantly. I'm told she's a chronic patient and this is a chronic ward. She may be young, but there's nowhere else for her to go. Those patients on 'Ones' (neurotic admissions) are in and out in six weeks; Olivia has been here for years. She has had her fair share of ECTs, her narcosis therapy and her insulin, and they even tried the new Largactil, but nothing worked.

From her spleen-venting outbursts I gather she used to be a promising opera singer, twice married and divorced, and had either swindled or been swindled by both husbands, her agent, and sundry others. Her verbal attacks on the world in general and husbands in particular are so vitriolic and obscene I wonder if her entire story is pure confabulation (a word recently learned in training school and injected into my conversation given any opportunity). But I am wrong. Later she shows me some Italian newspaper clippings about her imminent debut at La Scala. The financial scandal broke a few weeks before her big night and her Anglo Italian family abandoned her to her fate. Here.

We know when she is going to erupt. Her hair is loose and wild and her eyes flash with menace. She tears down the aisle at great speed, knocking over any obstacles in her path, human or otherwise, rams on the brakes at its end, and swivels round to glare at us nurses, feeding or toileting each patient in rotation. Despite her tiny body she has a voice like a foghorn. "Look at 'em. *Look*!" she bellows, "Nothing but piss and shit, snot and pus and smelly sores, all dribbling and gaga. How can you bear to touch them? No mind, no art, no nothing. Useless bastards all. They should be taken out and shot! Put 'em out of their misery!" (This of course is a projection onto them of her own self precept and is an indicator of her suffering; but at this time projection is a concept still unborn in me.) We nurses quietly carry on with our work, awaiting the inevitable storm of tears that will follow. Sister fetches the chloral – another inevitability.

Yet at other times she trails after us nurses, passing us a clean pillowcase or fetching us clean dressings from the steriliser. She even offers up her quality talc: "You can't subject the old nag to that bloody NHS Harpic stuff. Or d'you *want* to kill her off, eh? Lighten your load wouldn't it?"

Sometimes she goes mute for days and disappears into a disused washroom far along the corridor outside the ward, desperate for a bit of privacy presumably, so we leave her alone. One day I pass by the door of that washroom, taking a note from Sister to the pharmacy. Olivia's chair has its brakes on and her back is towards me. She faces the blank cream wall above six tapless sinks, her back very straight, her body still as death. It seems wrong somehow to interrupt her state of concentration or meditation or whatever it is, so I pause, not sure what to do.

Then, out of the silence, there floats the most pure and lovely sound I have ever heard from any human creature. This is before I come to know opera myself, so I do not recognise Bellini's sublime 'Casta Diva' (Chaste Goddess), the druid high priestess singing a prayer to the moon. I am spellbound.

I think at the end I must sigh, for she whirls round, her snarl ready – but I see her face is awash with tears. Seeing my rapt expression she is mollified and quickly dons her superior air. "Such acoustics in here don't you think? One can't resist exercising one's lungs a bit." She rubs her face dry. "But now, back to the old biddies I think. Short staffed today. Those nurses could use a bit of help, even from this old hack."

After that, during my breaks we somehow find ourselves together in the washroom, if only for a few minutes. She sings me all the big arias in a foreign tongue – Lucia, Tosca, Turandot, Madame Butterfly, the Marschellin, Dona Elvira, Carmen, Salome. I don't understand a word but I am captivated. A disused washroom in a loony bin must be a poor substitute for Milan's great opera house, not to mention the audience of one; but for me it is a very heaven.

She takes me to what she ironically calls her *boudoir*, an old store room converted for her use, a concession to her age. She shows me her theatre trinkets, old programmes with her name on, an ostrich feather fan, a silver hairbrush, decaying stage cosmetics. There's a companion silk dressing gown, pale blue, still in its tissue paper. It was being kept for her debut night and she has never worn it. She says she is wont to take it out sometimes and just stroke it.

Towards the end of my three months stint, I decide I have to challenge her. "Look Olivia, you've got to fight, get back on stage, use your gift. Get a new agent and let him manage your earnings till you're out of bankruptcy. You're completely sane if a bit, well okay *very*, temperamental, but hell you're an *artiste*!"

"Look kid, I'm dead as yesterday's newspaper, haven't seen a stage in ten years. There's a new generation out there queuing up to star at Covent Garden and La Scala. Anyhow who the hell wants to see Tosca leaping to her death from the Castello Sant' Angelo in a ruddy wheelchair? I couldn't even get up on the parapet."

I'm not giving up. "You could do concerts, recordings. You could get one of those fancy steel wheelchairs and put spangles all over the spokes. Your chair would become your trademark! You could throw away all those granny rugs and wear long slinky slithery gowns. Wow, you'd be a sensation!"

Her countenance suddenly darkens and she crouches back in her chair like an animal about to pounce. Her face is an ugly sneer. "Slinky gowns, you barmy kid? Slinky gowns, with *these*?" She flings back all the rugs in one fierce gesture and I gasp in horror. Her hips are wasted, practically non-existent, and her legs are two shrivelled matchsticks set for all eternity at crooked angles. If you touched them they would snap and crumble to dust.

"I win," she cackles bitterly and gathers up her rugs.

All us nurses are forbidden to have relationships with patients after our ward term is finished, but it isn't that which keeps me away after I leave 'Thirteens.' It's shame at my own ignorance and impotence.

If I could but bend time, Olivia, so that you visited me now, fifty years on, I just might help you face and come to some kind of terms with your triple tragedy -- a wrecked body, an incarcerated life, and a wasted gift. At the very least I could show you that your grief is understood and that I know my three months' worth of admiration and respect represented not even one drop in the ocean of your need.

Summing up

Custodial care and narcotic drugs were the best you three could expect. In such a setting there was no time, knowledge or personnel for psychotherapy. The concept of care in the community just loomed on the far horizon. We owe it to you and your fellow inmates to go on developing ourselves and our treatments so that such suffering as yours should never be repeated.

Author's Note

I wish to make very clear that though I am frank in this article about conditions in the 1960s, I have no desire to criticise the NHS, its staff or its practices at that time. We were overwhelmed by vast numbers of chronic or seriously disturbed patients with very few treatments to hand. That generation of patients has now died off, whilst new drugs – antipsychotics, tranquilisers and antidepressants – have proliferated, enabling psychiatry to operate much more in the ordinary community and prevent the sad chronicity which I have recounted.

Despite the odds, I never once witnessed cruelty, abuse or wilful neglect in all my five years at three mental hospitals including the one above. The staff varied in intelligence and aptitude, as they did in country of origin and level of education and language. We generally worked in pairs or fours on the chronic and geriatric wards and the collaborative bonds quickly forged within these units would have to be seen to be believed. I am proud to have been a member of that workforce and I only wish there was more of that team spirit in some of our care homes and hospitals today.

BIOGRAPHY

Wyn Bramley is semi-retired and runs a small private practice in rural Oxfordshire. She began her career as nursing sister at the Cassel therapeutic community in the 60's. She then moved into student counselling at University of Westminster and later at University College London. Over this 15 year period she helped to arrange in service training for herself and colleagues, and participated in the setting up of the Association for Student Counselling. In 1976 she qualified at the Institute for Group Analysis and Family and Marital Therapy (now Institute of Group Analysis). She moved to Oxfordshire in 1986 as freelance trainer / therapist / consultant in the NHS, including work in GP practices. In 1996 she designed and directed the 4 year Oxford University Masters Programme in Psychodynamic Studies. Pertinent to this book are *The Broad Spectrum Psychotherapist* and *The Supervisory Couple in Broad Spectrum Psychotherapy*, published by Free Association Books.